Durability
of
Geotextiles

Durability
of
Geotextiles

RILEM
(The International Union of Testing and Research
Laboratories for Materials and Structures)

LONDON   NEW YORK
CHAPMAN AND HALL

First published in 1988 by
Chapman and Hall Ltd
11 New Fetter Lane, London EC4P 4EE
Published in the USA by
Chapman and Hall
29 West 35th Street, New York NY 10001

© 1988 RILEM

Printed in Great Britain at the
University Press, Cambridge

ISBN 0 412 30660 3

British Library Cataloguing in Publication Data

Durability of Geotextiles = Durabilité des
    géotextiles.
    1. Synthetic fabrics in building
    I. RILEM
    624.1'897   TA668

    ISBN 0-412-30660-3

Library of Congress Cataloging in Publication Data

Durability of geotextiles = Durabilité des
    géotextiles.

    English or French.
    Includes index.
    1. Geotextiles. I. International Union of Testing and
Research Laboratories for Materials and structures.
II. Title: Durabilité des géotextiles.
TA455.G44D87   1988   620.1'97   87-31971
ISBN 0-412-30660-3

Contents

Foreword

How can we define the problems of durability in correct terms so as to ensure long service life in economically acceptable conditions? This question is being constantly asked, and probably too late, judging from the state of a number of civil engineering structures in many parts of the world.

So it is quite a healthy attitude to be concerned about materials of which we only have recent experience, such as geotextiles, without waiting for the long term to reveal the mistakes made and the lack of study of local conditions. It is certainly preferable to set up a practice on a firm basis of knowledge, rather than belatedly to investigate the causes of irreversible disorders and to learn costly lessons from degradation which we have not known how to avoid.

There could be no better motive and reason for bringing together experts from the chemical industry, from civil engineering and various research institutes to cast light on the different aspects of long-term behaviour of geotextiles and lift the veils from the future.

Although this book contains the most up-to-date information, it is not so much a compilation of what is known, or thought to be known, but more a marking out of the territory still to be explored.

Maurice Fickelson
Secretary General of RILEM

This work is the result of contributions to a seminar organized by RILEM and the International College of Building Science with the support of the International Geotextile Society. It took place in Saint-Rémy-lès-Chevreuse, France, 4–6 November 1986.

Contributors

Ph. Delmas Laboratoire Central des Ponts et Chaussées (LCPC), 58 bd Lefebre, 75732 Paris Cedex 15

G. Den Hoedt ENKA Research Institute B.V., Arnhem.

Y. Faure IRIGM (Institut de Recherches Interdisciplinaires de Géologie et de Mécanique de Grenoble), BP 68, 38402 St. Martin d'Heres Cedex.

M. Fickelson RILEM, 12 rue Brancion, 75737 Paris Cedex 15.

K. Gamski Université de Liège, Institut du Génie Civil, 6 quai Banning, B 4000 Liège.

T. S. Ingold Mulberry Lodge, St. Peters Close, St. Albans, Hertfordshire AL1 3ES.

B. Leclercq Institut Textile de France (ITF), BP 79, 92105 Boulogne Billancourt.

E. Leflaive Laboratoire Central des Ponts et Chaussées (LCPC), Orly Sud n° 155, 94396 Orly Aerogare Cedex.

A. McGown University of Strathclyde, Dept of Civil Engineering, John Anderson Building, 107 Rottenrow, Glasgow G4 0NG.

R. T.Murray Transport and Road Research Laboratory, Dept of Transport, Old Wokingham Road, Crowthorne, Berkshire RG11 6AU.

J. Perfetti Rhone Poulenc Textiles, Dépt Non Tissés, BP 80, 95871 Bezons Cedex.

P. R. Rankilor Manstock Geotechnical Consultancy Services Ltd, 1 North Parade, Parsonage, Manchester M3 2FB.

J. M. Rigo Institut de Génie Civil, Service Laboratoire des Matériaux de Construction, 6 quai Banning, B 4000 Liège.

A. L. Rollin Ecole Polytechnique, Dépt de Génie Chimique, BP 6079, succursale 'A', Montréal, Québec H3C 2A7.

F. Saathoff   Franzius-Institut für Wasserbau und Küsteningenieurwesen, Universität Hannover, Callinstrasse 32, FRG 3000 Hannover 1.

L. C. E. Struik   Kunstoffen en Rubber Instituut KRI – TNO, Postbus 71, 2600 AB Delft.

J. Verdu   Ecole Nationale Supérieure d'Arts et Métiers (ENSAM), 151 bd de l'Hôpital, 75640 Paris Cedex 13.

J. D. M. Wisse   Kunstoffen en Rubber Instituut KRI – TNO, Postbus 71, 2600 AB Delft.

INTRODUCTION

K. GAMSKI

Institut de Génie Civil, Université de Liège

The International Symposium organized in Paris in 1977 by the Laboratoire Central des Ponts et Chaussées and the Ecole Nationale des Ponts et Chaussées on the use of textiles in Geotechniques stimulated the setting up of the RILEM Technical Committee 47 Synthetic Membranes (TC 47 SM).

Between 1980 and 1985 TC 47 SM concentrated activity on Geotextiles and Geomembranes, two fields in full development. By placing emphasis on the priority given to Geotextiles, the Committee prepared a special issue of Materials and Structures n° 82 1981 devoted to Geotextiles.

TC 47 SM worked to a programme aiming at the preparation of Rilem recommendations related to test methods. This included :

- Definitions related to Geotextiles and Geomembranes,

- Recommendations most easy to apply for testing mechanical and hydraulic characteristics implied in these definitions,

- Recommendations to define the behaviour of immediate interest for the study of the practical use of Geotextiles and Geomembranes in the search for solutions to geotechnical problems.

This work resulted in the publication in Materials and Structures by TC 47 SM (May-June 1984 n° 99) of the following draft Recommendations for woven and non-woven geotextiles :

SM G 0   Scope

    G 1   Therminology

    G 2   Identification data sheet

    G 3   Characteristics of geotextiles and constituent materials

    G 4   Sampling

    G 5   Conditioning atmosphere

    G 6   Weight per unit area

    G 7   Nominal thickness

    G 8.1 Dry porometry

G 8.2 Porometry by wet process

G 9   Hydraulic permittivity

G 10   Transmissivity

G 11   Tensile strength and elongation tests under maximum stress

G 12   Tearing strength

G 13   Resistance to slip in the soil.

In May 1985, in compliance with an agreement signed between RILEM and ISO, these recommendations were forwarded to ISO and the newly set up ISO Technical Committee was entrusted with drafting ISO standards.

Since TC 47 had given priority to the study of recommendations for Geotextiles, the topic of Geomembranes had been left aside but will be taken up shortly by a new RILEM technical committee.

At present winding up its work in the field of Geotextiles, TC 47 SM aims at bringing together data and opinions on the aspect of Geotextiles not yet studied, that is Durability. The subject is of extreme importance but it is also difficult and must therefore be dealt with frankly and cautiously.

The durability of Geomembranes presents very different aspects from those encountered in the study of Geotextiles. Whereas up to now the diversity of materials used in the manufacture of Geotextiles is quite restricted and limited to thermoplastics such as polypropylene, satured polyester, polyethylene, polyamide, on the contrary Geomembranes are produced from a wide range of thermoplastic and thermosetting resins and elastomers, even mixtures of these. Geotextiles are always manufactured before placing, whereas certain Geomembranes can be produced in situ using reactive resin. Finally, Geotextiles in service are in contact essentially with loose soil and water, whereas Geomembranes are often designed to be placed in a polluted medium containing very different industrial waste. It is however true that in many cases Geotextiles are used together with Geomembranes, especially to protect the Geomembranes from perforation or to ensure drainage of underlying layers. Woven or unwoven geotextiles are made of complex fibres, processed mechanically and thermally, hence their excellent mechanical behaviour. Some special Geotextiles are however manufactured like certain Geomembranes from a calandered sheet. With the exception of Geomembranes produced in a continuous layer in situ from reactive resins, normally Geomembranes manufactured as a sheet will be assembled in situ by bonding or by welding. This raises the problem of the mechanical and hydraulic durability of these joints in addition to the mechanical and hydraulic durability of the sheet itself.

The set of problems outlined above brought the TC 47 SM to propose organizing a first Seminar devoted to Durability of Geotextiles and planning further study in a second seminar on Durability of Geomembranes. The date of the second seminar is not yet settled but might be held in a years time.

After each of these seminars, RILEM intends to set up a small study group to propose a precise programme of work for a Technical Committee with the following scope :

- study of aspects of durability,

- study of methods of selecting the most appropriate material for each given case,

- improvement of methods of observation in situ of Geotextiles and Geomembranes or of a combination of these.

As for Durability of Geotextiles, apart from the aspect related to the stability of their internal structure, there is a need to examine the durability of their mechanical and hydraulic behaviour.

The term Durability expresses the preservation in time of the characteristics or performance of a material, which are checked at the time of delivery or before placing and service.

So the degree of durability can be expressed by a physical or chemical change which occurs :

- spontaneously in the composition or in the internal structure of the material examined,

- following the action of placing or service, such as mechanical load, acid or basic medium, medium loaded with solid fragments, temperature, etc ...

- through the very nature of the process, these spontaneous induced changes sum up -even if we wish to analyse them separately, we should take into account their synergy and their cumulative effect.

There can be numerous causes of a spontaneous change in the internal structure or depolymerization. Breaking of chains and lateral grouping, photochemical decomposition, thermooxydation have been studied for many years and their different aspects will be surveyed during this seminar.

The change in initial properties of Geotextiles due to placing and service conditions becomes obvious through a measurable modification in the mechanical and hydraulic performance of a given material as recorded on delivery. This aspect of Durability of Geotextiles which also includes the spontaneous development of their internal structure is of prime importance to engineers and designers. It also interests the producers of basic materials and manufacturers of Geotextiles who endeavour to supply materials in compliance with builders requirements.

The degree of sensitivity of Geotextiles to loads will vary as a function of the type of basic material, the manufacturing process (weaving, needling, thermal action), confering a specific external structure on the material. Localized mechanical stresses exerted on nodes of reduced curvature under strong tension between small stones can subject the yarn to stress-cracking especially in the presence of salts.

A structure formed of multiple fibres will behave better than membranes under tension or calendered grid. This is because the local failure of a fibre will induce the transfer of mechanical forces to neighbouring fibres so that the continuity of the overall structure be not implicated. On the contrary, localized excess tension in a calandered membrane where the strength is directional could set up the rapid propagation of brittle fracture, without deformation in the direction of processing tension.

This mechanical aspect of Durability is important in almost all the practical uses of Geotextiles. In certain specific applications liable to set up high tensile stresses, creep strength becomes a predominant criterion in the choice of a Geotextile.

The study of the durability of the hydraulic properties of Geotextiles includes the problem of interaction with the surrounding soil. There is a risk that the permittivity perpendicular to the layer or the transmittivity in the geotextile plane, which are the intrinsic characteristics of a material when supplied, be subjected to a modification once the geotextile is placed in the soil. This deterioration will result from infiltration of fine particules into the porous structure of the geotextile. The application of filtration laws can help in the choice of a geotextile of defined porosity, taking into account the type of soil and the drainage rate of flow.

The RILEM recommendations at present used as a basis in ISO work form a reference to assess the modification in the initial mechanical and hydraulic characteristics and thereby provide a means of evaluation of durability.

This RILEM seminar fits into this general framework of investigation. The organization of this meeting was entrusted to the International College of Building Science in order to emphasize the scientific aspect of the subject, wider than the more restricted field adopted by the RILEM Technical Committees.

We trust that the proceedings of this Seminar will bring together a wealth of scientific data on which further study of durability can be based, the final objective being to provide criteria with which engineers can make a discerning choice of the Geotextiles best suited to the specific technical function imposed by the designer.

THE DIFFERENT ASPECTS OF LONG-TERM BEHAVIOUR OF GEOTEXTILES

E. LEFLAIVE
Laboratoire Central des Ponts et Chaussées, Orly

This seminar is organized with the support of the International Geotextile Society (IGS), which establishes a link worldwide between people and organizations interested in the development of geotextiles, geomembranes and related products.

IGS has been created fairly recently and has not yet undertaken any specific action dealing with the long-term behaviour of geotextiles ; however, the Inventory of Geotextile Testing Methods published this year indentifies some testing methods on creep, clogging and ageing. Also papers on these topics have been presented at the second and at the third International Conferences on Geotextiles. IGS is fully aware of the importance of long term behaviour of geotextiles in view of a long-term development of these materials and particularly for a number of fields of application where long life duration and safety are essential. This is why this RILEM seminar is encouraged and its conclusions will be considered with great interest, although it is known that such problems require years of observations and work.

The relevance of a comprehensive approach of long term behaviour of geotextiles results from the increasing use of these new materials and from the fact that civil engineering projects are built for very long life durations.

As a matter of fact, present experience of geotextiles as well as current knowledge from chemistry does not lead in any way to be apprehensive about their long term stability. However, authorities bearing the responsability of large scale projects must have a clear view of conditions to be met to rule out any chance of substantial failure or of unexpectedly fast ageing of large investments.

Therefore, chemical industry and civil engineers promoting geotextile techniques must put together the informations and data that are necessary for decision makers to engage into new applications or into a larger scale utilization of these materials.

The study of long-term behaviour of geotextiles is characterized by several features :

- life duration of civil engineering works is much longer than those usually required for synthetic textiles ;

- working conditions are particularly severe, specially in reinforced systems where stress is permanent ;

- the soil environment, while being favourable under some aspects (protection from light, temperature stability) is different from one site to another, of complexe nature and not always well known.

° ° °

The purpose of studies on long-term behaviour is to be able to give to users, whatever the contemplated use and life duration required, indications on product selection, working conditions and construction requirements to guarantee a degree of reliability of the work at least equal to that obtained from other and better known techniques.

It may probably be considered that for a number of applications of geotextiles the reliability of these materials is totally satisfactory, taking into account all observations made on existing constructions and considering the low level of risk involved in these applications.

In other situations, decisions to be made have such far reaching consequences that answers we can give today are still inadequate.

It is therefore necessary both to gather all information and knowledge on the subject, and to clearly identify orientations and procedures which will enable us, during the coming years, to make positive progress.

Thus, the purpose of this seminar is essentially to lay down correctly the problem of long-term behaviour of geotextiles, in order to launch the programs that will really bring new data in the future.

The conclusions drawn from the seminar will, particularly, have to be presented in the form of recommendations for research, field observations and working methods to be used to arrive at guidelines for the use of geotextiles in all fields.

Stating properly the question of long-term behaviour requires to approach it in an extensive way without limiting the question to one aspect or another ; the seminar has, therefore, been organized as a collective

6

discussion on all aspects of durability. At the same time, to be efficient, conclusions must be precise, practical and realistic in view of
available research means.

The main points of view under which the seminar program will approach
material changes with time are the mechanical point of view, the hydraulic and the physico-chemical, leaving for the final session some time
for a summary discussion on interactions between these three aspects.

The mechanical aspect is dominated by the questions of creep and behaviour under repeated loading.

The hydraulic point of view is centered around the risk of clogging
with the simultaneous change in permeability.

The physico-chemical aspect is that of ageing of materials, that is,
to use the words of J. Verdu, any slow and irreversible evolution, in
operating conditions, of one or several properties of the material, evolution which may result from structural modifications of macromolecules, and/or composition or morphological modifications of the material.

Interactions between these phenomena are numerous : stress may modify
ageing, ageing may have an effect on creep, surface characteristics
modifications may act on clogging, there may a link between strain on
one hand and clogging and permeability on the other hand, and so on.

o
o   o

From another viewpoint, the seminar organizers made an effort to get an
input from the three groups involved : the producers, the users and the
researchers.

The technical and economical conditions of industrial production of materials create a set of limitations the producers have to deal with :
it is desirable that other parties are well aware of these constraints.

Users have problems and requirements that are depending upon the type
of application. All parties must be in a position to evaluate the nature and importance of the specific considerations of each field of use.

Researchers represent a sum of knowledge and investigation means that
has to be analysed to identify the most appropriate elements for the
study of geotextile durability.

The purpose of the workshops scheduled during the first day is somehow
to make an inventory of all these viewpoints and all these data, to pre-
pare the discussions and the work of the following days with a good understanding between all groups. Other sessions will allow a deeper approach of each aspect before the conclusions.

The workshops will have to answer to a number of questions such as :

- what should be the objectives of studies on long term behaviour of geotextiles :

- . to predict a life duration ?
- . to compare products ?
- . to define favourable and unfavourable conditions of use for each
  family of materials ?
- . or else ?

- what are the methods, techniques and means available for such studies ?

- what are the data presently available ?

- what are the priorities ?

- agreement on terminology.

° °
 °

THE PRODUCERS' POINT OF VIEW

J. PERFETTI*
Rhone Poulenc Fibres

M. FICKELSON*
RILEM

Met together in discussion, the producers had no difficulty in fixing the two registers in which to make their voices heard : the present needs of an industry developing in rapid strides and the actions necessary to meet them in the short term. With such a clear situation, the producers were able to express the point of view requested of them as a straihgt-forward enumeration :

NEEDS

1) Test methods of short duration :

    - according to the type of structure,
    - according to the service life,
    - easy to carry out,
    - representative of the soil/textile interaction,
    - with international acceptation.

2) Definition of sharing responsibility :

    - liability of producers in respect to the behaviour of geotextiles
      a) product data sheets (in the plural because of the different standards)
      b) measurement of characteristics - by means of standardized test methods

    - liability of users defined in specifications
      a) precise knowledge concerning placing and working,
      b) drafting of specifications (reference to standards)
      c) strict application of specifications

    - involvement of research scientists which would ensure :
      a) the validity of the results of their work,
      b) the compliance with service conditions of the test methods drawn up for durability.

(*) The Producers Debate was conducted by J. PERFETTI and the drafting of his conclusions was carried out by M. FICKELSON

3) Knowledge of materials

   - bibliographic data bases (polymers)
   - objective drafting of a document on the behaviour of geotextile
     basic constituents.

PRIORITY ACTIONS

1) Inventory of all structures where geotextiles have been sampled

   Records to list : - type of structure
                     - service life
                     - results, assessment of residual strength

2) Inventory of research topics

   - planned,
   - in progress,
   - ready for publication.

3) assessment of research projects

   - definition of scope
   - means of financing
   - time scale
   - dissemination and use of results.

The advantage of such a down-to-earth statement is that it defined the
implicit conditions of a clearer exchange of view with the users, also
it transmitted certain signals which research could easily interpret,
making the beginnings of a response to the purpose of the seminar.

THE USERS' POINT OF VIEW

R. T. MURRAY

Transport and Road Research Laboratory, Department of Transport

The workshop on durability of geotextiles gave particular consideration to the following:

a.   Concept of structural life

b.   Factor of safety

c.   Specification procedures

d.   Nature and extent of additional information required for making greater use of geotextiles in civil engineering.

It was recognised that the required life of a geotextile or related product could vary greatly from important works of a permanent nature which could require properties to be maintained for periods in excess of 100 years and examples were cited of retaining walls, bridge abutments and earth dams as falling into this category, to the other extreme of temporary works involving geotextiles requiring a relatively short duration life of perhaps 2-10 years and the case of an embankment founded on soft compressible soils was referred to in this context. In this latter situation the geotextile might be included in the embankment to ensure short term stability until sufficient consolidation had taken place to give an adequate gain in shear strength such that the embankment was self-supporting without the need for geotextile reinforcement, It was recognised also that traditional materials may have a relatively short life span which could affect performance but are not always subject to the same constraints as geotextiles.

An example of a traditional type of drain of granular material or porous concrete was referred to which may have a life of some 20-25 years, a rather shorter period than might have been expected by the designer.

The contentious subject of safety factor was then discussed and consideration given to the approach which might be adopted in relation to geotextiles.   There was general concensus of opinion that the use of separate partial factors for each of the following factors would best account for geotextile and related product variability and thereby provide a more cost effective design:

(i)   Time-dependent properties

(ii)   Site damage to manufacturing tolerance

(iii)   Unfavourable deviations in loading

(iv)   Assumptions involved in the design and calculation process.

The approach to Specification was then discussed and it was agreed that the difficulties encountered with geotextiles and related products were sometimes exacerbated by the lack of an adequate specification.   It was

considered that the USERS could make an important contribution to the development and greater use of geotextiles
by applying greater effort to the development of suitable
specifications which would effectively interface with
civil engineering contracts.

There was general agreement among the USERS that the information provided by the PRODUCERS was inadequate and to
enable USERS to make more effective use of geotextiles and
related products, as well as to permit designs to be
carried out with greater confidence, the following information should be provided:

1.   A more comprehensive description of a product
and its constituent polymers to include:

   a.   Structure and fibre details
   b.   Any fillers incorporated and associated
   properties.

2.   Comprehensive test information on mechanical and
physical properties including creep, time-dependent
load characteristics, joint strengths etc.

3.   Advice on the use of a product, where it is most
appropriately used and where its use should be
avoided.

4.   Engineering bulletins or news letters providing
additional information on product properties and

behaviour from time-to-time as this becomes available.

There was also a need for further studies to be carried out by the RESEARCHERS and the following areas of particular interest were highlighted:

1. The formation of an International Data Bank which incorporates information on all aspects of geotextile properties and behaviour both in isolation and in the civil engineering environment.

2. Comprehensively instrumented full-scale studies to enable all aspects of geotextile behaviour to be monitored.

3. The Researchers should attempt to identify those factors associated with the constituents in polymers and the processes of manufacture which will provide indicators, perhaps of an indirect nature, relating to the ageing process in geotextiles and related products.

4. To develop suitable test procedures which will reliably assess long term and durability properties of geotextiles and related products such that they can be interfaced with appropriate engineering calculations.

THE RESEARCHERS' POINT OF VIEW

J. M. RIGO
Institut de Génie Civil, Université de Liège

1. Introduction

This workshop has been conceived to gather all those
present at this symposium in hope to determinate :
- the needs;
- the priorities;
- the possible actions.

It is the first time that a symposium is organized about
this subject and it was very important to be able to determinate and compare the advices of the different "cor-
porations" interested by the problems met with geotextiles.

2. Relations between the researchers and the group of manufacturers-users

It is possible, with the help of the next page diagram to
visualize the interactions between these three groups. We
place the researchers purposely in the center of the
diagram because that group is truing to find its definition.
The researchers are placed in the middle of the diagram
with, as possible inputs, the data coming from the manufacturers and the users.

2.1. The inputs
The researchers must meet the arrival on the market of
products of which the constitutive polymer nature and
different parameters change regularly. The time needed for
the study of such a product is longer than the time during
which this product is sold.
As far as users are concerned, the main problem is to know
exactly what they want to get. Often, and because of the
problem complexity , users don't always know it themselves. Manufacturers often say to users : "tell us what
you want and we'll do it".
Besides, geotextile users in civil engineering are very
specific; the geotextile service life changes from case to
case and new applications appear regulary.

Input

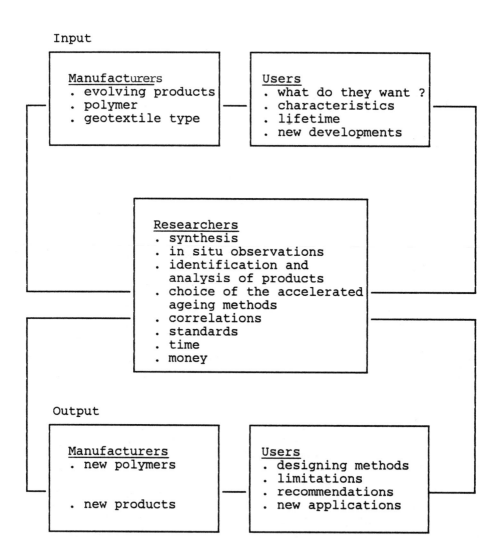

Manufacturers
. evolving products
. polymer
. geotextile type

Users
. what do they want ?
. characteristics
. lifetime
. new developments

Researchers
. synthesis
. in situ observations
. identification and
  analysis of products
. choice of the accelerated
  ageing methods
. correlations
. standards
. time
. money

Output

Manufacturers
. new polymers

. new products

Users
. designing methods
. limitations
. recommendations
. new applications

2.2. The researchers

About geotextile durability, and taking in account the variability in nature and complexion of products, researchers want to develop methods for identifying and analysing the products. The R.I.L.E.M. 47-SM Commission has conceived a filling index card for identifying geotextiles for users. The description the researchers want should be more complete. A keener need of in-situ observations comes up. An effort must be made in the field of work instrumentation. This instrumentation should permit the choice of accelerated ageing methods in laboratory, even though, in that field, precise correlations are not easy to find out. An important effort for the observation synthesising has to be made under the form of expert systems or data banks. One of the purpose of these works is the making up of standards to harmonize the works but it is expensive and takes time.

2.3. The output

The results of this works must lead to the definition of improved profile in matter of geotextiles (polymer and manufacturing methods).
These designing methods appear progressively. They include at this present time important safety factors.
New developments and experimentation tend to refine these methods but the number of in certainties is big.
Face to the complexity of the problems met, some people think that researchers work should be limited at the present time to the elaboration of recommendations for the different uses of geotextiles or insisting on the limitation of their uses.

3. Comments following the discussions

3.1. Definition of ageing

A special attention must be brought to the definition of a state of reference. Do we have to choose as reference the geotextile leaving the factory, when arriving in the gard, before or after being brought into place ?
As a general rule, for geotextiles on which in-situ observations were made, no reference data is available. There is a risk of separating the geotextile damaging when brought into place and the long term behaviour. Indeed, this last point can be affected by geometrical modifications or by excessive local stresses.
The geotextile community should also take as a pattern the works on durability load on other materials.

Finally, in the matter of durability, it may not be for-
gotten that the constitutive polymer structure may play an
important part, for instance when the temperature raising
is used to accelerate the ageing process. This
temperature raising may lead to another damaging process
rather than accelerating ageing.

3.2. Ageing methods
The results obtained in laboratory are essentially function of the ageing method used and function of the operating conditions. The tests in laboratory should be used
for comparison of products but not as simulation of in-
situ conditions.

3.3. Service life and life time
Service life is the time during which a product plays the
part it has to play.
Life time of products is the time during which it is present in the work. That difference must be kept in mind.

3.4. Instrumentation of the applications
This should be subjected to attention in future.
Specific devices must be developped to measure forces and
displacements but also for the measure of residual permeability, degree of chemical attack...
So, a clear definition of the state of references is important.
Our colleagues have also insisted on the necessity of
defining a method of sampling of the aged samples.

3.5. Era of pioneers
Geotextiles, because of the recent developments, oblige
engineers to innovate and guarantee simultaneously, which
in a certain way belongs to the era of pioneers

4. Needs, priorities and possible actions

Conerning researchers, the situation may be summerized by
the following diagram :

18

```
User            ┌────────────────────────────────────────┐
need to         │  the performance requirements of the   │
define          │  whole structure as function of time   │
                └────────────────────────────────────────┘
                         │
                    ┌────────────────────────────────────────┐
                    │  the performance requirements of geo-  │
                    │  textiles in the structure as a func-  │
                    │  tion of time                          │
                    └────────────────────────────────────────┘
                         │
Researchers     ┌────────────────────────────────────────┐
need to         │  determinate the effects of property   │
define          │  changes of geotextiles on structure   │
                │  performances (including observations  │
                │  in existing structures and the deve-  │
                │  lopment of prediction technics based  │
                │  on correct data)                      │
                └────────────────────────────────────────┘
                         │
Manufacturers   ┌────────────────────────────────────────┐
                │  geotextile performances in soil       │
                │  as a function of time                 │
                └────────────────────────────────────────┘
```

19

CIVIL ENGINEERING REQUIREMENTS FOR LONG-TERM BEHAVIOUR OF GEOTEXTILES

T. S. INGOLD
Consulting engineer, St. Albans

1.0 INTRODUCTION

The civil engineer deals with a wide range of applications of geotextiles where the required long term behaviour will vary according to the particular application and the function which the geotextile fulfills in this application. For example in a reinforced soil dam there may be one grade of geotextile used as reinforcement and another as a filter. Clearly the long term behaviour required for the reinforcing function would be very different from that required for the filtration function.

In designing for long term performance, it must be remembered that this will be affected by the handling, storage and installation of the geotextile. This means that at the design stage the engineer has to define short term properties, which are required to ensure the geotextile survives the installation process, as well as long term properties which are required to ensure the geotextile fulfills the design function over the required design life. An excellent example of this dual need is a geotextile filter. To assess the design function, the engineer must know the hydraulic properties of the geotextile such as permeability, physical properties such as pore size, and how these might be affected by normal stress, clogging, blocking or the chemistry of the ground and groundwater which may cause the polymer of the geotextile to deteriorate.

In designing for the filtration function reference is never made to mechanical properties such as tear strength or puncture strength. In practice, however, these properties are vital since if the geotextile is ruptured by the installation process, its subsequent performance in the design function of filtration could be rendered useless.

It becomes apparent then that the required long term behaviour of a geotextile will vary according to the particular application and design function. Consequently the following sections give separate consideration to the four prime geotextile functions of separation, filtration, drainage and reinforcement. Before embarking on this it is worth considering some items of nomenclature with a view to possible definitions.

First there is the question of "service life" and "design life". It would be logical to apply the term service life to the geotextile itself with the term design life applying to the soil-geotextile system which may be a filter, reinforced soil structure or whatever. Obviously it is a pre-requisite that the service life of the geotextile be equal to, or greater than, the design life of the soil-geotextile system. However, in assessing the service life of the geotextile it is important that any testing fully reflects the environments to which the geotextile is exposed before, during and after installation.

A second consideration is the definition of durability. This is generally understood to mean the ability of the geotextile to maintain its integrity, and a high degree of initial mechanical performance, over a long period of time when subjected to its operational environment. Perhaps this definition more accurately applies to the durability of the geotextile alone. It should be recognized, however, that the use of a durable geotextile does not necessarily lead to a durable soil-geo- textile system. An example of this is a geotextile filter used in a groundwater regime rich in iron, where iron oxide deposits may clog the geotextile, so rendering the system defunct before the design life is realised. So although the geotextile may be durable, the soil-geotex- tile system may not be.

21

2.0 SEPARATION

Separation is perhaps one of the most ill-defined functions of a geotextile. In general this is taken as the ability to prevent inter-mixing of two different solids such as an unbound pavement material and an underlying soft formation soil. A prime requirement is that the geotextile should maintain its physical integrity throughout its service life, in which case the greatest demand is probably made during installation when the geotextile must resist the rigours of handling, placing and filling. The objective here is to ensure the "survivability" of the geotextile by providing adequate resistance to puncture and tear. These properties may be severely impaired by careless wrapping or storage which allow the fabric to be exposed to ultra-violet light attack or combinations of natural environments such as UV and salt-water spray which can act in concert to devastating effect on certain polymers and fabric structures.

Once the geotextile is installed, there is a degree of protection against such natural environments in which case the only chemical environ-ments to be resisted are those generated by the fill, especially if this is industrial waste, or by the end use; for example if the geotex-tile is used as a separator in a storage area for chemicals or other industrial products which may be aggressive. Where a separation function is to be performed under dynamic loading such as traffic or wave action, then the separator must be resistant to abrasion and fatigue. The latter is particularly important in certain fabric structures such as non-woven staple fibres. It should be remembered that the separation function rarely applies alone and usually one or more of the other prime functions are simultaneously in operation.

3.0 FILTRATION

Once more there is a need for a geotextile which is sufficiently robust to withstand the loads applied by handling and installation. In addition the polymer of the geotextile must be resistant to attack by any chemicals in the liquids passing through the filter. This is particularly important in any waste containment applications where various mixtures of aggressive fluids may make contact with the geotextile. Under dynamic loading abrasion resistance again becomes an important feature. Where the geotextile is used as a long term filter, perhaps in a dam or as a drain behind a retaining wall, there may be a sustained normal stress. In certain fabric and mesh structures, this may cause significant compressive creep leading to a loss of water permeability normal to the plane.

Fundamental to the filtration function is the ability to maintain the required design level of permeability whilst retaining the appropriate fraction of fine base soil. The latter can prove particularly difficult under reversing flow or dynamic hydraulic conditions where there is no opportunity for the development of a stable bridging or filter cake network at the interface of the base-soil and geotextile. For both these conditions and steady state uni-directional laminar flow conditions it is the long term performance of the soil-geotextile system which must be assessed. Little or nothing can be gained by investigating the geotextile in isolation. The performance of the geotextile will be very much affected by soil type and grading as well as the structure of the fabric. For example with a given soil a very different performance would be obtained for say a heat bonded non-woven and a monofilament-on-monofilament woven. In either case what is important is the residual permeability and retention capability of the geotextile after all possible clogging and blocking has occurred. Impairment of permeability may be a function of more than the simple interaction between base soil and geotextile. As mentioned earlier, there may be the deposition of water borne chemicals such as iron oxide which can cause clogging. Also severe clogging can be caused at the construction stage. Examples of this include contamination by clay slurry, or even worse cement slurry, both of which can cause total clogging of the affected areas. Particular care must be taken where the geotextile is installed as part of a horizontal filter or drainage blanket. If the geotextile is in contact with a cohesive soil and is trafficked by construction plant, then this can cause extrusion of the cohesive soil through the geotextile. As well as being a function of the applied pressure and undrained shear strength of the cohesive soil, this particular mechanism is a function of the open area ratio of the geotextile as opposed to its absolute pore size.

4.0 DRAINAGE

The drainage function of a geotextile is generally associated with its ability to transmit liquid, or gas, in plane. For transmission of liquids the pressure in the geotextile may be above or below atmospheric. The latter condition, of course, applies to capillary suction. It is usually only the thicker felt fabrics which have a useful transmissivity, however, in recent years there has been the introduction of a wide range of meshes, mats and deformed sheets, such as cuspated styrene, which are used as high transmissivity cores in composite drains. As well as inertness to the fluids being transmitted and sufficient robustness to withstand handling and installation two important long term requirements can be defined. The first, which applies only to the felts, is the sustained ability to freely transmit gas and or liquid. Problems have arisen in the past with some fabrics prone to "air-locking" by gas which subsequently impedes liquid transmission. In assessing any such phenomenon it is important that tests are carried out at the relevant normal stress level since this will affect the porosity, and indeed pore-size, of a felt.

The problem of compressive loading applies to both felts and specialized core structures, including those used in association with thin geotextiles to form composite fin-drains. This requires close consideration in long term applications such as wall drainage or under-drainage to geomembranes where sustained compressive load can lead to a loss of transmissivity induced by creep.

24

5.0 REINFORCEMENT

Of all the geotextile functions reinforcement is perhaps the most diversely applied and most technically demanding. Applications vary from comparatively short term, low risk, installations such as unpaved roads to long-term, high risk applications, such as vertical walls and bridge abutments. Clearly the ramifications of failure in these two different applications are orders of magnitude apart. As well as soil reinforcing applications, there are of course applications of geotextile fabrics and grids to the reinforcement of asphaltic paving materials which involve high laying temperatures and subsequently the application of cyclical loading. For the sake of illustration two examples are taken from this wide field of application. These are the construction of embankments on soft, low compressibility, ground and vertical rein- forced soil walls.

These two applications have very different design lives. In the case of embankments on soft ground these are best designed to be stable in the long term, once the foundation soil has consolidated, without any support from the geotextile. On this basis the geotextile, which is inserted as full-width reinforcement at the base of the embankment, is only needed to give stability in the short and intermediate term. Totally different requirements prevail for a vertical reinforced soil wall where the geotextile is needed to provide a stabilising force for the entire design life. For permanent structures the design life varies from country to country, and in the United Kingdom may be as long as 120 years.

Used in the construction of embankments on soft ground a basal layer of geotextile must serve several functions which vary according to the stage reached in construction. In the initial stages of construc- tion, when the geotextile is first laid over the surface of the soft ground, it initially acts as a separator between the soft ground and the embankment fill. It is quite likely that the first layer of fill will be a granular drainage medium used to aid the dissipation of pore- water pressure generated in the foundation soil. In this case the geotextile would need to act as a filter as well.

Clearly the prime function of the geotextile would be to reinforce.

25

To achieve this successfully the geotextile must comply with two basic criteria.

    i) The reinforcement must not rupture.

    ii) The reinforcement must prevent excessive movement.

The first of these criteria is the most important since this is the basis of design against out-right collapse of the embankment. Allied to this of course the geotextile needs to be rough enough to prevent any form of soil-geotextile bond failure. To prevent collapse of the embankment by rupture of the geotextile, the geotextile must make available the restoring force required by the embankment. The restoring force required by the embankment will vary with time such that this required force decreases as the embankment consolidates. Indeed when a sufficiently high degree of consolidation has been achieved in the foundation soil, no restoring force is required from the geotextile. Since the required force decreases with time, it follows that the available geotextile force can also be allowed to decrease with time. The only requirement is that at any time the available geotextile force should always be greater than the required force to keep the embankment stable.

This criterion is linked with the second major design criterion which states that the geotextile must prevent excessive movement in the embankment. This requirement is a serviceability criterion. To achieve this it is adequate to limit the axial strain in the geotextile to some predetermined level. An acceptable level would be approximately 5% strain which would be the upper limit on strain for the entire design life of the geotextile.

These two criteria of collapse, which calls upon the geotextile to provide a required stabilising force which decreases with time, and serviceability, which requires the geotextile to maintain an approximately constant strain with time, can be modelled using a stress relaxation curve for the geotextile. Alternatively, if the performance of the geotextile is not stress path dependent, an isometric curve constructed from creep loading tests would give the same data. Either way a curve can be constructed which would show the force in the geotextile, at constant strain, decreasing with time. This effectively is a plot of available geotextile force against time for a constant strain.

The counter-part of this plot is a plot of the required restoring force against time which can be obtained using well established soil mechanics theories. Provided at any time this force is less than that indicated by the stress-relaxation curve, or isometric creep curve, for the geotextile then both the collapse criterion and serviceability criterion would be satisfied. In either case it is important that the geotextile is tested in the condition, and environments likely to prevail on site. For most applications of embankments on soft ground the geotextile would not be in service for much more than one year and consequently there is little need for accelerated testing. Clearly in this case the service life of the geotextile is likely to exceed the design life of the basal reinforced embankment.

A much more demanding situation arises for vertical walls where the force required to maintain stability remains constant with time and must, therefore, be supplied by the reinforcement for the entire design life of the wall. In this case the design life of the wall is dictated by the service life of the reinforcement whether this be metal strip, geotextile fabric or polymer geogrid. As for an embankment on soft ground there are two sets of requirements for long term behaviour of the reinforcement. It must not rupture nor must it allow excessive movement in the wall.

Since some extremely long design lives, up to 120 years, are required it is vital to make an assessment of the time dependent failure strength of the reinforcement and its time dependent stiffness. For metallic reinforcement time dependent failure strength is largely governed by prevailing rates of corrosion and this type of reinforcement is considered no further.

For polymeric reinforcement the time dependent rupture strength will be affected by a wide variety of parameters not least of which is the exact polymer used and its physical form. Other very important factors are the soil environment in which the reinforcement must operate and, of course, any damage caused to the reinforcement during handling and installation. Included in this category would be short term exposure to ultra-violet light during site storage, since this may well have

27

an effect on long term behaviour. All of these factors must be taken into account in testing the reinforcement especially any synergism which may prevail in composite environments. Where long design lives are involved there may be the temptation to extrapolate test data too far. If tenuous extrapolations are attempted, then the resulting rupture loads must be reduced by a partial factor which increases as the degree of extrapolation increases. Of course this factor would be in addition to any conventional factor of safety employed.

As well as determining the variation of rupture strength, and mechanism, with time it is necessary to determine the variation of reinforcement axial stiffness with time. This time dependent stiffness would be employed to evaluate wall deflections at various times to ensure that these comply with the serviceability requirement for the wall. Testing techniques used to determine stiffness must, of course, reflect the "as placed" condition of the reinforcement and the environment in which the reinforcement must operate.

6.0 CONCLUSIONS

Geotextiles and related products may be used in a wide range of applications where they may be required to perform one, or a combination, of design functions. Different functions, and different operational environments, will make different demands on the geotextile. It follows from this that no meaningful assessment of long term, or short term, behaviour can be made unless full account is taken of application and environment. In general the two broad requirements of a geotextile are that it must be robust enough to survive short term environments as well as maintaining adequate properties in the long term to fulfill the required design function. In all cases care must be taken in laboratory testing to ensure that installation and operational environments are fully reflected. Particular attention must be paid to any synergism which prevails between various components of the operational environment. Due to the possible effects of synergism it is not acceptable to directly add the effects of different discrete environments assessed in separate tests.

It is beyond doubt that these requirements would involve extensive testing which needs to be product-specific, and system specific. Due to the time and expense involved in this, it would be necessary to classify soil-geotextile systems according to the ramifications of failure. Where the consequences of failure are slight it may be considered acceptable to dispense with any laboratory based assessment of long term behaviour in the belief that this would be identified in due course from direct field experience. Where the ramifications of failure are more severe then every effort must be made to accurately predict long term behaviour from laboratory tests which model all aspects of the installations and operational environment. As test data and subsequent field performance data are amassed and analysed the laboratory test techniques may be simplified to include only first order environmental effects.

An alternative, and perhaps more pragmatic, approach is less sophisticated laboratory testing combined with the use of high partial load factors to give conservative design parameters. Again the acquisition and analysis of subsequent field data could be used to progressively reduce these partial factors as the performance of various products in various environments becomes better understood. Although these approaches may seem conservative, they are commensurate with the general degree of conservatism exercised by the civil engineer who is ultimately responsible for design liability.

PREDICTION OF LONG-TERM CREEP AND RELAXATION OF PLASTICS

L. C. E. STRUIK

Plastics and Rubber Research Institute TNO, Delft

The message of my talk is: for unoriented plastics such as PVC, PP, PETP, etc., the problem of predicting the long-term creep and relaxation over say 50 years has been solved (Struik (1978-1986)). Simple methods could be developed, based on rather sound theory and these methods have been checked experimentally.

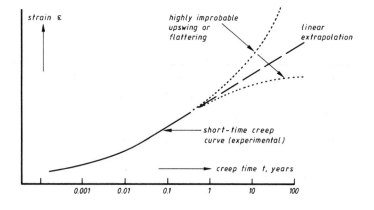

Fig. 1   Linear extrapolation method used to obtain the long-term creep; for explanation see text.

The essentials are summarized in Fig. 1, which shows a creep curve at 20°C (full curve). After some period of creep, the curve (strain ε vs log creep time) becomes almost straight. Theory predicts that it will remain straight over many decades of time. Consequently, the long-term creep can simply be obtained by a linear extrapolation (dashed) of the short-time creep (full curve); there is no risk for an upswing or flattening after long times (dotted curves). Even for extrapolation factors of 100-1000 on time scale, the errors remain acceptably small (see chapter 10-11 of Struik (1978)).
Another important point is outlined in Fig. 2. Often the creep at the working temperature (here 20°C) is predicted from tests at higher temperatures (here 40, 50 and 60°C). It could be shown, theoretically as well as experimentally, that this method is wrong in gener-

30

al; the predicted creep is (much) larger than the actual creep (see e.g. Fig. 126 of Struik (1978)). The inapplicability of such time-temperature superposition methods does not induce problems; we can use the much simpler method of Fig. 1.

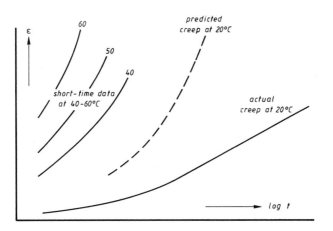

Fig. 2   On the use of tests at higher temperatures (40-60°C) for the prediction of the creep at the working temperature (20°C); for explanation see text.

The time-temperature superposition method basically fails because the creep is not primarily determined by temperature but by the <u>age</u> of the material. In simple cases (rapid cooling from the molten or rubbery state to the working temperature) the age is defined as the time t_e elapsed at the working temperature T after solidification during cooling (see Figs 3 and 4). In general, the age depends on the entire temperature-deformation history after solidification and the definition of an aging time becomes very complicated (Struik (1986)).

Figs 3 and 4 give some data for rigid PVC, quenched from above glass-temperature T_g (~80°C) to the measuring temperature (20°C in Fig. 3, 0, 20 and 40°C in Fig. 4). Fig. 3 shows that the aging effects are important, in fact the creep is delayed by about a factor of 10 for each increase in aging time t_e with a factor of 10. Fig. 4 shows that the aging effects can be more important than a change in temperature of 40°C, the creep of a "young" sample at 0°C is faster than that of an "old" sample at 40°C. Consequently, aging time t_e is an important parameter specifying the behaviour of the material.

The aging effects are not independent of the simple extrapolation method outlined in Fig. 1. Actually, it is the aging which is the origin of the logarithmic creep law; during use, the material gradually stiffens (aging) and it is exactly for this reason that strain ε varies linearly with log t.

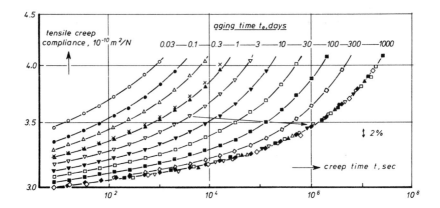

Fig. 3   Small-strain tensile creep curves of rigid PVC quenched from 90°C (i.e. about 10°C above T_g) to 20°C and further kept at 20 ± 0.1 °C for a period of 4 years. The different curves were measured for various values of time t_e elapsed after the quench. The master curve gives the result of a superposition by shifts which were almost horizontal; the shifting direction is indicated by the arrow. The crosses were found when, after 1000 days of aging, the sample was reheated to 90°C, requenched to 20°C, and remeasured for a t_e of 1 day. They show that the aging is thermoreversible.

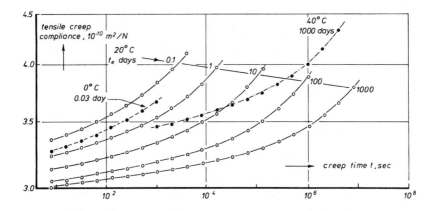

Fig. 4   Small-strain tensile creep of rigid PVC, quenched from 90°C to 0, 20 and 40°C, respectively. For details, see the text and the caption to Fig. 3.

32

The long-term creep prediction methods were originally developed for amorphous glassy polymers such as PVC, PC or PMMA at roomtemperature; later the methods were extended to semi-crystalline polymers such as PP, HDPE, PETP, etc. (Struik (1987)). Not much work has been done on oriented polymers as used in geotextiles, but most probably, the methods will also apply to this class of materials.

References

L.C.E. Struik (1978) Physical Aging in Amorphous Polymers and Other Materials. Elsevier, Amsterdam-New York.
L.C.E. Struik (1985) Aging, Physical, Article in Vol. 1 of the Second Ed. of the Mark-Bikales-Overberger-Menges: "Encyclopedia of Polymer Science and Engineering", Wiley, New York.
L.C.E. Struik (1986) Physical Aging: Influence on the Deformation Behaviour of Amorphous Polymers, in "Mechanical Failure of Plastics", Brostow & Corneliussen, Eds. Hanser, Munnich-Vienna,
L.C.E. Struik (1987) The Mechanical Behaviour and Physical Aging of Semi-crystalline Polymers", sequence of papers accepted for publication in Polymer.

PRINCIPLES OF CREEP AND RELAXATION

G. DEN HOEDT
ENKA Research Institute, Arnhem

Preface

Regarding the preceding lecture by Professor Struik, we have doubts about the importance of age of the polymer for oriented, semi-crystalline polyester.

We have never looked especially into the influence of age, but in our numerous creep measurements on polyester yarns we have not observed either any unexplained "irregularities" which might have induced us to start these investigations.

During the seminar we agreed upon performing some research in that direction.

1. Defining the problem area

All important mechanical properties of a geotextile are related to strength and elongation.

For long-term behaviour these properties are represented more or less by stress relaxation and creep. Creep represents the long-term elongation behaviour (mostly under a constant stress) and stress relaxation is the long-term stress behaviour (generally at a constant elongation).

Physically, both phenomena are strongly interrelated.

Problems with creep and/or relaxation of geotextiles can arise only in those applications where certain limits regarding displacement or elongation must not be exceeded.

This is mainly the case in reinforcement applications. For separation layers the problem is not relevant at all, while for filters and drains it is only of minor importance.

In the majority of cases a designer will select a polymer-construction combination on a technical basis from the following scheme:

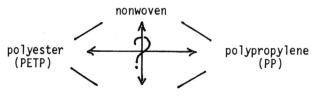

Together the 4 possible combinations form at least 95% of the geotextile market.

A small minority is formed by other materials (polyamide-PA, polyethylene - PE) and by other constructions (extruded grids, braided fabrics, etc.)

2. The visco-elastic behaviour of geotextiles

Creep is the most important feature of the visco-elastic - i.e. time-dependent - behaviour of synthetic materials. In principle, one should not use the term "elastic limits" for geotextiles, as mentioned in the IGS Inventory on Test Methods. All types of geotextiles show creep, but the extent varies considerably and depends mainly on:

- the material (the type of polymer and its processing conditions)
- the construction (nonwoven, woven, type of weave, grid, etc.)

Long-term elongation generally consists of:
- instantaneous polymer elongation ("stress-strain curve of the yarn").
- creep of the polymer
- instantaneous construction-elongation
- constructional creep.

For all materials and constructions the creep rate increases with temperature.
For most materials and loading conditions the creep rate increases with specific load.
For all materials creep increases with time, sometimes linearly on a logtime scale, but then the linearity is not per se constant over a large number of decades. (The log-log relation, as formulated by Nutting, in general does not apply to drawn polymers).

3. Influence of the polymer

Drawn, melt-spun polymers consist of long chain molecules arranged in crystalline regions alternated with amorphous regions (Figure 1).

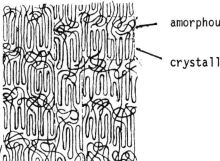 amorphous region

crystalline region

Figure 1.
Model of the two-phase structure of a drawn, melt-spun polymer

Although the short-term stress-strain behaviour is almost
exclusively determined by the deformation of the amorphous part,
the crystalline part may become important in long-term creep
behaviour.
Distinct differences between different polymers will then become
manifest.

Figure 2.
Physical models of molecular
chains of polyethylene,
polypropylene and polyester.

Polyethylene (PE) consists of long, slender molecules without any
cross-links.
In polypropylene (PP) the chains are less slender and smooth (CH_3
side groups), but in principle no cross-links are present.
The molecular structure of polyester (PETP) is far more intricate
than that of polyolefins. Apart from the C-6 rings in the chains,
acting as thick plugs, the oxygen atoms in the side chains enter
into dipolar interactions with the neighbouring molecules. (For
physical models, see Figure 2)

This molecular structure is indeed reflected in the creep behaviour.
In the case of PE and PP the chains slip along one another in the
crystalline regions under prolonged loading.
In the case of PETP this slippage in the crystalline regions hardly
occurs if at all.
The creep of PETP is much lower than that of PP and PE under
comparable loading conditions.

4. Influence of the construction

The yarns in a geotextile are rarely straight and exactly positioned in the direction of the tension applied. In nonwovens this phenomenon holds almost by definition, but in most wovens, too, the yarns are wavy, i.e. they show <u>crimp</u> (Figure 3).

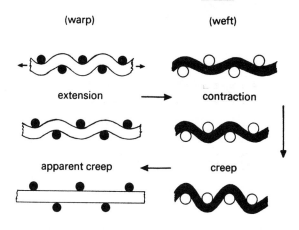

Figure 3

In a uniaxial tensile test this leads to a contraction in lateral direction.
When this cross contraction is restricted (biaxial loading, or friction by the soil), creep in the cross yarns also causes an apparent creep in the main direction (retarded construction-elongation).
To prevent both instantaneous and retarded construction-elongation, it is advantageous to position the yarns beforehand as straight as possible in the fabric (e.g. straight warp woven).
In the case of nonwovens these constructional phenomena are even more pronounced.

5. Conclusions
- Both the polymer properties and the constructional aspects have their own influence on the elongation and creep behaviour of a geotextile.
- The sensitivity to creep of polymers increases considerably in the sequence: PETP - PP - PE.
- When a fabric shows cross contraction, the creep should, in principle, be measured under loading conditions where this contraction is prevented.

- At the present state of knowledge it is difficult and dangerous to give exact figures for the relative influence of polymer and construction on the creep, especially because of the indistinct dividing line between instantaneous and retarded construction elongation.
- Nevertheless, the following figures will serve as a rough guideline:

total construction elongation (%)		creep (%) due to polymer	
grid	0		
straight warp woven	0 - 2	PETP	< 2
woven with crimp	5 - 10	PP	5 - 20
stiff nonwoven	abt. 25	PE	> PP
loose nonwoven	abt. 50		

Which part of the total construction elongation is instantaneous depends on construction and loading; probably the instantaneous part is of the order of a few % (abs.) and the remainder is retarded.

- For reinforcement applications a polyester straight warp fabric functions best.

Reference:
G. den Hoedt, Creep and relaxation of geotextile fabrics.
Geotextiles and Geomembranes 4 (1986), 83-92.

FLUAGE COMPARÉ DE FILS DE POLYESTER ET DE POLYPROPYLÈNE

B. LECLERCQ *Institut Textile de France, Paris*

1 - Avant-propos

Le sujet de cet exposé est le résultat de la thèse (1) de
M. MIR-ARABCHAHI conduite sous la direction de M. BIAREZ, Professeur
à l'Ecole Centrale de Paris, et de M. LEFLAIVE, chargé d'affaires au
laboratoire Central des Ponts et Chaussées à Paris et réalisée au laboratoire de l'Institut Textile de France - Paris.

2 - Introduction

On appelle fluage la déformation en fonction du temps d'un système
sous contrainte ou sous charge constante. Les essais de fluage sont
généralement conduits sous charge constante car, étant donné la déformation subie par le système au cours de l'essai, il est difficile
de maintenir une contrainte constante. Un essai de fluage consiste à
établir pour une contrainte initiale donnée σ_0 une fonction $\varepsilon = f(t)$
qui décrit la courbe expérimentale de fluage. Une telle courbe peut
généralement se décomposer en 3 partiès (Fig. 1).

Fig. 1 - Allure générale d'une courbe de fluage.

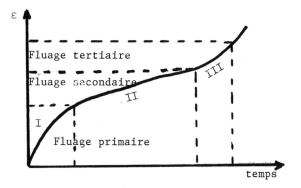

La partie I correspond au fluage primaire pendant lequel la vitesse
de déformation $\dot{\varepsilon}$ est décroissante.

La partie II correspond au fluage secondaire pendant lequel la vitesse de déformation $\dot{\varepsilon}$ est constante.

La partie III correspond au fluage tertiaire pendant lequel la vitesse de déformation $\dot{\varepsilon}$ est croissante. Le fluage tertiaire se termine
par la rupture en fluage de l'échantillon.

Suivant le niveau de la contrainte initiale de l'essai de fluage seules les parties I et II de la courbe représentative peuvent être décrites. Si la déformation tend vers une limite, le fluage est dit stabilisé. D'une façon générale et plus particulièrement dans le cas des géotextiles, la fonction fluage s'exprime par une relation du type :

$$\varepsilon = \varepsilon_0 + A\, f(t) \text{ où } A \text{ est une constante.}$$

Suivant les auteurs la fonction f (t) est soit logarithmique (2), soit exponentielle (3).

Des essais de fluage peuvent être conduits sous différentes températures. Il en résulte que les différents paramètres à prendre en compte dans une expérience de fluage sont :

- la contrainte ou la charge initiale
- la déformation
- la vitesse de déformation
- la température.

Dans cet exposé sont présentés des essais de fluages sur fil polypropylène et polyester sous différentes charges initiales et à diverses températures.

3 - Conditions d'essais et représentations graphiques

Deux fils, l'un polyester T 105 280/60 dtex et l'autre fil polypropylène 330/60 dtex, dont les résistances à la rupture sont respectivement 18 et 13,9 N ont été soumis à des essais de fluage en prenant une longueur entre pinces égale à 5 cm. L'une des pinces est accrochée à un portique tandis qu'à l'autre pince est suspendu un poids connu P pour que l'essai soit mené avec une contrainte initiale bien déterminé. La distance entre pince est mesurée en fonction du temps avec un cathétomètre . Les essais ont été menés soit dans le laboratoire conditionné à une température constante de 20° C soit dans une enceinte climatique dans un domaine de température compris entre 40 et 100° C. Une attention particulière était apportée à la mise en charge des fils de manière à ce qu'ils ne soient pas soumis à un effet de choc.

La déformation au cours de l'essai de fluage est définie par la relation

$$\varepsilon = \frac{\Delta l}{l_0}$$

dans laquelle Δl est l'allongement et l_0 la longueur initiale.

Considérons un fil de section initiale S_o ; au début d'un essai de fluage, il est soumis à une contrainte initiale $\sigma_o = \frac{P}{S_o}$. Au cours de l'essai, le fil s'allonge et par suite sa section S diminue. En considérant que le volume de matière reste constant, on peut écrire :

$$V = S_o \, l_o = S \, (1 + \varepsilon) \, l_o$$

d'où $S = \dfrac{S_o}{1 + \varepsilon}$

La contrainte instantanée devient $\quad \sigma = \dfrac{P}{S} = \dfrac{P \, (1 + \varepsilon)}{S_o}$

La contrainte instantanée est donc liée à contrainte initiale par la relation :

$$\sigma = \sigma_o \, (1 + \varepsilon)$$

Considérons σ_r comme la contrainte de rupture du fil ; on peut définir le niveau de contrainte instantanée par $q = \dfrac{\sigma}{\sigma_r}$, le niveau de contrainte initiale étant $q_i = \dfrac{\sigma_i}{\sigma_r}$ où σ_i est le niveau de contrainte initiale.

Le niveau de contrainte instantanée est ainsi lié au niveau de contrainte initiale par la relation $q = q_i \, (1 + \varepsilon)$ qui peut encore s'écrire :

$$\varepsilon = \frac{q}{q_i} - 1.$$

Dans un plan de référence $(\varepsilon - q)$, un essai de fluage de contrainte initiale q_i sera donc représenté par une droite. Les courbes représentatives de divers essais réalisés sous différents niveaux de contraintes initiales q_i formeront un faisceau de droites convergentes dont les coordonnées du point de convergence sont $(0 - 1)$ (Fig. 2).

Fig. 2 - Chemins d'essais pour différents niveaux de contraintes initiales.

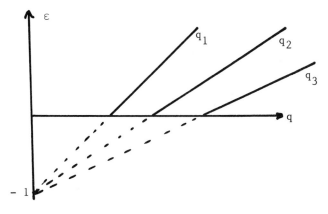

La courbe de la figure 1 représente l'allure générale d'une courbe de fluage dans le plan (ε, t). Dans ce même plan, des essais de fluage sous différents niveaux de contraintes q_1, q_2 .... q_n seront représentés par une série de courbes comme le montre schématiquement la figure 3.

Fig. 3 - Représentation schématique d'une série d'essais de fluage.

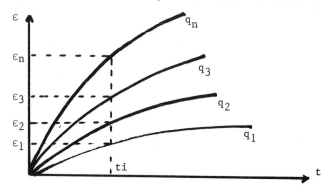

Pour une valeur du temps donnée, à chaque niveau de charges q_1, q_2... q_n correspond une valeur de déformation $\varepsilon_{i,1}$, $\varepsilon_{i,2}$, $\varepsilon_{i,n}$. Si les couples de points q_n, $\varepsilon_{i,n}$ sont reportés dans le plan (ε, q) on obtient une famille de courbes isochrones qui sont représentées schématiquement sur la figure (4).

Fig. 4 - Représentation schématique des courbes isochrones dans le plan (ε, q).

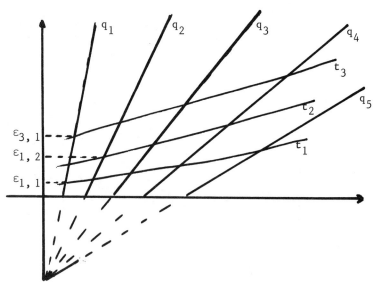

Les conditions des essais de fluage sur fil polypropylène sous des températures et des niveaux de contraintes différents sont consignées dans le tableau 1 tandis que celles relatives aux essais sur fil polyester sont résumées dans le tableau 2.

Tableau 1 - Essais de fluage sur fil polypropylène

Températures	Niveaux de contraintes initiales q_i		
20° C	0,20	0,45	0,60
80° C	0,25	0,30	0,35
100° C	0,25	0,30	0,35

Tableau 2 - Essais de fluage sur fil polypropylène

Températures	Niveaux de contraintes initiales q_i		
20° C	0,60	0,75	
40° C	0,70	0,75	0,80
60° C	0,65	0,70	0,75
80° C	0,60	0,65	
100° C	0,50	0,60	0,65

Certaines températures d'essais peuvent paraître élevées compte tenu de la température d'utilisation des géotextiles. Elles ont cependant été retenues pour voir dans quelle mesure des fluages accélérés par l'effet de la température peuvent être raccordés à des fluages à la température ambiante. Il est à noter que dans le cas du polypropylène les températures d'essais sont supérieures à sa température de transition vitreuse qui est inférieure à 0° C, alors que dans le cas du polyester elles encadrent la température de transition vitreuse de ce dernier qui est de l'ordre de 70° C.

Pour minimiser les effets des défauts éventuels de la structure sur les résultats, chaque essai a été répété au moins trois fois.

4 - Résultats

Bien que le tracé des courbes de fluage dans le plan (ε, t) permette de visualiser le point d'inflexion entre le fluage secondaire et tertiaire, le tracé de ces courbes dans le plan $(\varepsilon, \log t)$ a été préféré pour avoir une échelle de temps moins étendue.

Figures 5 et 6, sont représentées à titre indicatif quelques courbes de fluage de fils polypropylène et polyester à des températures d'essais et à des niveaux de contraintes différents. A partir de ces courbes, on constate que l'augmentation de la température produit une accélération du fluage. On remarque également que les courbes ε, logt sont sensiblement linéaires pour les fils polyester alors qu'elles présentent une forte concavité pour les fils polypropylène. Cela signifie que l'évolution du fluage est plus rapide pour les fils polypropylène que pour les fils polyester.

A partir des données expérimentales, les courbes isochrones pour des valeurs de temps de 10^0 à 10^6 minutes ont été tracées dans les plans de référence ε, q et sont représentées figures 7 et 8 respectivement pour les fils polypropylène et les fils polyester. L'observation de la figure 7 fait apparaître que ces courbes isochrones sont des faisceaux de droites qui ont le même point de convergence quelle que soit la température d'essai. La figure 8 fait ressortir que pour les polyesters les courbes isochrones sont également des faisceaux de droites convergentes qui sont répartis à partir de deux points de convergence. L'un correspond aux températures d'essais inférieures à la température de transition vitreuse T_g du polyester, l'autre aux températures d'essai supérieures à cette température de transition.

Les coordonnées de ces points de convergences sont données dans le tableau 3.

Tableau 3 - Coordonnées des points de convergences

	ε_s	q_s
Polypropylène	0,01	0,1
Polyester T < Tg	0,114	0,52
Polyester T > Tg	0,095	0,275

De l'observation des droites isochrones des figures 7 et 8, on peut également remarquer que l'angle fait par ces droites avec l'axe q varie linéairement avec le logarithme du temps.

Fig. 5 - Fluage de fils polypropylène.

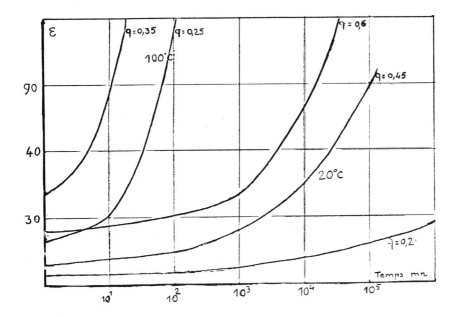

Fig. 6 - Fluage de fils polyester.

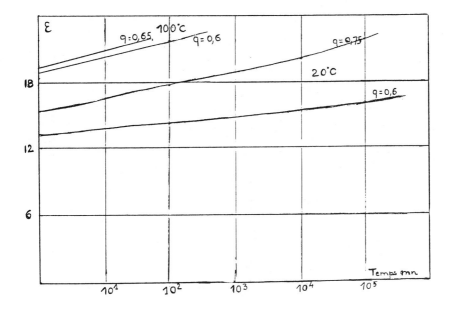

Fig. 7 - Faisceaux de courbes isochrones des fils polypropylène.

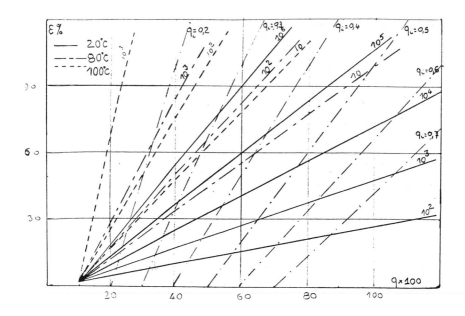

Fig. 8 - Faisceaux de courbes isochrones des fils polyester.

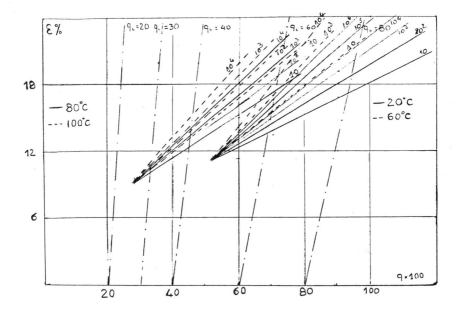

En considérant que ces courbes isochrones sont des faisceaux de droites convergentes dont les arctangentes de leurs pentes varient linéairement avec le logarithme du temps, on peut proposer comme formulation du fluage l'équation suivante :

$$\varepsilon = \frac{(q_i - q_s) \times tg\ \alpha + \varepsilon_s}{1 - q_i\ tg\ \alpha} \quad (1)$$

où ε_s et q_s sont les coordonnées du point de convergence.

L'angle α est donné par la relation

$\alpha = m\ Ln\ (t) + C\ (2)$ où m et c sont des constantes.

Les courbes représentatives de α en fonction du logarithme du temps sont représentées sur les figures 9 et 10 pour les différentes températures d'essais. L'étude analytique de l'équation 1 montre qu'elle peut représenter les différentes phases du fluage.

Fig. 9 - Variation de α en fonction du temps pour les fils polypropylène.

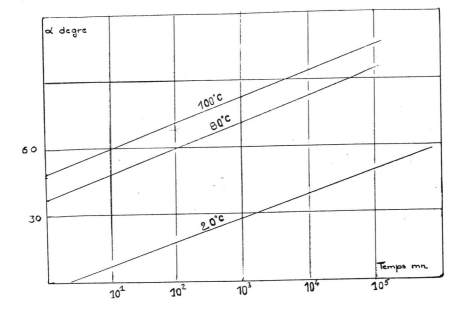

47

Fig. 10 - Variation de α en fonction du temps pour les fils polyester.

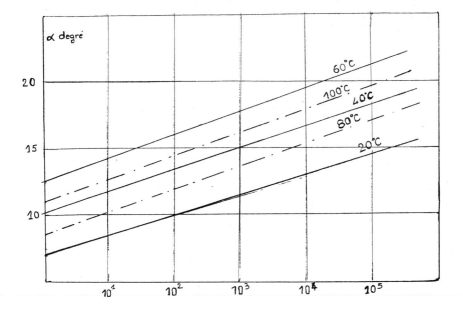

Les valeurs des paramètres des équations (1) et (2) ε_s, q_s, m et c sont données dans les tableaux 4 et 5 respectivement pour les fils propylène et polyester. On remarque que m est caractéristique du matériau alors que c dépend de la température.

Tableau 4 - Paramètres des équations (1) et (2) pour le fil de poly-propylène.

Températures	ε_s	q_s	m	c
20° C	0,01	0,1	4,8	- 5,4
80° C	0,01	0,1	4,8	37
100° C	0,01	0,1	4,8	46,5

Tableau 5 - Paramètres des équations 1 et 2 pour le fil polyester

Températures	ε_s	q_s	m	c
20° C	0,114	0,52	0,688	6,9
40° C	0,114	0,52	0,688	10,3
60° C	0,114	0,52	0,688	12,7
80° C	0,095	0,275	0,688	8,7
100° C	0,095	0,275	0,688	11,5

Les valeurs de déformation à la rupture par fluage ont été comparées à celles obtenues par un essai de traction. Les déformations sont identiques pour le fil polyester (21 % en traction et 23 en fluage) tandis qu'elles sont très notablement différentes pour le fil polypropylène (21 % en traction et 135 % en fluage). En introduisant ces données dans l'équation de fluage on peut comparer les temps de rupture calculés et ceux obtenus expérimentalement (tableau 6).

Tableau 6 - Temps de rupture en fluage des fils polypropylène et polyester

Temps de rupture	Polypropylène 20° C $q_i = 0,45$	Polyester 20° C $q_i = 0,60$
1 essai	218 jours	26 jours
2 "	181 "	
3 "	145 "	27 "
Moyenne	181 "	30 "
Calculé	182 "	29 "

On peut remarquer une bonne concordance entre les temps expérimentaux et les temps calculés.

L'influence de la température sur le fluage pourrait être abordée par une loi du type Arhenius :

$$\frac{d\varepsilon}{dt} = K\, e^{-\frac{Q}{RT}}$$

dans laquelle Q est l'énergie d'activation du système.

Cependant si on regarde les paramètres des équations (1) et (2), on remarque que seul le coefficient c de l'équation 2 varie avec la température. Ceci traduit le fait qu'une augmentation de température provoque une rotation des courbes isochrones autour du point de convergence.

Si on considère deux essais conduits à des températures différentes T_1 et T_2 avec T_2 supérieure à T_1, pour avoir la même déformation, il faut, d'après l'équation (1), que $\alpha_{T_1} = \alpha_{T_2}$. Selon l'équation (2) cela conduit à Ln (α_{T_1}) = Ln $(\alpha_{T_2}) + \dfrac{C_2 - C_1}{m}$,

c'est-à-dire à Ln (α_{T_1}) = Ln $(\alpha_{T_2}) + C^{te}$.

Par suite, si on considère les courbes de fluage dans le système de coordonnées $(\varepsilon - \log t)$, la courbe de l'essai à température T_1 se déduit de la courbe de l'essai à la température T_2 par une translation de cette dernière parallèle à l'axe $\log t$. On peut donc, comme le montre la figure 11 à partir d'un essai mené à une température T_1 jusqu'à un temps t_1, extrapoler la courbe au-delà de ce temps par translation de la courbe obtenue à partir d'un essai conduit à une température T_2.

Fig. 11 – Superposition Temps – Température .

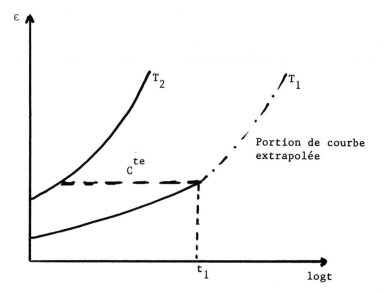

5 - Conclusions

Les essais de fluage réalisés sur des fils polyester et polypropylène ont permis de proposer une équation de fluage, fonction du temps et de la température, qui permet de décrire les trois phases primaire, secondaire et tertiaire du fluage.

La représentation graphique dans le plan (ε, q) a mis en évidence un point de convergence des droites isochrones. Ce point représente la frontière entre le fluage stabilisé et le fluage non stabilisé qui évolue vers la rupture. Pour des contraintes correspondant au fluage stabilisé, c'est-à-dire $q < q_s$, le matériau tend vers une déformation limite égale ou inférieure à ε_s. Pour des contraintes $q > q_s$, la déformation croît avec le temps jusqu'à la rupture.

La surperposition Temps-Température permet d'extrapoler par une simple translation une courbe de fluage à partir de la courbe des essais réalisée à une température plus élevée.

D'autre part, des essais réalisés sur des géotextiles non tissés semblent autoriser une généralisation de cette loi de fluage.

Bibliographie

1) - MIR ARABCHAHI,
     Fluage des matériaux textiles utilisés dans les ouvrages de
     génie civil. Thèse 1985

2) - FINNIGAN J.A.
     The creep Behaviour of high tenacity yarns and fabrics used in
     civil engineering applications - 1er Congrès International des
     Geotextiles - Paris 1977

3) - KABIR M. H.
     In isolation and in soil Behaviour of Geotextiles. Thèses,
     Université de Strathclyde - Glasgow - 1984.

ASSESSMENT OF THE TIME DEPENDENT BEHAVIOUR OF GEOTEXILES FOR REINFORCED SOIL APPLICATIONS

R. T. MURRAY
Transport and Road Research Laboratory

A, McGOWN
University of Strathclyde

Abstract

Geotextiles and related products are being used increasingly for soil reinforcement purposes. Such materials are often cheaper than conventional metallic reinforcements and may be more durable in chemically aggressive soils. However, as they are manufactured from polymers, their load-strain behaviour is both time and temperature dependent. In major structural applications geotextile reinforcements are sometimes required to sustain their design loads in excess of 100 years without rupturing or inducing unacceptably large strains in the structure. Therefore for safe and economic construction of reinforced soil structures it is essential that the long-term load-strain behaviour of geotextile reinforcement be reliably assessed.

This paper gives consideration to the strain and stiffness characteristics of soils and geotextiles and describes procedures which assist in ensuring strain compatibility of the two materials. Methods of testing the time dependent load versus strain characteristics of geotextiles and procedures for more reliably determining the long term behaviour are described. An alternative technique for assessing creep behaviour is introduced which is based on a mathematical interpretation of the visco-elastic and plastic strain behaviour generally considered to characterize polymers. The paper concludes with a discussion on the methods of design of reinforced soil structures taking into account the load-strain properties of geotextiles.

1. Introduction

It has long been recognised that granular soils are strong in compression but have little or no tensile strength. Cohesive soils on the other hand exhibit tensile strength, but as such strength is most commonly associated with negative porewater pressures, some or all of it will be lost in the longer term when an equilibrium porewater pressure condition is attained.

Because of this strength deficiency it is rarely possible, with the exception of some types of naturally cemented soils, to construct significant heights of embankment or cutting at a greater slope than the natural angle of repose of the soil. Until recently the support for steeper slopes or vertical cuts was generally provided by conventional retaining walls of mass or reinforced concrete.

With the development of reinforced soil concepts (Vidal, 1966) an entirely different approach became available in which tensile resistance was imparted to the soil by the incorporation of reinforcement, usually metal strips, at appropriate spacings and direction to achieve the required composite strength. The technique of reinforced soil has been in use for over twenty years and a large number of structures based on this principle have been constructed worldwide. More recently attention has been given to the use of polymeric materials, ie. geotextiles or related products, in place of metallic reinforcement as such materials are often cheaper and may be also more resistant to attack by aggressive soils so that lower quality backfills may be employed leading to further economies.

Much of the development of geotextiles and related products has taken place very recently and it is necessary to develop reliable methods of assessing their load-strain properties when subject to the influence of time, temperature and the soil environment.

This is particularly the case for major structural applications in which the reinforcement layers may be required to sustain their load carrying capacity for periods of 100 years or more without rupturing or inducing unacceptably large strains in the structure.

This paper describes test apparatus and procedures for the assessment of the load-strain properties of geotextiles and related products taking account of their time dependent behaviour, the influence of temperature and confinement in soil. Consideration is also given to the interpretation of the test data and how such data may be extrapolated for extended time scales and employed in the design of reinforced soil structures.

2. Strain considerations in soil and reinforcement

It is not always appreciated that the interaction between reinforcement and soil may be profoundly influenced by the different stiffnesses and strain characteristics of the two materials. This lack of appreciation may be attributable in part to the widespread use of metal reinforcement which strains much less than the soil. Generally, therefore, the strain characteristics of the reinforcements may be ignored and only the strain and corresponding deformation behaviour of the soil need be considered. Moreover, it is reasonable to anticipate that a significant proportion of the tensile strength of such reinforcement will be mobilised at strains that are small in relation to typical soil values.

In contrast, the stiffness characteristics of geotextiles and related products, hereafter referred to simply as geotextiles, ranges from materials with significantly higher stiffness to much lower stiffness than the soil. Moreover, their strain to rupture in relation to the soil can be described as varying from brittle to extremely ductile or extensible. Thus an assessment of the load-extension properties of a geotextile is only meaningful over a range of strains compatible with that for the soil. This can imply that the useable tensile strength of a geotextile can be significantly less than its ultimate strength.

A further consideration is that the relations between stress and strain for soils are frequently quite different in character from the load-strain characteristics of geotextiles. Fig. 1(a) shows schematically the relations between mobilised friction angle and lateral strain for a triaxial compression test carried out on both a dense and a loose sand. The relation for the dense sand shows a rapid increase in strength at small strain to reach a "peak" strength value. During the post-peak stage, shear strength reduces to ultimately attain a constant value at large strains. In contrast the relation for the loose sand shows a gradual increase in strength up to a maximum value at large strain.

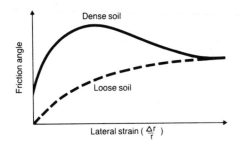

Fig. 1(a) Triaxial test on granular soil

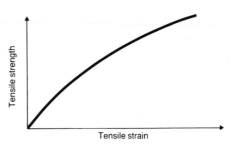

Fig. 1(b) Tensile test on geotextile

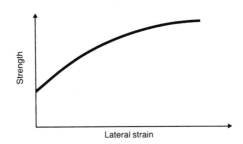

Fig.1(c) Combined strength versus strain relation
for geotextile reinforced soil

The relation between tensile load and strain for a geotextile is shown schematically in Fig. 1(b). The development of the tensile load takes place gradually and continues to increase at large strain until rupture occurs. As can be seen by comparing Figs. 1(a) and 1(b), the peak strength of a dense sand may be associated with a relatively small proportion of the ultimate strength of the geotextile. It is evident on this basis that the commonly employed design procedure for reinforced soils of combining the peak strength of the soil with the ultimate tensile strength of the geotextile and dividing by a factor of safety, may lead to an unsafe design. If, on the other hand, the mobilised strengths of the two materials are combined at equal values of strain, as shown schematically in Fig. 1(c), then the resulting strength versus strain relation provides a more rational basis for design.

A difficulty with the above method is that comprehensive information on the lateral strain behaviour of the soil is required from tests which should correctly represent the stress-strain paths in the reinforced soil structure. An alternative and simpler approach which could be developed is based on the ultimate friction angle at large strain, usually referred to as the friction angle at constant volume ($\emptyset'_{cv}$), indicated in Fig. 1(a) and shown in detail in Fig 2.

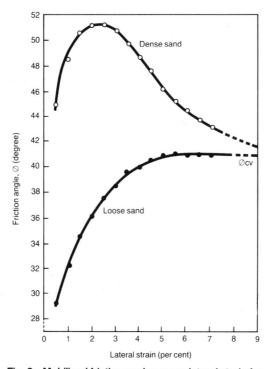

**Fig. 2 Mobilised friction angle versus lateral strain for
Leighton-Buzzard sand from plane-strain test**

As can be seen from this latter figure, after an initial small strain has been developed, the friction angle in the dense sand is always equal to or greater than $\emptyset_{cv}$. Moreover, even with soils in a loose condition (Fig. 1(a)) induced strains produce a gradual increase in mobilised friction angle until the ultimate value of $\emptyset_{cv}$ is attained at large strain. The results of plane strain tests on specimens of dense and loose soil support this pattern of behaviour as shown by the tendency of the data in Fig.2 to converge at large strains. Thus the use of $\emptyset_{cv}$ in design calculations will produce generally safe results with reasonable strain compatibility between the soil and geotextile at both the working and limiting conditions. Failure of dense soils and extensible reinforcement is likely to occur in the post-peak phase of the strength versus strain relation for the soil, whereas the most critical conditions with loose soils and high modulus, relatively brittle reinforcement, are likely to be at small strains.

To enable reliable designs to be produced therefore, it is essential when assessing the load-extension properties of geotextiles to give consideration to the state and characteristics of the soils in which they are to be used.

3.   Strain characteristics of reinforcement and permissable loads

The design of reinforced soil structures employing high modulus reinforcement, with small strains to rupture, such as steel, is generally based on a permissible load approach which does not consider strain in the reinforcement.

ie. Permissible design load = $\dfrac{\text{Yield Load of reinforcement}}{\text{safety factor}}$

For such types of reinforcement this approach is satisfactory as both the immediate and long term strains are very small.

Geotextiles, however, are much more susceptible to strain under load and moreover a significant proportion of strain is frequently time dependent so that a different approach to the determination of permissible load is needed for permanent structures. Thus the interpretation of the interaction between geotextiles and soil is considerably more difficult than for steel or similar "rigid" re-inforcements, particularly where significant creep takes place. However, current practice in design generally does not attempt to evaluate in detail how the materials interact over the life of the structure. Instead the design approach is based on the determination of a "safe" load in the geotextile which ensures that specified strain limits are not exceeded in the longer term. The permissible load is thus calculated from:

Permissible design load

$$= \dfrac{\text{Limit load based on allowable long-term strain}}{\text{Factor of safety}}$$

It is apparent that the permissible load determined on the above basis may be only a small proportion of the short term rupture load of the geotextile.

It should be noted that where a geotextile is characterized as being inextensible relative to the soil, the permissible load would be determined on the same basis as the high modulus materials having small strain to failure.

It may well be that the polyaramids fall into this category although, as far as is known, such materials have not been used yet for major reinforced soil structures in the United Kingdom.

4.   Apparatus and test methods

Because geotextiles are polymeric products, their load carrying capacity is both time and temperature dependent. It is therefore necessary to establish their load-strain behaviour in controlled temperature environments appropriate to the specified application. Moreover, many geotextiles have physical structures which are in-fluenced by the lateral confinement of soil such that their relations between load, strain and time can be significantly altered from the unconfined state. Tensile tests, carried out over a wide range of strain rates, at appropriate temperature may be employed to indirectly obtain these data but involves complex interpretation. A simple, more direct and cost effective technique is the sustained load (creep) method of testing (Andrawes et al, 1986; Murray and McGown, 1987). The test may be carried out on either unconfined or soil-confined specimens using the apparatus shown in Figs 3(a) and 3(b) respectively.

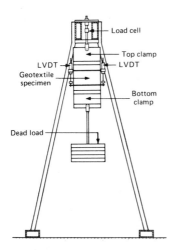

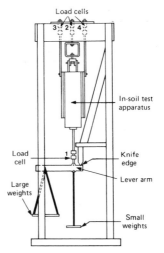

Fig. 3(a) Apparatus used in sustained load test on unconfined geotextile specimen

Fig. 3(b) Apparatus used in sustained load test on confined geotextile specimen

Details of the apparatus and test method are provided in an earlier publication (Murray and McGown, 1987). The procedure involves monitoring the deformation of a geotextile specimen, generally 200 mm wide by 100 mm in length, when subjected to a sustained load. The assessment of the strain-time behaviour should be carried out for a sufficient range of loads to significantly exceed those anticipated for the structure. The minimum number of loads for the assessment should be five, although more will be often required and the maximum load should induce failure in about 1000 hours. Each load is applied rapidly and smoothly to a different specimen of the geotextile and sustained for periods of between 1000 hours for the maximum load and more than 10,000 hours for smaller loads.

5. Test results and their interpretation

Examples of the relations between total strain and time for tests carried out on specimens of a geotextile, plotted to linear scales are shown in Fig.4. The tests were carried out at a constant temperature of 20°C and for periods up to about 8,000 hours. Each curve shown in the figure corresponds to a specific value of sustained load applied during a test.

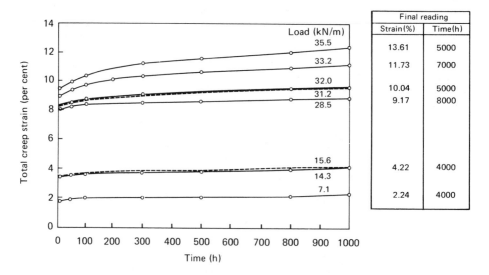

Fig. 4 Creep curves for geotextile at constant temperature of 20°C

The relations shown in Fig.4 are fairly typical of those obtained from sustained load (creep) testing of geotextiles in that during the initial stages of a test the strains develop very rapidly. This is followed by a transition period showing relatively sharp curvature of the relation between strain and time leading into an apparently asymptotic or steady creep rate of long duration.

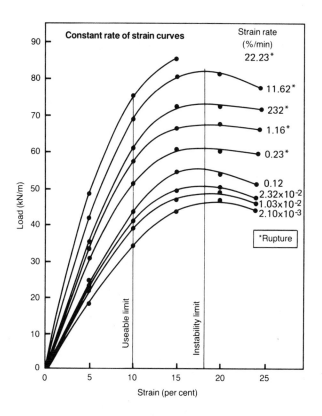

Fig. 5 Constant rate-of-strain test data from tests on geotextile

It has been previously pointed out that constant-rate-of-strain tests can provide data which may be interpreted to produce the same information as obtained from sustained load tests. The results of a series of such tests on the same geotextile as before are shown in Fig. 5. The similarities of the different curves shown in the figure suggests that the data may be normalised with respect to the peak value of load obtained in a test. Although there is some scatter, this tends to be confirmed by Fig.6 in which the normalised data are shown.

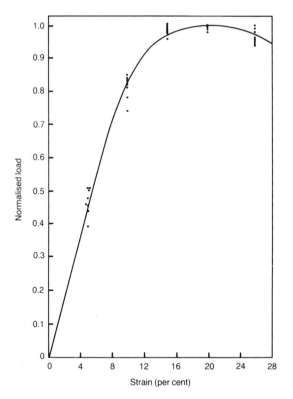

**Fig. 6 Normalised load versus strain results from constant
rate-of-strain tests**

Recent studies referred to by Ward (1984) have concluded that creep of
oriented polymers is associated with visco-elastic behaviour during
which the creep rate reduces with time. However, a further mechanism
may also operate in which permanent plastic flow takes place at a
constant rate ultimately leading to failure. It appears that the
latter process may be avoided with polymers of high molecular weight,
such as are used in the manufacture of geotextiles, provided that the
applied stresses are below a particular level for specific temperature
conditions.

It is essential for polymer reinforcement to operate at a tensile load
significantly below that which would ultimately induce failure within
the required life-span of the structure. The use of Sherby-Dorn plots
(1956) in which log.strain rate is plotted versus total strain, is a
valuable technique for establishing the presence of a steady state
rate of creep and can thus assist in the avoidance of long-term
instability. For such a technique to be effective, however, a
sufficiently long period of testing must be carried out for a range of
tensile loads.

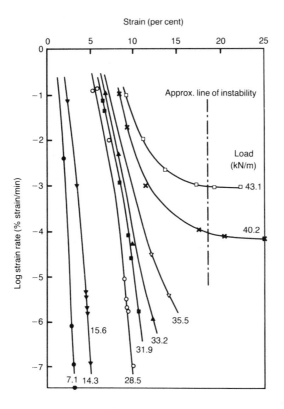

Fig. 7 Sherby-Dorn plots for geotextile at constant temperature of 20°C

The results shown in Fig.4 have been re-plotted in Fig.7 as Sherby-Dorn plots and at the higher testing loads the curves indicate that a steady-state creep rate has been virtually established. In contrast, tests carried out at relatively low tensile loads show no evidence of a constant creep rate developing. A difficulty is that, even with the smaller loads, such a condition could develop at a much later stage of the test.

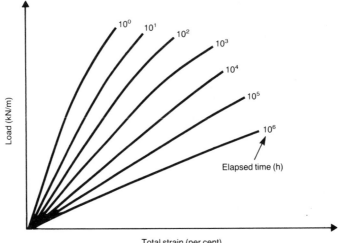

Fig. 8 Load versus strain relations for specific values of time

It is convenient to obtain the relations between load and strain for specific values of time as shown schematically in Fig. 8 as then the appropriate design values to achieve the required life of structure can be selected directly. However, a difficulty is encountered for the larger values of time as the creep data from tests will rarely be of sufficient duration to correspond to the extended life requirements of 100 years or more for major structures in the United Kingdom. To ensure safe and economic designs it is important that extrapolations of the data are reliable.

Estimation of long term creep behaviour for various types of geo-textile can be obtained by a method developed by Findley et al. (1976). The method is referred to as the multiple integral model (Kabir 1984) and the general form of equation for uni-axial loading is as follows:

$$\varepsilon(t,P) = \varepsilon_{t=o} + \varepsilon_t t^n \qquad (1a)$$

where t = elapsed time
P = tensile load

$$\varepsilon_{t=o} = \varepsilon_o = \mu_1 P + \mu_2 P^2 + \mu_3 P^3 \qquad (1b)$$

$$\varepsilon_t = \omega_1 P + \omega_2 P^2 + \omega_3 P^3 \qquad (1c)$$

The constants μ and ω are material functions and are dependent on confining pressure while the exponent n, although a function of the material, may or may not be influenced by other factors.

The method is essentially a polynomial curve fitting technique which attempts to include sufficient terms to allow for the various factors which induce strain in geotextiles. For a linear visco-elastic material only the first order terms would be non-zero. Note that as discussed earlier, separate terms for visco-elastic and plastic modes of creep deformation have not been included as the above expression has only a single component relating to time. In this regard, therefore, it cannot be considered as providing a proper mathematical description of creep behaviour but nonetheless may provide reasonable estimates because of the large number of terms employed in curve fitting.

To apply the method it is necessary to first convert the strain versus time data to the equivalent instantaneous loading case by assuming that application of the tensile load to the specimen occurred linearly over time t_L and that the time t_o corresponding to the instantaneous load case occurred at half this value of time (Fig.9(a). The equivalent relation between strain and time for instantaneous loading is obtained from the recorded data plotted on logarithmic scales as shown in Fig.9b. In all subsequent analysis it is this equivalent relation between strain and time which is used.

Re-arranging Eqn. (1a) and taking logarithms produces the following expression:

$$\log (\epsilon - \epsilon_o) = \log \epsilon_t + n \log t \qquad (2)$$

The above equation indicates that with the proper choice of ϵ_o, a linear relation will be obtained on a plot of $\log (\epsilon - \epsilon_o)$ versus $\log t$ with slope n and intercept $\log \epsilon_t$. Separate linear relations will be obtained for each value of tensile load applied in creep tests on a specific material.

The values of ϵ_o and ϵ_t can be determined on the basis of selected pairs of values of ϵ and t from the instantaneous load relation as follows:

Taking three values of time t_1, t_2 and t_3 and the corresponding

strains ϵ_1, ϵ_2 and ϵ_3

where $t_2 = 10 \, t_1$
and $t_3 = 100 \, t_1$

then $\log (\epsilon_3 - \epsilon_o) = \log \epsilon_t + n \log 100 t_1 \qquad (A)$

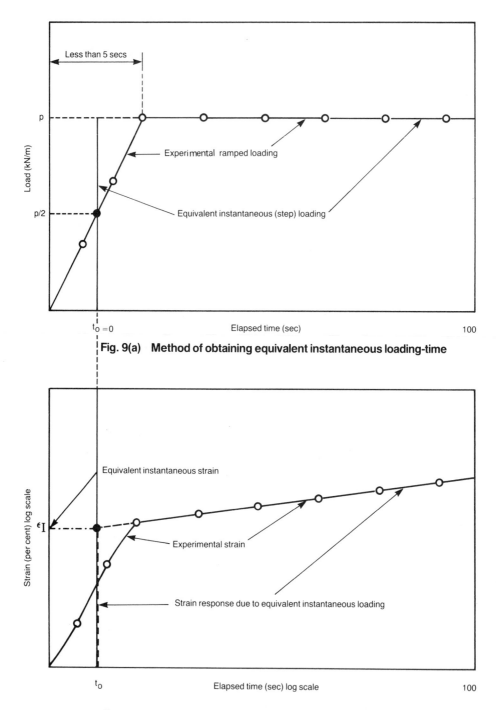

Fig. 9(a) Method of obtaining equivalent instantaneous loading-time

Fig. 9(b) Method of obtaining equivalent instantaneous loading strain

$$\log\left(\varepsilon_2 - \varepsilon_o\right) = \log \varepsilon_t + n \log 10t_1 \qquad \text{(B)}$$

$$\log\left(\varepsilon_1 - \varepsilon_o\right) = \log \varepsilon_t + n \log t_1 \qquad \text{(C)}$$

Subtracting (B) from (A) and (C) from (B) after re-arranging gives:

$$\log \ \frac{\varepsilon_3 - \varepsilon_o}{\varepsilon_2 - \varepsilon_o} \ = n \log 10$$

and $\quad \log \ \dfrac{\varepsilon_2 - \varepsilon_o}{\varepsilon_1 - \varepsilon_o} \ = n \log 10$

$$\frac{\varepsilon_3 - \varepsilon_o}{\varepsilon_2 - \varepsilon_2} = \frac{\varepsilon_2 - \varepsilon_o}{\varepsilon_1 - \varepsilon_o}$$

i.e $\varepsilon_o \ = \dfrac{\varepsilon_2 - \varepsilon_3\varepsilon_1}{(\varepsilon_1 - \varepsilon_3)}$ \qquad (2a)

Note also that for t equal to unity, log t equals zero

$$\varepsilon_t = \varepsilon_{(t=1)} - \varepsilon_o \qquad \text{(2b)}$$

Incorporating the values of ε_o and ε_t obtained from Equation (2) into (A), (B) and (C) and re-arranging allows the exponent, n, to be determined.

ie. $n = [\log \{(\varepsilon - \varepsilon_o)/\varepsilon_t\}]/\log t.$ \qquad (2c)

An alternative procedure for obtaining the values of ε_o and ε_t is based on the differentiated form of Equation (1a).

ie. $\dfrac{d\varepsilon}{dt} = \varepsilon_t . \ nt^{n-1}$ \qquad (3)

Taking logarithms gives:

$$\text{Log}\left(\frac{d\varepsilon}{dt}\right) = \log(n\varepsilon_t) + (n-1) \log t \qquad \text{(4)}$$

Thus a plot of $\dfrac{d\varepsilon}{dt}$ versus t on logarithmic scales (Fig.10a) produces a linear relation of slope (n-1) and intercept $(n\varepsilon_t)$. Once n and ε_t have been determined the value of ε_o can be obtained for the strain relation at unit time (Eqn. 2b):

ie. $\varepsilon_o = \varepsilon_{(t=1)} - \varepsilon_t$ \qquad (2d)

As previously pointed out, different values of ε_o and ε_t will be obtained for the various tensile loads employed in testing and to allow Eqn. (1a) to be used for estimating the creep versus time relation for general load conditions, the terms μ and ω in Equations (1b) and (1c) must be obtained. These values are determined by

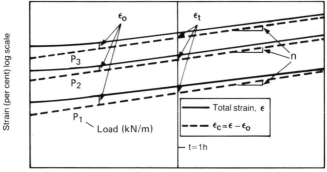

Fig. 10(a)   Curve fitting method to obtain creep parameters

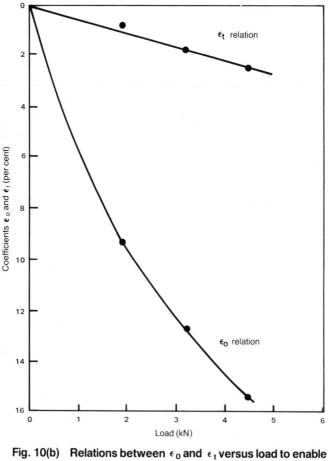

Fig. 10(b)   Relations between ϵ_0 and ϵ_t versus load to enable curve fitting parameters μ and ω to be obtained

fitting a third order polynominal in terms of load P to each of the relations shown in Fig.10b to obtain the respective coefficients μ and ω corresponding to ε_o and ε_t.

The application of this technique to three dissimilar types of geotextile is shown in Fig.11 where it can be seen that fairly reasonable agreement has been obtained.

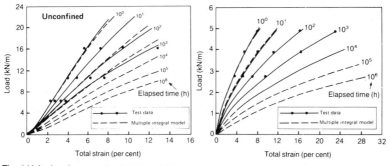

Fig. 11(a)   Isochronous load strain relations
for Geotextile 'A'

Fig. 11(b)   Isochronous load-strain
relations for Geotextile 'B'

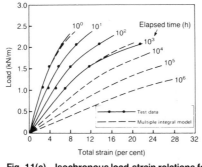

Fig. 11(c)   Isochronous load-strain relations for
Geotextile 'C'

An alternative method of assessing long term creep deformation involves the application of an equation which attempts to consider the visco-elastic and plastic modes of creep deformation separately. The assumption that visco-elastic creep diminishes with time suggests that this behaviour may be described by the equations.

$$\frac{\varepsilon_v}{P} = m_e \; \ell n \; (t - t_o) + C \qquad\qquad (5)$$

where ε_v = creep strain due to visco-elastic behaviour

P = sustained load during a test

m_e = slope of relation due to visco-elastic creep

t_o = time to end of "instant" strains

C = a constant

Now the creep resulting from plastic deformation is constant with time:

ie. $\dfrac{\varepsilon_p}{P} = m_p t$ (6)

where ε_p = strain due to plastic deformation

m_p = slope of relation due to plastic deformation

Thus the total strain (ε_T) is the combination of the two forms of strain:

ie. $\dfrac{\varepsilon_T}{P} = \dfrac{\varepsilon_v}{P} + \dfrac{\varepsilon_p}{P}$

ie. $\dfrac{\varepsilon_T}{P} = m_e \ln (t - t_o) + C + m_p t$ (7)

and $\dfrac{1}{P} \dfrac{d\varepsilon_T}{dt} = \dfrac{m_e}{(t-t_o)} + m_p$ (8)

A plot of strain rate ($\frac{d\varepsilon_T}{dt}$) versus the reciprocal of time ($1/(t-t_o)$) for a particular load (P) should enable the strain rate due to visco-elastic deformation (m_e) and that due to plastic deformation (m_p) to be determined from the slope and intercept respectively of the resulting linear relation (Fig.12).

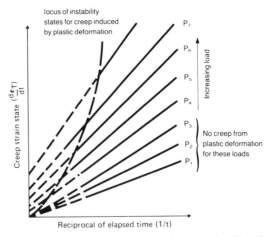

Fig. 12 Relations between creep strain rates and reciprocal of elapsed time shown schematically

A comparison of m_p so obtained with the appropriate load curve on the Sherby-Dorn plot would then allow an estimate to be made of the required test duration. Moreover, the plot could also provide a convenient method of determining the critical load below which creep due to plastic deformation does not occur. In addition, it may prove possible to indicate on the curves the elapsed time at which creep instability occurred in specimens which failed, so allowing the data to be extrapolated to tests in which failure did not occur as shown schematically in Fig.12. Applying the method to data obtained from long term test on the same geotextile indicates that when the sustained load is small (Fig.13a) there is no evidence of steady-state creep. In contrast, when a relatively large sustained load is applied, a steady-state creep rate of 0.015 is obtained (Fig.13b). These results, therefore, provide support for the theory.

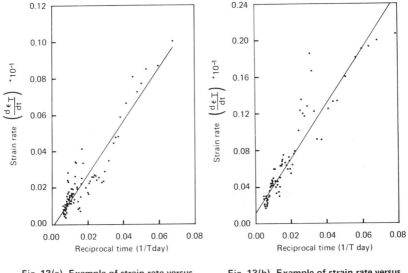

Fig. 13(a)   Example of strain rate versus 1/time relation for geotextile subjected to a load of 7.1 kN

Fig. 13(b)   Example of strain rate versus 1/time relation for geotextile subjected to a load of 44.3 kN

6.   Safety factor considerations in the design of reinforced soil structures

Test are normally carried out on ex-works quality specimens to take account of variations in material properties during manufacture, but for design purposes consideration must be also given to variations which result from construction and environmental damage.

The conventional approach in geotechnical engineering projects for taking account of such variations in material properties as well as the influence of other factors such as construction tolerances, deviations in loads and errors or inaccuracies in design, is to apply an overall factor of safety to the properties determined in testing. However, this approach is not readily applicable to geotextiles because their wide range of strength and deformation behaviour requires that the selection of an appropriate value of safety factor will be specific to the structural requirements and the properties and characteristics of the geotextile to be employed. For this reason it is proposed that partial factors of safety be used to concentrate attention in design to the various factors affecting behaviour. The partial factors that should be considered for this purpose are listed in Table 1. The values of the partial factors γ_{fl} and γ_{f3} are normally provided in Codes of Practice in relation to the many other materials used in civil engineering (eq. B.S. 5400, 1980). However, γ_{m1} and γ_{m2} are product related and must be determined for a specific material in a particular application, eq. soil reinforcement. The value of γ_{m1} is determined from the variation in properties between control specimens and normal production material under strictly controlled laboratory conditions and should include constant rate of strain tests and sustained load (creep) tests to assess strength variability in both the short and long term.

The partial factor γ_{m2}, which is a reflection of strength variation due to site damage and several other factors associated with con- struction and environmental effects, is also best evaluated from comparisons with the strength of control specimens. The data should be supplemented by results of tests on geotextiles subjected to appropriate site damage trials and exposed under stressed conditions in the anticipated environmental conditions.

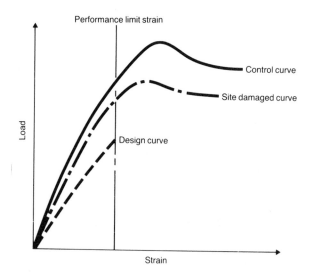

Fig. 14 Relations between load and strain shown schematically to demonstrate site damage effects

Fig.14 shows schematically how the load versus strain relation for a specific value of time may be affected by site damage. It is important to note that although a significant reduction in ultimate strength has occurred, because the value employed in design is governed by limitations of strain the effect on the design load is less dramatic. This point should be considered when a value of γ_{m2} is being determined.

Table 1.   PARTIAL FACTORS CONTRIBUTING TO THE OVERALL FACTOR OF SAFETY

PARTIAL FACTOR	PURPOSE
γ_{m_1}	To cover the possible reductions in material properties compared to the properties of control specimens.
γ_{m_2}	To cover for site damage and construction or manufacturing tolerance on site, such as mis-alignment, undulations and mis-shaped products.
γ_{fL}	To cover unfavourable deviations in loads.
γ_{f3}	To cover errors or inaccuracies in the design method.

Overall Factor of Safety = $(\gamma_{m_1} \times \gamma_{m_2} \times \gamma_{fL} \times \gamma_{f3})$

7.   Conclusions

1.   The differences in the strain and stiffness characteristics of soil and geotextiles have been considered and the importance of ensuring strain compatibility between the two materials discussed. It was pointed out that the present method of employing the peak friction angle of the soil together with the ultimate tensile strength of the geotextiles could lead to unsafe design. The use of the constant volume friction angle ($\emptyset_{cv}$) offers greater load and strain compatibility between the two materials and avoids the dangers of rapid post-peak failure which could result from a combination of peak soil strength and highly extensible reinforcement.

2.   Methods of testing and interpreting the time-dependent behaviour of geotextiles have been described together with procedures for obtaining more reliable predictions of long term behaviour. These procedures have been used for determining the time dependent behaviour of three widely dissimilar geotextiles and it

71

has been shown that reasonable agreement can be obtained with their observed behaviour.

3. It is generally recognized that the long term deformation behaviour of geotextiles is associated with both visco-elastic and plastic strain mechanisms. It was considered that the equation describing long term behaviour should incorporate separate terms for each of these strain mechanisms. As the procedure employed for predicting long term behaviour and referred to as the multiple-integral method only accounts for a single strain mechanism, the success of the method was attributed to the large number of terms used in curve fitting.

4. An alternative to the multiple-integral method of determining long term load-strain behaviour involved the introduction of an equation which attempts to provide a better mathematical des-cription of time dependent behaviour by incorporating separate terms for visco-elastic and plastic strain mechanisms. Con-ceptually, the method seems to offer greater scope for obtaining the parameters controlling time-dependent strains but will require further study to assess its validity.

5. It was considered that the use of partial factors in design could have advantages over the overall (or lumped) factor of safety method employed with conventional reinforced soil struc-ture design involving steel reinforcement. In particular, partial factors allow account to be taken of the influence of the variations in material properties, site damage, construction and design tolerances. They may also take account of long term load strain behaviour so that more rational values can be used for design purposes.

8. Acknowledgements

The work described in this report was carried out in the Ground Engineering Division of the Structures Group of the TRRL and in the Department of Civil Engineering of the University of Strathclyde. The Authors would like to acknowledge the contribution of BE Division of the Department of Transport who also advocated the use of partial factors of safety. This paper is published by permission of the Director, TRRL.

9. References

Andrawes, K Z. McGown, A. and Murray, R T. (1986) - The load-strain-time temperature behaviour of geotextiles and geogrids. Proc. Third Int. Conf. on Geotextiles. Vol III, Session 7A, Vienna, pp. 707-712.

British Standards Institution (1980) BS.5400 - Steel, concrete and composite bridges. British Standards Institution, London.

Findley, W.N. LAI, J.S. and Onaran, K. (1976) - Creep and relaxation of non-linear visco-elastic materials. North Holland Publishing Company, Oxford.

Kabir, M.H. (1984) In isolation and in-soil behaviour of Geotextiles. PhD Thesis, University of Strathclyde, Glasgow.

Murray, R.T. and McGown, A. (1987) Testing of geotextiles and related products. Dept. of Transport, TRRL Application Guide AG5, Crowthorne (Transport and Road Research Laboratory).

Sherby, O.D. and Dorn, J.E. (1956) Anelastic creep of polymethylmethacrylate. Journal of Mech. Physics, Solids, Vol. 6, pp. 145.

Ward, I.M. (1984) The orientation of polymers to produce high performance materials. Proc. of Conference on Polymer Grid Reinforcement, March 1984, London.

Vidal, H. (1966) La Terre Armée, Annales de I'Institut Technique du Batiment et des Travoux Public, France, Nos 223-226, pp. 887-938.

LE COMPORTEMENT MÉCANIQUE À LONG TERME DES GÉOTEXTILES ET SA PRISE EN COMPTE DANS LE DIMENSIONNEMENT D'OUVRAGES

PH. DELMAS

Laboratoire des Ponts et Chaussées, Paris

1. Introduction

Dans le cadre de cet article, on n'abordera que le comportement des ouvrages dans lesquels les géotextiles sont soumis à des charges permanentes. On ne traitera pas des charges dynamiques ou cycliques (pistes de chantier, ouvrages soumis à séismes,...).

Les recherches sur le renforcement des sols par les géotextiles réalisées depuis une dizaine d'années ont permis de mettre en évidence, d'étudier et de caractériser l'aptitude des géotextiles à renforcer le sol, c'est-à-dire à limiter ses déformations sous un chargement déterminé, ou à augmenter sa capacité de chargement, en particulier lors des déformations élevées.

En comparaison aux armatures à haut module de déformation, les géotextiles entraînent un comportement très spécifique du massif renforcé. Ainsi de nombreux auteurs (Mc Gown et al.,1978; Blivet et al.,1979) ont montré l'importance de la raideur du géotextile, ainsi que du niveau de déformation du sol renforcé, sur la rhéologie de ce matériau composite soumis à des chargements instantanés.

De manière analogue, on a pu montré l'influence du déplacement relatif sol-géotextile sur la loi de mobilisation de l'adhérence et du frottement ainsi que celle de la raideur du géotextile sur les résultats d'essais d'extraction (Delmas, 1979; Collios et al. 1979).

Ces deux exemples de comportement particuliers sont l'image d'un comportement plus général qui a conduit de nombreux auteurs (Holtz, 1977; Gourc, 1982) a mettre l'accent sur l'importance de la prise en compte de la relative déformabilité des géotextiles. D'une manière générale, on retiendra donc que les méthodologies de dimensionnement amènent à définir un nouveau concept de rupture, dont le critère n'est pas lié uniquement à la résistance en traction du renforcement, mais aussi à la déformation admissible de l'ouvrage.

Il s'en suit que la connaissance du comportement à long terme du géotextile, et en particulier au fluage, est un élément nécessaire au dimensionnement des ouvrages définitifs de renforcement. Cependant dans les nouvelles approches qui peuvent être élaborées dans ce sens, il est important de garder une vue globale du phénomène et en particulier de ne pas oublier qu'un ouvrage renforcé est constitué d'un matériau composite. Une modélisation optimale devra prendre en compte, outre le comportement au fluage du renforcement, la rhéologie à long terme du sol (consolidation et fluage) ainsi que celle de l'interface. On notera en outre que dans l'hypothèse d'emploi d'un sol argileux à teneur en eau élevée l'utilisation d'un géotextile multi-fonction (renforcement - drain) pourra s'avérer judicieuse. Ceci nécessitera donc la prise en compte simultanément des propriétés mécaniques et hydrauliques des géotextiles. En conclusion, compte tenu de la complexité des phénomènes en jeu, l'emploi de méthode de calcul en déformations, et en particulier le recours à la méthode aux éléments finis, sera pratiquement indispensable pour arriver à une modélisation fine du comportement des ouvrages. Cependant, cela n'exclut pas la mise au point de méthodes de calcul opérationnelles simples pour les dimensionnements courants.

2. Réflexions sur l'étude du fluage des matériaux : sol, géotextile

Pour être validée, la modélisation choisie devra s'appuyer sur deux approches distinctes:

- la première visera à caractériser in-situ ou sur modèles réduits le comportement global d'ouvrages renforcés.

- la deuxième cherchera à connaître la réponse propre des matériaux dans le but d'en déterminer des modèles rhéologiques satisfaisants, ainsi que les paramètres correspondants.

Concernant la première approche, on dispose actuellement de très peu de données. Les ouvrages de renforcement existants datent au plus de 15 ans et cette période est encore courte pour tirer des enseignements. D'autre part les premiers ouvrages ont été construits avec des sols de bonnes caractéristiques mécaniques peu susceptibles de fluer.

Or, il faut noter que l'avenir du développement des
géotextiles se situe dans l'emploi de sols peu élaborés,
voire de récupération, et donc de caractéristiques mécaniques médiocres, en particulier à long terme. D'autre part
les taux de travail, et donc les niveaux de déformation des
géotextiles, utilisés jusqu'ici dans les ouvrages de
renforcement définitifs restent très faibles (ϵ <4%). Les
risques d'apparition d'un fluage important du renforcement
entraînant des déformations sensibles sont donc assez res-
treints sur les ouvrages existants.

La deuxième approche, quant à elle, a déjà fait l'objet d'un certain nombre d'investigations en laboratoire
tant en ce qui concerne les sols que les géotextiles.

* En ce qui concerne les sols, de nombreux auteurs (plus
de 60 en trente ans) se sont attachés à étudier en laboratoire le comportement au fluage déviatorique. Cependant
actuellement bien que le comportement des sols soit mieux
connu, il n'existe pas de loi contrainte-déformation-temps
universellement admise. Parmi les difficutés rencontrées on
notera:

- Le caractère multiphasique du matériau sol. Sur ce
point en particulier l'étude des ouvrages renforcés par
géotextiles sera d'autant plus délicate qu'en général le
sol utilisé en remblai est non saturé et que la mécanique
des sols non-saturés est encore embryonnaire.
- Les conditions expérimentales sont très délicates, et
dépendent entre autres du mode de préparation des échantillons, du type d'essai, etc ...

* En ce qui concerne les géotextiles, les études sur le
fluage sont plus récentes. Aussi, au stade actuel, on se
contentera d'encourager les recherches s'appuyant sur des
essais de laboratoire aussi représentatifs que possible des
conditions de travail in-situ (déformations planes, température, hygrométrie, etc ...).

3. Généralités sur la modélisation du comportement au
   fluage des matériaux

De manière générale, et ceci vaut autant pour les géotextiles que pour les sols, bien que les moyens de calculs
actuels soient relativement puissants et poussent à définir
des lois de calcul complexes, il s'avère souvent difficile
de déterminer à posteriori en laboratoire les paramètres
correspondants. Il sera important dans le choix des lois de
modélisation choisies de garder à l'esprit le fait qu'elles

devront être à la fois suffisamment simples pour pouvoir être employées couramment, et suffisamment complexes pour rendre compte correctement des résultats expérimentaux.

L'expérience acquise sur la rhéologie des matériaux a permis de mettre en évidence que la variation de pression hydrostatique n'a pratiquement pas d'influence sur les courbes de fluage des matériaux. Aussi on admet généralement que seule la contrainte déviatorique peut entrainer une déformation plastique. C'est pourquoi on se limitera dans la suite à l'étude des matériaux soumis à une contrainte déviatorique.

La formulation de la loi de comportement du matériau nécessite certaines hypothèses simplificatrices pour être applicable. En ce qui concerne les théories, on distingue principalement deux approches:

- la formulation différentielle qui relie le tenseur des contraintes aux dérivées successives du tenseur du gradient des déformations,

- la formulation intégrale qui relie le tenseur des contraintes aux déplacements correspondant à l'intégration des déformations dans le passé (théorie de Boltzman par exemple).

Dans la pratique, on retiendra que les théories de type différentiel sont adaptées à des mouvements lents, alors que les théories de type intégral sont adéquates pour décrire les petites déformations. Dans le cas des ouvrages de renforcement par géotextiles on se situera dans la deuxième hypothèse.

Un échantillon de matériau, soumis à un état de contrainte déviatorique constant, subira dans le temps une déformation du type présenté sur la fig. 1. Bien que le comportement de l'interface sol-géotextile n'ait fait l'objet à ce jour de nombreuses recherches, on pourra considérer à priori que la modélisation du fluage du contact est similaire.

On définit trois phases de fluage: le fluage primaire (vitesse décroissante), le fluage secondaire (vitesse constante), le fluage tertiaire (vitesse croissante conduisant à la rupture). Ces trois phases ne sont pas atteintes systématiquement, le comportement dépend en effet, non seulement de la durée de l'essai et du type de matériau, mais aussi du niveau de contrainte. Ainsi certains auteurs ont mis en évidence une limite de fluage en dessous de laquelle le matériau se comporterait comme un solide visqueux (vitesse nulle pour un temps infini): ainsi pour les sols Ter-Stepanian (1963) et Biarez et Boucek (1973), et pour les géotextiles Mir-Arabchahi (1985). Sans vouloir être exhaustif, on pourra retenir les généralités suivantes.

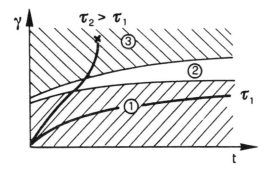

Fig. 1. Courbes de fluage schématiques. Distorsion en fonction du temps pour une contrainte constante.
Fluage primaire (1), secondaire (2), tertiaire (3)

En ce qui concerne le fluage amorti, de nombreux auteurs ont défini des lois, cependant beaucoup s'accordent
pour appliquer la loi de Singh et Mitchell (1968):

$$\gamma(t) = A \cdot e^{\alpha \, (\tau / \tau_r)} \cdot (t_1/t)^m$$

Des valeurs des paramètres (A, α, m) ont été déterminées pour de nombreux matériaux sols ou géotextiles en
particulier. Si cette loi reproduit bien les essais de
laboratoire, elle présente l'inconvénient de donner une
vitesse infinie au temps t = 0. De plus elle ne modélise
qu'un déviateur constant dans le temps.

Parmi les autres formulations présentées, on citera
entre autres la loi exponentielle proposée par Kabir(1984)
pour interpréter ses essais de fluage sur géotextiles:

$$\epsilon = \epsilon_0 + \epsilon_t \cdot t^n$$

La phase de fluage secondaire permet, lors de la
modélisation, de relier directement les vitesses de déformation aux contraintes. Parmi les lois existantes, on citera
en particulier la loi de Bingham(1916):

$$\dot{\gamma} = (\tau - \tau_0) / \mu \qquad \text{si } \tau > \tau_0$$

$$\dot{\gamma} = 0 \qquad \text{si } \tau \leqslant \tau_0$$

Le point faible de cette loi se situe surtout au niveau de l'hypothèse de linéarité faite pour les valeurs de τ supérieures à τ_0. On notera que pour les sols on propose généralement de prendre la résistance résiduelle comme valeur de seuil.

La phase de fluage tertiaire est plus délicate à aborder. En effet la rupture n'est pas toujours simple à définir: déformation arbitraire ou vitesse de déformation arbitraire. Il semble toutefois que dans le cas des sols, d'après Singh et Mitchell (1969), on puisse définir le produit du temps jusqu'à la rupture par la vitesse moyenne de déformation déviatorique comme paramètre intrinsèque du sol. En tout état de cause la connaissance de cette troisième phase sera importante dans le dimensionnement des ouvrages définitifs afin de s'assurer qu'elle ne puisse être atteinte pendant la durée de vie de l'ouvrage.

4. Approches de la prise en compte du temps dans les ouvrages renforcés par géotextile

Dans la pratique, et compte tenu de l'état des connaissances sur les caractéristiques à long terme des sols et des géotextiles, il ne semble pas possible d'envisager dans un proche avenir de réaliser pour des études courantes des calculs en déformation.

Actuellement, les méthodes de dimensionnement opérationnelles sont principalement des méthodes à la limite; (on exclura volontairement la méthode des déplacements (Delmas et al., 1986) qui fera l'objet d'une analyse particulière).

Le dimensionnement se fait en supposant la rupture simultanée du sol et des renforcements. La tenue de l'ouvrage est assurée par la prise en compte de coefficient de sécurité sur les paramètres du calcul. Le calcul de stabilité vérifie que l'équilibre de l'ouvrage est assuré moyennant la réduction des paramètres par les coefficients de sécurité. Dans ce cas, la prise en compte du fluage ne pourra donc être réalisée que par une réduction forfaitaire de la résistance en traction des géotextiles. En outre, il ne permet de tenir compte ni des déformations du sol dans le temps ni d'un éventuel fluage au niveau du contact sol-géotextile.

Plusieurs démarches sont alors envisageables:

- ne pas solliciter les géotextiles au delà du seuil de fluage; c'est la démarche suivie par Delmas et al.

(1986) qui s'appuyant en particulier sur les résultats de la thèse de Mir-Arabchahi (1985) propose des coefficients réducteurs différentiés suivant le type de polymère:

polyester	T/T_R	0.20
polypropylène	T/T_R	0.10

- tolérer des contraintes dans les géotextiles supérieures au seuil de fluage et appliquer des coefficients réducteurs qui garantissent une vitesse de fluage suffisamment faible pour ne pas entraîner des déplacements inadmissibles pour l'ouvrage. Cette approche nécessite de pouvoir se fixer à priori une déformation admissible du géotextile qui n'entraine pas de déplacements ou de déformations intolérables pour l'ouvrage. Elle suppose alors de pouvoir déterminer, pour cette déformation admissible du géotextile et le temps correspondant à la durée de vie de l'ouvrage, l'effort de tension dans le géotextile employé (Andrawes et al., 1986). Cet effort peut alors être pris en compte dans un calcul de stabilité à la rupture. Cette approche reste cependant délicate d'utilisation dans la mesure où le calcul ne permet pas de relier les déformations dans le géotextile aux déplacements du massif et prend en compte implicitement une adhérence parfaite sol-géotextile.

Dans le même ordre d'idées, on pourra citer l'approche de Koerner (1980) qui propose une relation empirique entre les caractéristiques au fluage du sol et celles souhaitables pour le géotextile (Tableau 1).

Tableau 1 - Valeurs de coefficients de fluage proposés par Koerner (1980)

Geotextile Reinforcement Application	Ratios of Creep Equation Constants (f refers to fabric; s refers to soil)		
	$\dfrac{m_f}{m_s}$	$\dfrac{\alpha_f}{\alpha_s}$	$\dfrac{A_f}{A_s}$
Roadway Subgrade Reinforcement			
soft (CBR < 5)	1.2	.5	.3
medium (5 ≤ CBR ≤ 20)	1.1	.7	.5
firm (CBR > 20)	1.0	.9	.7
Slope Stability Reinforcement			
shell	1.0	.9	.8
core	1.0	.7	.6
foundation	1.0	.8	.7
Retaining Wall/Containment Systems			
soft	1.2	.5	.3
medium	1.1	.7	.5
compact	1.0	.9	.7

La méthode des déplacements: prise en compte du temps.

A la frontière entre les méthodes de calcul à la limite et les méthodes en déformation, la méthode des déplacements (Delmas et al.,1986; Gourc et al.,1986) permet une exploitation différente des lois de comportement au fluage des géotextiles.

Dans son principe de base il s'agit d'une méthode à la à la limite qui suppose l'existence d'une surface de rupture dans le sol le long de laquelle se génèrent des déplacements. Ces déplacements entraînent des déformations dans les géotextiles et par conséquent une mobilisation d'efforts résistants. Dans la pratique le calcul est réalisé en prenant en compte un comportement élastique linéaire du géotextile et en supposant que la loi de contact est de forme élasto-plastique.

Dans la perspective de travaux futurs sur la prise en compte du temps dans les ouvrages renforcés, plusieurs lois de comportement au fluage des géotextiles ont été essayées. Le principe même du calcul impose de supposer que le sol a un comportement rigide plastique, et donc ne flue pas. De même, on supposera que la loi de contact n'est pas modifiée dans le temps, que le fluage des géotextiles ne modifie pas l'état de contrainte dans le sol et que la surface de rupture n'est pas modifiée.

Les différents essais de modélisation ont montré que la loi exponentielle permettait une exploitation simple de la méthode des déformations (programme CARTAGE). Si l'on suppose donc que le géotextile est régi par une loi de la forme:

$$\epsilon (\alpha,t) = \epsilon_0 + \epsilon_t . t^n$$

il est possible de coupler facilement la loi de comportement du géotextile à la loi de comportement du contact. Or pour un niveau de déformation initial faible, il est en outre possible de considérer que ϵ_0 et ϵ_t sont des fonctions linéaires de l'effort de traction α. La résolution devient alors très simple, on a alors:

$$\epsilon = A_0.\alpha + A_t.\alpha.t^n$$

ce qui permet de définir une raideur en traction J équivalente, pour un textile soumis à un effort de traction T, durant un temps t:

$$J (t) = (A_0 + A_t.t^n)^{-1}$$

A titre d'exemple si on s'appuie sur les résultats obtenus par Kabir (1985) pour un nontissé aiguilleté de polyester de 300g et pour un tissé de polyprylène de caractéristiques mécaniques équivalentes, on peut écrire:

pour le non tissé de polyester (NTAPES)

$$J(t) = (0.04 + 0.005\, t^{0.08})^{-1} \qquad \text{avec} \qquad \alpha_R = 18 \text{ kN/m}$$

pour le tissé de polypropylène (TPP)

$$J(t) = (0.008 + 0.014\, t^{0.15})^{-1} \qquad \text{avec} \qquad \alpha_R = 16 \text{ kN/m}$$

Le programme CARTAGE permet alors de faire un calcul à la limite, pour un temps donné, et en particulier d'évaluer le déplacement induit sur le massif renforcé. A titre d'exemple, si l'on considère l'ouvrage présenté sur la fig. 2, dans l'hypothèse d'une rupture du sol ($F_{sol} = 1$), on peut calculer l'évolution du décrochement en tête en fonction du temps (fig.3).

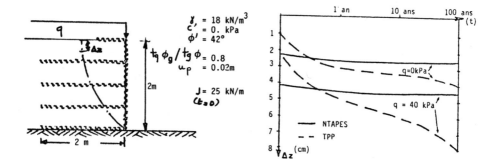

Fig. 2. Exemple de calcul.

Fig. 3. Déplacement en tête fonction du temps pour 2 géotextiles et pour 2 surcharges

Cette première tentative encourageante pour prendre en compte le temps dans l'étude des ouvrages renforcés par géotextiles demandera à être approfondie et validée sur des observations d'ouvrages expérimentaux ou de modèles réduits en laboratoire.

5. Conclusion

La généralisation de la construction d'ouvrages définitifs renforcés par géotextile nécessite la mise au point
de méthodes de dimensionnement qui permettent de tenir
compte du comportement dans le temps des différents matériaux constituants, sol et géotextile, ainsi que celui de
l'interface.

Cependant au stade actuel des connaissances, on ne
dispose pas de moyens simples et opérationnels de détermination des paramètres de comportement des matériaux à
entrer dans les calculs. D'autre part les outils de calculs
en déformation sont encore souvent d'un emploi très lourd,
et on ne peut envisager de les utiliser pour des études
courantes.

Il conviendra donc en attendant les résultats des
recherches en cours d'évaluer le poids respectif des propriétés de chaque matériau dans les déformations à long
terme des ouvrages. Ainsi, dans l'hypothèse où le sol
utilisé possède de bonnes caractéristiques mécaniques, en
particulier à long terme, le comportement au fluage du
géotextile deviendra prépondérant dans celui de l'ouvrage.
On pourra alors proposer des développements des méthodes
présentées ci-dessus (méthode en déplacement, par exemple).

Par contre l'emploi de sols aux caractéristiques médiocres susceptibles de subir des déformations importantes
à long terme (consolidation ou fluage) nécessitera de
limiter leur utilisation à des ouvrages susceptibles de
supporter ces déformations. On notera en particulier que
l'emploi de géotextiles multifonction, qui permettra sans
aucun doute des développements très intéressants de la
technique du renforcement, nécessitera le couplage de la
modélisation mécanique et hydraulique en fonction du temps.

Si des modélisations sont d'ores et déjà envisageables
par le biais des calculs en éléments finis en particulier,
il est important de garder à l'esprit que le développement
de la technique ne pourra se faire que sous réserve de la
mise au point d'outils de calcul d'emploi simple et largement diffusables.

Bibliographie

Andrawes K.Z., McGown A., Murray R.T., (1986)"The load
strain time temperature behaviour of geotextiles and
geogrids." C.R. IIIè Int. Conf. Geotextiles, Vienna, vol.3,
pp.707-712.

Biarez J., Boucek B., (1973),"Viscoplasticité de l'argile in-situ et en laboratoire." C.R. VIII^{è} ICSMFE, Moscou, vol.1, pp. 51-56.

Blivet J.C., Gestin F.,(1979),"Etude de l'adhérence entre le phosphogypse et deux géotextiles." C.R. Coll. Int. Renf. sols, vol.2, Paris, pp.403,408.

Collios A., Delmas Ph., Gourc J.P., Giroud J.P. (1980) "Experiments on soil reinforcement with geotextiles. The use of geotextiles for soil improvement", ASCE Nat. Conv., Portland, pp. 53-73.

Delmas Ph., (1979), "Sols renforcés par géotextiles. Premières études." Thè. Doct. Ing. IRIGM Uni. Grenoble, p. 202.

Delmas Ph., Berche J.C., Gourc J.P., (1986),"Le dimension-nement des ouvrages renforcés par géotextile - le programme CARTAGE." Bul. Liai. P. et Ch., n°142, pp.33,44.

Gourc J.P., (1982),"Quelques aspects du comportement des géotextiles en mécanique des sols." Thè. Doct. ès sciences, Uni. Grenoble, p.249.

Gourc J.P., Ratel A., Delmas Ph., (1986) "Design of retai-ning walls: the 'displacements method'" C.R. III^{è} Int. Conf. Geotextiles, Vienna, vol3, pp. 289-294.

Holtz R.D. (1977) "Laboratory studies of reinforced earth using a woven polyester fabric." C.R. I^{r} Int. Conf. Geotex-tiles, Paris, vol. 3, pp.149-154.

Kabir M.H., (1985), "In insolation and in soil behaviour of geotextiles." Phd Uni. Strathclyde, Glasgow.

Koerner R.M., Rosenfarb J.L., Dougherty W.W., McElroy J.J.,(1980), "Strain stress time behaviour of geotextiles in uniaxial tension. Use of geotextile for soil improve-ment". ASCE Nat. Conv., Portland, pp.31-52.

Mc Gown A., Andrawes K.Z., Al-Hasani M.M., (1978),"Effect of inclusion properties on the behaviuor of sand." Géo-technique, (28), 3, 327-346.

Mir Arabchahi N., (1985), "Fluage des matériaux textiles utilisés dans les ouvrages de génie civil." Thè. Doc. Ing. Ecole Centrale Paris.

Singh A., Mitchell J.K., (1968), "General stress strain time function for soils." J. of Soil Mech. a Found. Div. ASCE, 94, SM1, 21-46.

Singh A., Mitchell J.K., (1969), "Creep potentiel and creep rupture of soils." C.R. VII^{è} ICSMFE, Mexico, vol.1, pp.379-384.

Ter Stepanian G. (1963),"On the long term stability of slopes." Norvegian Geot. Inst., Oslo, n°52, pp.1-13.

EXAMINATIONS OF LONG-TERM FILTERING BEHAVIOUR OF GEOTEXTILES

F. SAATHOFF

Franzius Institut für Wasserbau und Kusteningenieurwesen der Universität Hannover

1. Introduction

In a given application, a geotextile can perform several different functions, but in the majority of practical applications, the primary or secondary function of a geotextile is to serve as a filter. At every location where a filter forms a substantial part of the construction, the service life depends upon the maintenance of the phase separation functions of the filter. In general, all filters have to fulfill two basic requirements, a soil retention capability (mechanical filter efficiency) and a vertical water permeability (hydraulic filter efficiency). Common parameters for the filter design of geotextiles include the opening size of the geotextile, grain-size diameter and uniformity of the existing soil for the assessment of the mechanical filter efficiency and for a comparison of the water permeability coefficients of soil and geotextile.

During the filter stabilization phase, a reduction of the permeability of the virgin geotextile - as with mineral filters - is inevitably produced by soil contact (deep filtration, clogging, cake filtration, blocking). After the filter stabilization phase, the permeability normal to the plane of the soil-polluted geotextile must remain equal to or larger than the permeability coefficient of the soil present even in the boundary layer soil-geotextile in order to ensure an almost head-loss-free drain-off of water.

This paper gives a summary of the results from different research programmes of the FRANZIUS-INSTITUT FOR HYDRAULIC RESEARCH AND COASTAL ENGINEERING of the University of Hannover concerning the testing of the long-term filtration properties of geotextiles. Other properties such as mechanical or chemical ones will not be discussed here (results on long-term resistance of geotextiles based upon the investigations are given, for example, in Heerten (1982) and in the different reports of the FRANZIUS-INSTITUT).

All investigation programmes consist of three parts:

(a) Excavation of various geotextiles after many years of service.
(b) Investigation of the properties of the excavated geotextiles using testing methods.
(c) Comparison of the results from excavated and virgin geotextiles.

2. Test Procedures

The properties by which the filtering behaviour can be described are "the effective opening size" and the "water permeability coefficient normal to the plane of the geotextile". The testing methods used in Germany are based upon methods developed at the FRANZIUS-INSTITUT, and may briefly be described as follows (Saathoff and Kohlhase, 1986).

2.1 Determination of the effective opening size

The effective opening size, D_w, of the geotextile is determined by wet-sieving with a chosen test sand. During the test the fabric operates as a sieve, as shown in Figure 1. A grain-size analysis of the retained material and that of the material passing the geotextile leads to the effective opening size by a fixed equation method.

Due to wet-sieving with a test sand, the testing of soil-contaminated geotextiles which have been installed for many years is not possible. The passage of soil through the geotextiles must be determined on the basis of the grain-size distribution of the contacting soils and the soil deposition within the geotextile.

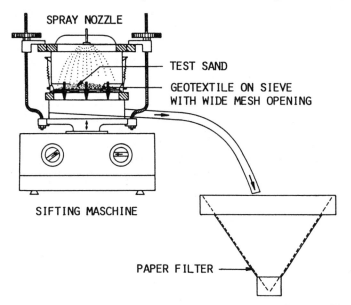

Fig. 1. Test equipment for the determination of the effective opening size (Saathoff and Kohlhase, 1986).

2.2 Determination of the permeability normal to the plane of the geotextile

The permeability value normal to the plane of the geotextile, k_v, is determined by a permeability test using a constant hydrostatic head generated by two overflow reservoirs and by making use of Darcy's law with a constant pressure head in the permeability cell acting on a packet consisting of several layers. Figure 2 shows the test equipment.

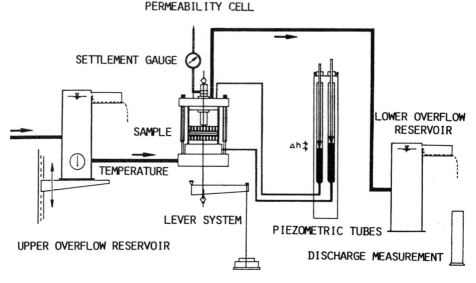

Fig. 2. Test equipment for the determination of the permeability
normal to the plane of the geotextile (Saathoff and
Kohlhase, 1986).

In addition, this testing method allows the determination of the
permeability of aged geotextiles in service within the structure for
several years which have been carefully excavated. In order to
ensure that there is no change in the clogging rate (the amount of
incorporated soil material) during transport and storage of the samples, attention is given to ensure that there is no variation in the
moisture content and that the samples are carefully handled.

3. Research Programmes of the Franzius-Institut

From several special investigation programmes, the following results
which are subdivided into coastal engineering and shore protection,
inland waterway and embankment dam constructions, and railway
and road applications, can be presented.

3.1 Coastal engineering and shore protection

The field investigations on coastal engineering structures were the
most important part of the different research programmes.
    The field of coastal engineering was the starting point for the
use of geotextiles in geotechnics in Germany in the 1950s. Pioneers
first used synthetic fabrics to form huge sand bags for building
groynes and closing dikes.
    Geotextiles today are commonly used, for example, in the con-
struction of seawalls, as a separation layer in groynes and break-
water constructions, and as flexible scour protection mats.

From 1978 to 1980 the FRANZIUS-INSTITUT has carried out extensive field investigations on the long-term behaviour of geotextiles in coastal structures on the German North Coast in order to safeguard the coast and to broaden knowledge on long-term resistance (Heerten, 1981 and Heerten and Kohlhase, 1986).

As the most important part of the investigation program, 39 samples of fabrics in service from 5 to 21 years were taken at 13 locations. 16 samples were excavated from seadike revetments and 23 samples were taken from sand bags and sand-filled tubes.

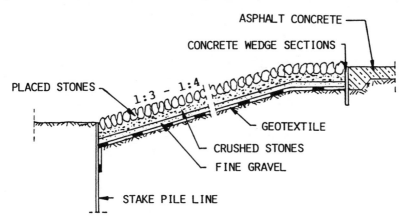

Fig. 3.   Layout of the seadike revetment on the Northfrisian coast (Zitscher, 1986).

Figure 3 shows the general layout of the revetment, Figure 4 gives an impression of the large revetment works for the sampling operation.   Figure 5 shows a non-woven fabric after removal of the covering layers.   An example showing the application of the sand-filled tubes as a stabilizing element for beach feeding areas endangered by erosion is shown in Figure 6.   Two differently loaded samples were taken from the tubes or sand bags: Samples from the top (weathered) and from the bottom (protected against UV-radiation).

For results of the long-term resistance in relation to the tensile strength see Heerten, 1981, and Heerten and Kohlhase, 1986.

A re-examination of the filtering properties of the geotextile samples excavated from seadikes and revetments led to the following basic results:

Mineral grain filter layers (crushed stone material and gravel) installed above the geotextile were clearly filled up with sand and mud particles.   Despite this, even those revetment sections remained stable which according to present day knowledge contained geotextiles with too high opening sizes.   This is due to the fact that the infiltration of marshy soil shields against dynamic loading and thus prevents the flushing-out of soil particles.

Although the excavated mechanically bonded non-woven fabrics did not show a compression in correspondence with the

89

Fig. 4.   Sampling operations at the seadike revetment, excavation of a geotextile.

Fig. 5.   Needle-punched non-woven fabric after removing the revetment cover layers.

Fig. 6.   Sand filled tube in a beach feeding area.

revetment loads, they did show thicknesses equal to or greater than the production thickness. This unexpected behaviour is influenced by the interaction between geotextiles and the soil from spontaneous grain-fibre-grain contact and has also been demonstrated in the meantime for the case of high road embankments and railway tracks (see Section 3.4 and 3.5).

Since the pores of the mechanically bonded non-woven fabrics and of the composite materials were partly filled with soil particles, in some cases the weight of the filtermats had risen tenfold by soil incorporation (mass of the soil to that of the fibre material from 1.5 to 9.0, on average 3.9). In this connection, a dependence could be found between soil incorporation and "porosity P" (Def. see Section 4.1). As the open pore structure of e.g. needle-punched non-wovens cannot attain the same density as the existing soil, the observed good hydraulic filtering efficiency of these soil-contaminated products is explained by the fact that they are 2 to 12 times (on average 6.0) more permeable than the existing soil with k-values of 1.3 to $9.4 \cdot 10^{-5}$ m/s.

In Figure 7, some data concerning the virgin non-woven fabrics (porosity n, permeability k_v) and the excavated fabrics (pores clogged by soil, remaining porosity n', remaining permeability $k_{v,s}$) are given. The permeability ratios between the flushed and soil-polluted samples were between 1.3 and 70, on average 12.8. The portion of pores of the non-wovens is still as high as $n' = 32$ to 74 % after many years of installation. This guarantees a sufficient long-term permeability.

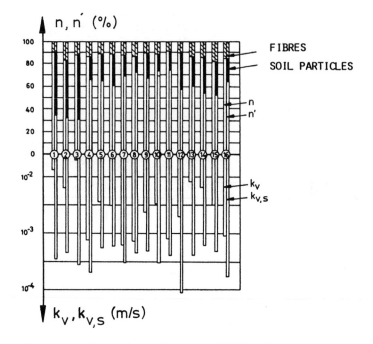

Fig. 7. Clogging of voids and permeability decrease of needle-
punched non-woven fabrics (Heerten and Kohlhase, 1986).

The permeability of the wovens partly fell below that of
the existing soil permeability. The ratios of the permeability of the soil-polluted woven geotextiles to the permeability
of the soils were in the range of 0.16 to 1.8 (on average 0.9).
This behaviour can be explained by the blocking of single
mesh openings by soil particles (sieve blockage).
Due to this effect, wovens react more sensitively to fluc-
tuations in the grain-size distribution of the existing soil
than non-wovens with a wider pore spectrum and a given filtration length.

In accordance with the recommendations of the German Committee
"Küstenschutzwerke" (Coastal Structures) of the Deutsche Gesellschaft für Erd- und Grundbau e.V. (German Society for Soil Mechanics and Foundation Engineering) and the Hafenbautechnische
Gesellschaft e.V. (Committee for Waterfront Structures) (Kramer,
1981) the following basic dimensioning formulation for the mechanical filter efficieny should be considered for existing fine and medium sands in coastal areas

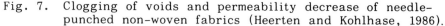

$$D_w \cong d_{50} \, .$$

In addition, an exact and stable installation of the geotextile has
to be ensured. An extensive, fixed placement of thin geotextiles
can in general only be achieved by installing an intermediate layer of e.g. crushed stone material or gravel (see Section 4.2).

3.2 Inland waterway constructions

Knowledge of the loads exerted on a canal bed by the passage of ships has grown in accordance with the type and extent of the resulting damage. This has made possible a clearly-defined classification of shipping traffic and resulting damage and has prompted clarifying investigations (Kniess, 1986). Figure 8 shows an example of the loading on the bank covering of a canal due to a fast-moving motorised cargo vessel in the vicinity of a canal bank.

In 1977/78 local defects revealed in inland-area revetments gave rise to the assumption that geotextiles used in such applications had inadequate long-term resistance. In an effort to clarify the problems, a representative selection of 22 samples in service from 1 to 14 years were excavated in 1980 from revetments of canals and rivers (Fig. 9). At the request of the BUNDESANSTALT FÜR WASSER-BAU (BAW) (Federal Institute of Waterways Engineering), the FRANZIUS-INSTITUT has investigated the filtration properties of these fabrics also (Partenscky, Heerten and Grabe, 1980, see H.-J. List, 1984, and Kniess and H.-J. List, 1982).

Fig. 8. Loading of the bank covering due to shipping traffic.

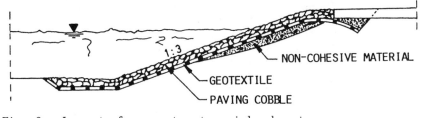

NON-COHESIVE MATERIAL

GEOTEXTILE

PAVING COBBLE

Fig. 9. Layout of a revetment on inland waterways (Zitscher, 1986).

Geotextile filters on the water-facing slopes of German canals which have become blocked have not been studied either by removal of samples or by other means.

In several of the removed geotextile samples, the mechanical filter effectiveness of the soil concerned was clearly underdimensioned. Cover layer damage was due for example to inadequate dimensioning of the mechanical filter effectiveness such as woven fabric with large mesh opening layed on the silty sand. It was apparent, however, that stable grain filters develop below non-filter-stable geotextiles provided non-uniform soils are present.

The geotextile filters were generally spread widely over the underlying material. Independend on the type of covering material, the load distribution over the boundary surface between the geotextile and the underlying material was mostly uniform and the contact between the geotextile and soil was good.

Very uneven slope surfaces or those with "spoilers" (old riprap or similar) prevented full contact of the geotextile filters. Beneath such hollow filter cavities, which were especially observed in the case of stiff, chemically bonded and thermally bonded non-wovens and tightly tensioned wovens, slight erosion damage was present.

As in the case of coastal protection, the layer thicknesses of mechanically bonded non-wovens were also equal to or larger than those of the retained samples in the majority of cases.

Although the permeability of the soil-polluted and mainly undisturbed excavated samples was significantly lower than that of the retained samples or the flushed samples (under a load of 2 kN/m^2, the permeability ratios between the flushed and soil-contaminated samples were between 4.7 and 53.0, on average 14.6), it was none the less significantly larger (5 to 12 times) than that of the soil to be filtered. Although the retained quantities of soil in the non-wovens sometimes increased the mass per unit area considerably above that of the virgin material (mass of the soil to that of the non-woven material from 1.33 to 3.67, on average 2.9), the remaining proportion of the open pores (pore space, total porosity) was in most cases still about 52 % to 79 % of the filter volume.

A similar investigation program to that carried out by Heerten has also been carried out in the Netherlands by Veldhuijzen van Zanten and Thabet (1982) for bank protection works. Samples were taken from 33 sites alongside the Dutch canals, rivers and coast. The minimum age of the structures sampled was 7 years. Their conclusions were as follows:

Changes in the composition of the subsoil usually extend some 40 to 70 mm below the geotextile in bank protection works, sometimes even down to 120 mm or more.

The largest changes take place in a thin layer (order of magnitude 5 mm) directly under the geotextile.

At the majority of sites investigated, the geotextile was found to be clogged, sometimes to a very large extent.

Appreciable uplift pressures may result due to blocking of the upper soil layer. Clogging of the geotextile was not the reason for this at any of the sites investigated, because its permeability is and remains larger than that of the subsoil.

3.3 Embankment dam constructions

Many failures of embankment dams have occurred as a result of erosion of the sealing element or of the subsoil. The cost of the damage in such cases is enormous. The use of geotextiles as filters is mostly able to prevent erosion by retaining the fine particles (self-healing) (F. List, 1984).

Geotextiles can also be used for control purposes, as for example for the measurement of the free water surface level in dams. This is the case in the 84 m high Frauenau dam/FRG.

The non-wovens installed in the core of the Frauenau dam are of particular advantage in that they not only provide additional protection against possible erosion but also enable the large-scale pressure condition in the core wall to be determined.

In the Frauenau dam, the non-wovens are subdivided into nine partitions by means of synthetic napped liners. By this configuration, it was possible to control the loss of head in the dam core (hydraulic grade line) as well as the corresponding infiltration rate (seepage water discharges). Figure 10 shows the head-loss in the form of isobars.

Up to the present, the control system has operated flawlessly. On the basis of the data obtained, prognoses concerning the long-term filter behaviour are expected.

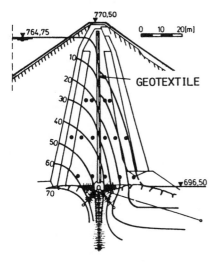
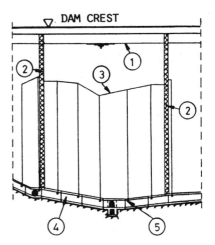

1	Water level	3	Water pressure in non-woven
2	Non-woven partitioning with napped liners	4	Control passageway
		5	Measuring point

Fig 10. Isobars of the pore water pressure and measured water pressure in the non-woven fabric in the longitudinal direction of the Frauenau-dam (F. List, 1984).

3.4 Track laying applications

The Deutsche Bundesbahn (German Federal Railway) have used geotextiles since 1973, for example, as a separation layer between
track bed ballast and railway substructures (Figure 11).

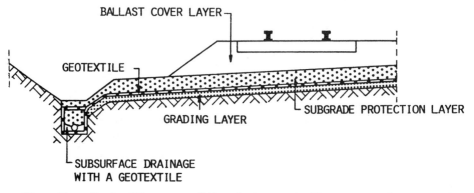

Fig. 11. Geotextile as a filter between ballast cover layer and
railway foundation layer (Martinek, 1986).

On many sections of the German Federal railway, the stability
of track foundations is jeopardized by inadequate foundation and
subsoil conditions. The subgrade protection layer consisting of
gravel sand must, in addition to other criteria, be filter stable in
comparison to the overlying ballast and the underlying natural
soil. In the case of clay soil with little silt and no sand fractions, this filter stability cannot always be ensured by gravel
sands which are frost-resistant.

By applying geotextiles, the cumbersome installation of graded
filters may be avoided.

Within the scope of investigation programmes, the FRANZIUS-
INSTITUT has been contracted on many occasions to remove samples
from various test sections in order to determine the characteristic
properties of the material (Partenscky and Grabe, 1983a and b, see
Martinek, 1986).

Test section at Neckarzimmern station/FRG
The test section was investigated after one year, five years
and ten years following installation of the geotextiles which
were installed as an alternative to a mineral graded filter
and in addition to a subgrade protection layer. Figure 12
shows the sampling of a geotextile and Figure 13 shows the
underside of an excavated sample. Fine material in the subsoil (silty clay, the fine-grained fraction for a grain size of
0.06 mm was 90 %) or the grading layer, where present, had
risen by about 1 cm into the subgrade protection layer.

Test section at Bruchsal-Bretten/FRG
The track subgrade required attention owing to the fact that
the natural subsoil had greatly contaminated the overlying
ballast.

Fig. 12.   Sampling of a geotextile, test section at
Neckarzimmern station.

Fig. 13.   Underside of an excavated sample, test section at
Neckarzimmern station.

For operational reasons, the geotextiles were laid directly onto the subsoil without a gravel sand layer and directly loaded with ballast, which was placed to a greater thickness than is usual.

The test section was investigated one year, four years and eight years after installation of the 13 different geotextiles.

The subsoil consists of a very fine-grained soil (clayey silt, the fine-grained fraction for a grain-size of 0.06 mm was above 95 %) whose largest grain diameter is smaller than the pore openings of the geotextiles. One year after installation, the following facts were established. Decisive factors for the overall poor effectiveness of the geotextiles (in some cases non-effective) are:

(a) Poor drainage of the subsoil beneath the geotextiles, which favours the accumulation of water in the absence of a subgrade protection layer.

(b) Absence of a gravel sand cover layer above the geotextiles; these were therefore quickly perforated by the sharp-edged ballast stones.

After eight years following installation, test pits show that the track bed ballast on top of the geotextiles was up to an average height of 10 cm (maximum height of 30 cm) mixed with clayey material of a pasty consistency. On the underside of the geotextiles, a fine water film was found. The underlying subsoil was of a stiff consistency which means that it had stabilized. The geotextile samples were very moist and contained clayey admixtures.

Figure 14 shows the exposure of a geotextile. The discolouration of the ballast is clearly apparent. Figure 15 shows a removed geotextile sample with perforations in the region of the tracks.

Concerning the performance of geotextiles below railway tracks, the following results of both test sections appear to be important:

Owing to the high dynamical loading and the simultaneous presence of water, the mass of the impregnated soil exceeded the fibre mass by 3 to 16 times.

The ratio of the permeability coefficients perpendicular to the geotextile plane between washed and soil-contaminated samples after 8 to 10 years of service was 23 on average (extreme values 2.5 and 75), i.e. through soil impregnation, the permeability was reduced on average by more than a factor of ten.

The ability to drain water in the geotextile plane is not as greatly reduced by soil impregnation as in the direction normal to the plane. For some products, the permeability in the geotextile plane of soil-contaminated samples was in fact larger than that of washed samples (ratio of the permeability coefficients in the geotextile plane between washed and soil-contaminated samples was between 0.2 to 12 under a load of 2 kN/m^2), which may be explained by the greater thickness.

Fig. 14.   Sampling of a geotextile, test section at Bruchsal-Bretten.

Fig. 15.   Excavated sample, test section at Bruchsal-Bretten.

In order to satisfy the hydraulic filter effectiveness, the soil-contaminated geotextiles only need to be slightly more permeable than the natural soil. The geotextiles employed in track laying applications should not be too stiff; the mass per unit area should lie between 250 and 400 g/m^2.

In summarizing, it can be concluded that the configuration shown in Figure 11 appears sensible (grading layer approx. 5 cm, sub-grade protection layer greater than 20 cm thick).

Seitz and Kany (1986) have investigated the filter behaviour of non-woven fabrics under cyclic dynamic loading between test soils under flow conditions in the laboratory. Noticeable quantities of soil of the clay and silt fraction could be found passing for thin non-woven fabrics and cohesive soils only under considerable strain and high cyclic loading. Thus, the reported results of the excavated geotextiles of the Deutsche Bundesbahn can be confirmed in the laboratory. In the case of cohesive soils, a certain amount of clay and silt material passing the geotextiles will more or less always be expected under dynamic loading. Under the testing conditions, a compacted filter cake was formed below the geotextile in the cohesive soils, and the permeability of the system was reduced. This result is confirmed by laboratory tests carried out at our institute. Provided low residual permeabilities are sufficient and the compaction effect is not effective over the entire surface, non-woven fabrics seem to be suitable for the cohesive test soils as a separation layer with filter effects, accounting for their strength and depending on the type of fill material.

3.5 Road constructions on soils of low bearing capacity

Geotextiles used for placing embankments on soils of low bearing capacity both prevent down punching of the sub-base by separation and upward pumping of fines and organic material from the subsoil into the embankment fill by filtration and thus ensure stability.

In the marshy areas around Brunsbüttel/FRG where poor load-bearing capacity soil layers exist up to a depth of 16 to 18 m, many geotextiles have been employed to provide a separation layer below sand fills from 1976 up to the present-day. This enabled on the one hand a reduction in the sand-bed layer thickness in temporary road construction, whilst on the other hand the migration of fines from the subsoil (silty clay) into the fill material was prevented (Partenscky and Grabe, 1982, see Huhnholz, 1984).

In order to establish the effectiveness of the geotextiles used, the FRANZIUS-INSTITUT was contracted to test, amongst other things, the filtering behaviour of 5 different non-wovens after a service time of 0.4 to 6.3 years under sand fills (coefficient of uniformity C_u from 2.5 up to 3.0) in the ground water or ground water fluctuation area.

Figure 16 shows a sampling operation and Figure 17 shows a geotextile sample which has been cut and opened out.

From the determined grain-size distribution, the soil particles washed out of the geotextiles originate predominantly from the fine to medium-grained sand of the fill material.

Fig. 16.   Sampling of a geotextile, test section at
Brunsbüttel.

Fig. 17.   Removal of sample, test section at Brunsbüttel.

The results showed that all the products tested had experienced a decrease in their original permeabilities.

If the ratio of the permeability coefficients between washed and soil-polluted non-woven geotextile sheets (soil mass/fibre mass = 0.5 to 5.8) is taken as a governing parameter to represent the influence of soil impregnation on permeability, values of 2 to 188 are obtained under a load of 2 kN/m^2, with a mean value of 56, i.e. about 1.5 orders of magnitude.

Nevertheless, the geotextiles considered above remain more permeable than the subsoil. A rise of fine-grained fractions into the embankment material has been prevented and the geotextiles have thus fulfilled their task as a separation layer.

Sotton (1984) has also reported on the filtering behaviour of geotextile separation layers which have been retested 5 to 12 years after installation. The results may be summarized as follows:

> The residual permittivity of all non-woven-samples contaminated by soil particles remains greater than the permeability of the soil.
>
> The permittivity of the samples decreases with increasing degree of contamination. The permittivity of the washed samples compared to the control samples, is a factor 5 to 10 less whilst that of the polluted ones is 30 to 60 times less. These values reveal the internal contamination of the geotextiles.
>
> The clogging of needled nonwoven geotextiles by clayey-muddy soil is always limited. Consequently geotextiles maintain high permeability compared to the natural soil and do not constitute a hydraulic continuity barrier between the natural soil and the fill material.

Brorsson and Eriksson (1986) have reported about a research program conducted by the Swedish National Road Administration. In 1973, nine different geotextiles were installed on a very frost susceptible road subgrade. Samples of the geotextile were excavated after 5 and 10 years and tested. Soil samples were also taken from the sub-base close to the fabrics. The function as a separator at the subgrade/pavement interface was quite satisfactory for all the geotextiles. No migration of the fine-grained subgrade soil (silt and clay) into the sub-base was noticed.

4. Selection of Geotextiles

4.1 Filter criteria

First of all it should be noted that dimensioning formulae as well as the following filter criteria must always be considered in relation to the chosen test method otherwise a comparison of different filter criteria is already cast in doubt on the grounds of the formulae used. Only when testing methods are in close agreement with one another it is possible to make comparisons between different filter criteria (Saathoff and Kohlhase, 1985).

In cases of testing geotextiles in combination with soil material, it has to be considered that the testing conditions in the laboratory are very different to natural conditions.

The methodology of the tests mentioned here on excavated products including the testing procedures outlined in Section 2 still have a number of shortcomings. If, however, the result, which in this case refers to the filter criteria, has shown itself to be successful, small deviations are also acceptable.

The results of the different research programmes of the FRANZIUS-INSTITUT are part of the "Empfehlung für die Anwendung und Prüfung von Kunststoffen im Erd- und Wasserbau" (Recommendations for the use of synthetic materials in soil and hydraulic engineering) of the German Working Group 14 of the "Deutsche Gesellschaft für Erd- und Grundbau e.V., (DGEG)" (German Society for Soil Mechanics and Foundation Engineering, GSSMFE) (Zitscher, 1986).

Figure 18 shows a reduced flow diagram which explains the procedure to select a fabric according to the characteristics of the subsoil and the construction.

In order to conduct the dimensioning, several parameters must be known (characteristics of the soil from the grain-size distribution, permeability coefficients as well as characteristics of the geotextile such as effective opening size, permeability coefficient of the virgin geotextile, degree of porosity, thickness). Uncertainties must be assessed and accounted for depending upon the case in question (Zitscher, 1986). An analysis of the tests conducted according to the FRANZIUS-INSTITUT standard testing procedures for determining the effective opening size and the permeability coefficient (load 2 kN/m^2) for geotextiles has shown that no noticeable (Heerten, 1981) or only a weak (Grabe, 1983) relationship between opening size and permeability coefficient exists. For this reason, a generally valid estimate of the filter effectiveness must include the dimensioning of both parameters.

In the first step, we have to estimate the effective opening size D_w. D_w is given by a filter criterion which is a function of the grain-size distribution of the soil and the load conditions. Static load conditions, for example, are given by laminar flow including a change of flow direction. Dynamic load conditions are given by high turbulent flow, wave attack or pumping phemonena.

In the second step, the hydraulic conditions have to be controlled. To prevent over-pressures in a revetment construction, the permeability of the filter fabric (k_v) has to be higher than the permeability of the subsoil (k).

Since only the permeability determined by the standard testing procedure is generally known for a geotextile to be selected, testing of the hydraulic filter efficiency relies on the assumption that a known relationship exists between the permeability of the geotextile delivered from the factory and the permeability of the soil-contaminated geotextile.

As a result of the investigations, it is possible to estimate a permeability reduction factor η as a function of fabric data and soil characteristics. The permeability of the fabric is sufficient when

$$\eta \cdot k_v \geqslant k.$$

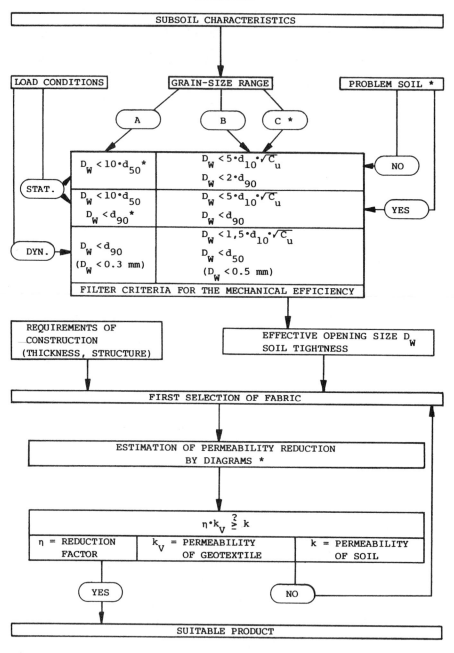

* Additional remarks see Zitscher (1986)

Fig. 18.   Flow diagram to check the filtration properties of geotextiles.

Examinations of long-term filtering behaviour of geotextiles

For relatively thin geotextiles (wovens and thin nonwovens with a thickness < 2.0 mm), whose filtering behaviour is comparable, a reduction factor η_G can be determined as a function of the permeability value k_v and the grain diameter d_{10} of the soil to be filtered. Figure 19 shows the diagram to estimate η_G. The application of this diagram is limited by the particle distribution of the investigated soils at the sampling locations ($0.01 \leqslant d_{10} \leqslant 0.50$ mm).

η_v is given as a function of the fabric parameters k_v and P (Fig. 20). k_v is the permeability value of a virgin geotextile determined under load conditions similar to those in the field and P is defined as a product of the porosity n, fabric thickness d (under a load of 2 kN/m^2), and effective opening size D_w.

It was surprising to find that there is no correlation between η_v and the soil parameters even though the soil parameters vary over a wide range.

It is known from investigations on needle-punched nonwoven fabrics installed many years ago that the hydraulic filtering efficiency of these geotextiles (thickness of filtering layer $30 \cdot D_w \leqslant d \leqslant 50 \cdot D_w$) for silts and sands is guaranteed if the permeability k_v of the virgin product measured under a load of 2 kN/m^2 exceeds the permeability coefficient of the soil by a factor of approximately 50 ($\eta \leqslant 1/50 = 0.02$)

$$k_v \geqslant 50 \cdot k.$$

As an additional boundary condition, it must be noted that for coarse soils, a significant reduction in the permeability of non-wovens and composite materials can only occur when the pore structure of the geotextile allows the infiltration of soil particles. The reduction factor may thus be set to $\eta_v = 1.0$ when non-wovens and composite materials are selected with such small opening sizes that the infiltration of soil particles is almost impossible. As a limiting condition for $\eta_v = 1.0$, the following is given here:

$$D_w \leqslant 0.5 \cdot d_{10}.$$

In the case of particular geotextile types (e.g. woven fabric with large mesh opening), a reduction in the permeability of between 3 and 4 orders of magnitude may be achieved. Basically the reduction in permeability is dependent upon the pore structure and the thickness of the geotextile as well as the grain structure of the surrounding soil. With regard to the hydraulic filter efficiency, the upper limits of the pore openings, which are allowable to ensure mechanical filter efficiency should be fully exploited - voluminous open pore structure is generally superior to a dense fine structure with respect to the filter effectiveness.

4.2 Additional requirements

Depending upon the subsoil and the covering layer, the thickness and pore structure of a geotextile can decisively influence the stability of the interface. In addition to the normal filter technical design, these aspects are also important.

Actual examples of a number of cases of damage to revetments, for example, have occurred as the result of soil migration beneath the geotextile (Fig. 21) (Mühring, 1984). Figure 22 illustrates the consequences which may result. Although for the revetment system, a correctly designed woven fabric was installed, downslope soil migration beneath the geotextile could not be avoided and damage to the revetment occurred (Heerten, 1986).

A possible solution involves the use of geotextiles including a stabilization layer for the prevention of soil movement and to stabilize surface susceptible to erosion.

The past experience of more than 10 years on German Waterways, for example on the Mittellandkanal (Saathoff, 1985), and short-term tests has shown that the multiple-layered structure of a geotextile filter as a composite material with a stabilization layer (roughness layer) provides a better filter effectiveness than that of a simple non-woven layer. According to circumstances, a composite material with a three-layered non-woven structure has the advantage over a single non-woven fabric in that a good filter effectiveness is provided over a wide range of grain sizes. Considering the difficult matching of the geotextile structure to the soil, this can provide an additional safeguard.

Under consideration of the factors mechanical and hydraulic filter effectiveness as well as stabilization of the soil, a multiple-layer, graded structure geotextile filter should be aimed at. A composition including a fine filter, pre-filter and roughness layer appears particularly meaningful, since the stabilization layer, as well as providing stability, can also supplement the filtering function of the other layers (Mühring and Saathoff, 1986).

According to today's knowledge, $0.3 \text{ mm} \leqslant D_w \leqslant 2.0 \text{ mm}$ can be taken as an approximate value for the effective opening size. The thickness of a stabilization layer should be a minimum of 5 mm. Corresponding geotextiles, as shown by excavated samples, form a stabilized interface geotextile/soil, which means a stable bridging of the hollow spaces beneath a rip-rap layer.

An additional research activity of the FRANZIUS-INSTITUT concerns the filtering behaviour of elongated geotextiles.

The knowledge obtained so far from laboratory tests (Saathoff, 1986) may be summarized as follows:

> The elongation influences the dimensioning parameters "effective opening size" and "permeability". Elongation can cause either an "increase in fibre density" or an "increase in fibre spacing". An increase in fibre density, which may also be achieved by loading, reduces the permeability and the effective opening size. An increase in fibre spacing increase both these parameters. The situation is complicated by the fact that both phenomena can occur simultaneously or sequentially depending upon many different influencing factors such as the type of elongation, the mass per unit area, thickness, bonding and loading.

All these aspects must also be considered as representing long-term filter behaviour if one is to retain the subdivision of the long-term behaviour in terms of filter effectiveness and mechanical and physical-chemical properties.

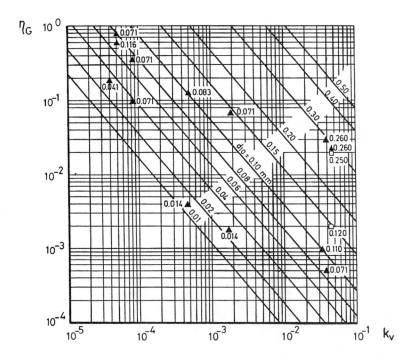

Fig. 19. Determination diagram for the permeability reduction factor (wovens and thin non-wovens with thickness up to approx. 2.0 mm) (Heerten, 1981).

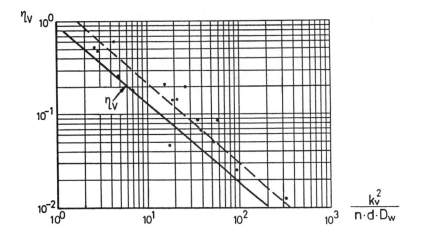

Fig. 20. Determination diagram for the permeability reduction factor (non-wovens with thickness greater than 2.0 mm) (Heerten, 1982).

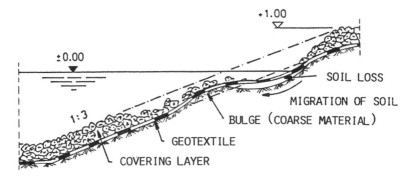

Fig. 21.   Revetment damage caused by migration of soil particles
beneath a geotextile without a stabilization layer
(Mühring, 1984).

Fig. 22.   Failure of a bank cover layer as a result of
insufficient filtering.

5. Conclusions

A successful long-term filter performance may be defined as a long-
term prevention of the failure of a filter. A failure can thereby
be identified by a blocking of the filter or by a flushing-out of
the grains of the soil to be protected. Predictions of the long-term
filter effectiveness as related to the age of the construction can
thus only be made from object tests on geotextiles installed for
many years.

In this paper, some fundamentals of the long-term filtering behaviour of geotextiles are given. The case studies of geotextile application show the necessity of knowing the geotextile performance for successful design and construction. In many cases, the geotextile, its suitable selection, its safe installation and its adequate long-term behaviour are of decisive importance for the service-time and safety of the whole structure.

Table 1 shows a summary of the results from the individual investigation programmes (Notation see Section 6).

Table 1. Proportionality factors.

Application	Geotextiles	$\dfrac{m_S}{m_F}$	$\dfrac{k_V}{k_{V,S}}$	$\dfrac{k_{V,S}}{k}$	$\dfrac{k_V}{k}$
Coastal Engineering & Shore Protection	16 NW	1.5- 9.0 (3.9)	1.3-70.0 (12.8)	2.0-12.0 (6.0)	7.9-684.0 (137)
	23 WF	-	1.3-2000* (296)*	0.2-5.0* (1.5)*	1.6-818.0 (197)
				0.2-1.8** (0.9)**	
Inland Waterway Constructions	16 NW	1.3-3.7 (2.9)	4.7-53.0 (14.6)	5.0-12.0	(>73.0)
	6 WF	-	-		-
Track Laying Applications	15 NW	3.0-16.0	2.5-75.0 (23.0)	>1.0 (>1.0)	(>23.0)
Road Construction	5 NW	0.5- 5.8	2.0-188.0 (56.0)	>1.0 (>1.0)	(>56.0)
Approx. Average of the values	52 NW	5.1	20.5	>4.8	>76.6
	29 WF	-	≈296	2.5	>171.3

The following average values are of particular interest:

The ratio of the permeability coefficients normal to the geotextile plane between brand new and soil-contaminated non-wovens and composite materials is about 20 on average, whereby the incorporated mass of soil exceeds the mass of the fabric by a factor of about 5.

The permeability distance-ratio (permeability of the soil-contaminated geotextiles to that of the soil) is at least 4.8 on average for non-wovens and about 2.5 for woven fabrics. For wovens, the ratio drops below 1 in some cases.

If one compares the permeability coefficients of brand new geotextiles to those of the soil, ratios of 7.9 to 684.0 are obtained for non-wovens, and ratios of 1.6 to 818.0 are obtained for woven fabrics, in other words an expected maximal reduction by about 2 orders of magnitude on average (non-wovens $>$ 76.6, woven fabrics $>$ 171.3).

The given filter criteria make it possible to select a geotextile according to the special requirements of the application given by the grain-size distribution and the permeability coefficient of the soil.

Owing to the absence of a relationship between the opening-size and the permeability of the geotextiles, a given dimensioning procedure which provides information on the mechanical filter efficiency and which compares the permeability coefficients of the soil to be filtered to that of the soil-contaminated geotextile will make it possible to check the filter efficiency under conditions of head-loss-free seepage water runoff.

Diagrams developed to estimate the reduction in permeability of virgin geotextiles separately for wovens/thin non-wovens and thick non-wovens/composite materials based upon collected data provide a complete formulation for solutions which take into consideration the interaction between geotextile and soil.

Neglecting the possibility of a secondary filter developing due to grain deposition in the boundary layer geotextile-soil, the filter effectiveness of woven fabrics is governed by the selected effective opening size D_w and the possible blocking of the pore openings due to the interfacial contact between grain particles and the fabric. The blocking of fabric pores can lead to a significant reduction in the permeability compared to the value obtained from tests on the woven fabric alone.

In the case of non-wovens and composite materials, a temporal change in the filter effectiveness is to be expected by the deposition of soil particles in the three-dimensional fabric structure, which means that the hydraulic filter efficiency of non-wovens and composite materials is possibly a long-term varying quantity. Non-wovens and composite materials in which soil deposition was many times larger than the mass of the fabric indicated that a head-loss-free runoff of seepage water was still provided.

When geotextiles were first introduced design information and classification concerning their use were not available. The choice of geotextiles was based upon intuitive judgement or upon the arguments of the manufacturers of different products. It should be noted that in judging the results presented, the products used are not quite representative for today's use. Many of the products have been changed by the manufacturers during the past years.

On the basis of the investigations, it can be concluded that there is no doubt at present concerning the sufficient long-term filter effectiveness of correctly designed geotextiles.

6. Notation

A,B,C	grain-size range, see Zitscher (1986)	
C_u	coefficient of uniformity	(-)
D_W	effective opening size of the geotextile	(mm)
d	thickness of the geotextile under a load of 2 kN/m²	(mm)
d_{10}	grain diameter of the soil at 10 % sieve passage	(%)
d_{50}	grain diameter of the soil at 50 % sieve passage	(%)
d_{90}	grain diameter of the soil at 90 % sieve passage	(%)
k	permeability coefficient of the soil	(m/s)
k_V	permeability coefficient normal to the plane of the virgin (or washed) geotextile	(m/s)
$k_{V,S}$	as for k_V, but soil-contaminated	(m/s)
m_F	fibre mass of the sample	(g)
m_S	mass of incorporated soil	(g)
n	porosity of the virgin geotextile	(-)
n´	residual porosity of the soil-contaminated geotextile	(-)
P	"porosity", product of n, d, and D_W	(mm²)
Δh	piezometric head loss through the sample	(m)
η	permeability reduction factor	(-)
$η_G$	permeability reduction factor for wovens and thin non-wovens with thickness up to 2.0 mm	(-)
$η_V$	permeability reduction factor for non-wovens with thickness greater than 2.0 mm	(-)

Table 1:

NW	non-woven fabrics
WF	woven fabrics
*	$k_{V,S}$ determined at system woven-soil
**	$k_{V,S}$ and k determined at system woven-soil
(...)	on average

References

Brorsson, I. and Eriksson, L. (1986) Long-term properties of geotextiles and their function as a separator in road construction. *Proc. of the Third International Conference on Geotextiles,* Vienna.

Grabe, W. (1983) Mechanische und hydraulische Eigenschaften von Geotextilien. *Mitteilungen des FRANZIUS-INSTITUTS für Wasserbau und Küsteningenieurwesen der Universität Hannover,* Heft 56.

Heerten, G. (1980) Long-term experience with the use of synthetic filter fabrics in coastal engineering. *Proc. of the 17th International Conference on Coastal Engineering,* Sydney.

Heerten, G. (1981) Geotextilien im Wasserbau - Prüfung, Anwendung, Bewährung -. *Mitteilungen des FRANZIUS-INSTITUTS für Wasserbau und Küsteningenieurwesen der Universität Hannover,* Heft 52.

Heerten, G. (1982) Dimensioning the filter properties of geotextiles considering long-term conditions. *Proc. of the Second International Conference on Geotextiles,* Las Vegas.

Heerten, G. (1986) Functional design of filters using geotextiles. *Proc. of the Third International Conference on Geotextiles,* Vienna.

Heerten, G. and Kohlhase, S. (1986) Geotextiles in coastal and harbour engineering, in *Port Engineering* (ed. P. BRUUN), Third Edition, Gulf Publishing Company.

Heerten, G. und Zitscher, F.-F. (1984) 25 Jahre Geotextilien im Küstenschutz - Ein Erfahrungsbericht -. *1. Nationales Symposium Geotextilien im Erd- und Wasserbau,* Forschungsgesellschaft für Straßen- und Verkehrswesen (Hrsg.), Köln.

Huhnholz, M. (1984) Geotextilien im Erdbau als Trennschicht zwischen Damm und wenig tragfähigem Untergrund. *1. Nationales Symposium Geotextilien im Erd- und Grundbau,* Forschungsgesellschaft für Straßen- und Verkehrswesen (Hrsg.), Köln.

Kniess, H.-G. (1986) Historische Entwicklung der Bauweisen für Auskleidungen von Binnenwasserstraßen. *Mitteilungen des FRANZIUS-INSTITUTS für Wasserbau und Küsteningenieurwesen der Universität Hannover,* Heft 62.

Kniess, H.-G. und List, H.-J. (1982) Langzeitbeständigkeit geotextiler Filter. Untersuchung von geotextilen Filtern aus Uferdeckwerken der Bundeswasserstraßen. *Bericht der Bundesanstalt für Wasserbau,* Karlsruhe.

Kramer, J. (Hrsg.) (1981) Empfehlungen für die Ausführung von Küstenschutzwerken (EAK 1981). *Die Küste,* Heft 36.

List, F. (1984) Technische Gesichtspunkte für die Anwendung von Geotextilien im Staudammbau. *1. Nationales Symposium Geotextilien im Erd- und Wasserbau,* Forschungsgesellschaft für Straßen- und Verkehrswesen (Hrsg.), Köln.

List, H.-J. (1984) Langzeitbeständigkeit geotextiler Filter aus Uferdeckwerken von Bundeswasserstraßen. *1. Nationales Symposium Geotextilien im Erd- und Wasserbau,* Forschungsgesellschaft für Straßen- und Verkehrswesen (Hrsg.), Köln.

Martinek, K. (1984) Erfahrungen mit der Anwendung von Geotextilien bei der Deutschen Bundesbahn. *1. Nationales Symposium Geotextilien im Erd- und Wasserbau*, Forschungsgesellschaft für Straßen- und Verkehrswesen (Hrsg.), Köln.

Martinek, K. (1986) Geotextiles used by the German Federal Railway - Experiences and Specifications -. *Geotextiles and Geomembranes*, 3.

Mühring, W. (1984) Die Entwicklung von Geotextilien beim Ausbau von künstlichen Wasserstraßen. *1. Nationales Symposium Geotextilien im Erd- und Wasserbau*, Forschungsgesellschaft für Straßen- und Verkehrswesen (Hrsg.), Köln.

Mühring, W. and Saathoff, F. (1986) Testing of filter characteristics of composite materials. *Proc. of the Third International Conference on Geotextiles*, Vienna.

Partenscky, H.-W. und Grabe, W. (1982) Untersuchung der Langzeitbeständigkeit von Geotextilien im Straßenbau. *Bericht des FRANZIUS-INSTITUTS für Wasserbau und Küsteningenieurwesen der Universität Hannover.*

Partenscky, H.-W. und Grabe, W. (1983a) Untersuchung der Langzeitbeständigkeit von Geotextilien im Eisenbahnbau, DB-Strecke Bruchsal-Bretten. *Bericht des FRANZIUS-INSTITUTS für Wasserbau und Küsteningenieurwesen der Universität Hannover.*

Partenscky, H.-W. und Grabe, W. (1983b) Untersuchung der Langzeitbeständigkeit von Geotextilien im Eisenbahnbau, DB-Bahnhof Neckarzimmern. *Bericht des FRANZIUS-INSTITUTS für Wasserbau und Küsteningenieurwesen der Universität Hannover.*

Partenscky, H.-W. u Heerten, G. (1979a) Untersuchung der Langzeitbeständigkeit von Kunststoffiltern im Seedeichbereich am Seedeich Speicherkoog Dithmarschen. *Bericht des FRANZIUS-INSTITUTS für Wasserbau und Küsteningenieurwesen der Universität Hannover.*

Partenscky, H.-W. und Heerten, G. (1979b) Untersuchung der Langzeitbeständigkeit von Geotextilien im Küstenschutz. *Bericht des FRANZIUS-INSTITUTS für Wasserbau und Küsteningenieurwesen der Universität Hannover.*

Partenscky, H.-W. und Heerten, G. (1980a) Untersuchung langjährig eingebauter Filtergewebe an Küstenschutzanlagen in Ostfriesland. *Bericht des FRANZIUS-INSTITUTS für Wasserbau und Küsteningenieurwesen der Universität Hannover.*

Partenscky, H.-W. und Heerten, G. (1980b) Ergebnisbericht zur Untersuchung der Filter- und Festigkeitseigenschaften langjährig ausliegender Geotextilien. *Bericht des FRANZIUS-INSTITUTS für Wasserbau und Küsteningenieurwesen der Universität Hannover.*

Partenscky, H.-W., Heerten, G. und Grabe, W. (1980) Untersuchung der Langzeitfilterwirksamkeit geotextiler Filter im Verkehrswasserbau. *Bericht des FRANZIUS-INSTITUTS für Wasserbau und Küsteningenieurwesen der Universität Hannover.*

Saathoff, F. (1985) Terrafix revetment systems used at the Mittellandkanal/FRG - A summary of experiences -. *Report for the PIANC Working Group 4 "Flexible Armoured Revetments"*, Hannover.

Saathoff, F. (1986) Filterwirksamkeit gedehnter Geotextilien. *Mitteilungen des FRANZIUS-INSTITUTS für Wasserbau und Küsteningenieurwesen der Universität Hannover*, Heft 64.

Saathoff, F. und Kohlhase, S. (1985) Zur Problematik der Bestimmung einer wirksamen Öffnungsweite. *Bericht des FRANZIUS-INSTITUTS für Wasserbau und Küsteningenieurwesen der Universität Hannover.*

Saathoff, F. und Kchlhase, S. (1986) Research at the FRANZIUS-INSTITUT on geotextile filters in hydraulic engineering. *Proc. of the Fifth Congress Asian and Pacific Regional Division, ADP/ IAHR,* Seoul.

Seitz, E. and Kany, M. (1986) Filter behaviour of ncn-woven fabrics under dynamic loading. *Proc. of the Third International Conference on Geotextiles,* Vienna.

Sotton, M. (1984) Durability of geotextiles. *23rd International Man-Made Fibres Congress,* Dornbirn.

Veldhuijzen van Zanten, R. and Thabet, R.A.H. (1982) Investigation on long-term behaviour of geotextiles on bank protection works. *Proc. of the Second International Conference on Geotextiles,* Las Vegas.

Zitscher, F.-F. (Hrsg.) (1986) Empfehlung für die Anwendung und Prüfung von Kunststoffen im Erd- und Wasserbau. *DVWK Schriften, Verlag Paul Parey, Hamburg/Berlin,* Heft 76.

ESTIMATION DU COMPORTEMENT HYDRAULIQUE À LONG TERME DES GÉOTEXTILES À PARTIR DES ESSAIS À COURT TERME

Y. FAURE

Institut de Recherche Interdisciplinaire de Géologie et de Mécanique Université de Grenoble

1. Introduction

Le comportement hydraulique des géotextiles dépend essentiellement des propriétés : permittivité, transmissivité et porométrie.

Actuellement, ces propriétés hydrauliques sont mesurées au laboratoire par des essais normalisés où le géotextile est testé seul, à l'état neuf. Depuis un certain nombre d'années, ont été développés à l'I.R.I.G.M., Université de Grenoble, des essais originaux de filtration et de drainage permettant de simuler le comportement hydraulique du géotextile au contact d'un sol.

Dans cet exposé sont présentés les moyens mis en oeuvre à l'I.R.I.G.M., pour observer et comprendre le comportement du système sol-géotextile en filtration, et les principaux résultats obtenus. L'objectif étant de répondre aux questions :

- les essais réalisés sont-ils significatifs du comportement à long terme ?

- peut-on prévoir le comportement hydraulique à long terme à partir d'essais à court terme et quel type d'essais faut-il réaliser?

Analyse du problème :

Nous devons étudier le comportement filtrant d'un système à deux composants :

- le sol : relativement bien connu par sa granulométrie (continue ou non, pourcentage de fines...) et ses propriétés mécaniques et hydrauliques, en particulier sa perméabilité et son coefficient de consolidation.

- le géotextile : si la perméabilité normale (ou transversale) du géotextile peut être connue expérimentalement sous compression et éventuellement sous tension, sa structure est moins bien connue, en particulier sa porométrie et même sa fibrométrie pour certains d'entre eux (tissé de bandelette par exemple). Or le comportement filtrant du géotextile est essentiellement conditionné par sa structure. C'est pourquoi une première partie de cet exposé est consacrée à l'étude de la porométrie des géotextiles, soit par observations de coupes transversales (dans le plan de la nappe) soit par l'application de modèles mathématiques.

Le système sol-géotextile est soumis à diverses sollicitations (hydrauliques et mécaniques) au cours desquelles le géotextile doit assurer la rétention du sol tout en laissant l'eau s'écouler le plus librement possible. L'évolution dans le temps du comportement hydraulique de ce système dépend bien sûr de la variation temporelle des propriétés hydrauliques du géotextile, mais est aussi conditionnée par le sol lui-même : Lorsque celui-ci aura formé une structure stable à l'interface avec le géotextile (consolidation, blocage des particules) l'évolution du système sera faible dépendant :
    - du comportement du sol lui-même,
    - des propriétés mécaniques du géotextile (compressibilité, résistance au fluage).

La deuxième partie porte donc sur une étude des conditions de formation d'une structure granulaire stable en amont du géotextile.

2. Etude de la porométrie des géotextiles

Pour comprendre les mécanismes mis en jeu, il faut connaître la structure des géotextiles et en particulier la porométrie dont dépendent fortement les propriétés hydrauliques comme la perméabilité et l'ouverture de filtration.

Cette étude a porté sur des non tissés, thermoliés ou aiguilletés, plus généralement utilisés dans les applications hydrauliques et a été abordée tant sur le plan expérimental que théorique.

2.1. Approche expérimentale :

Dans le cas des géotextiles minces, l'observation des pores peut être faite directement par transmission. On peut mesurer directement le diamètre des pores qui traversent le géotextile de part en part. Dans le cas des géotextiles épais, l'observation par transmission ne permet pas de voir des pores, dans la mesure où ceux-ci ne sont pas rectilignes ; cette méthode est donc peu significative. Il est nécessaire de réaliser des lames minces, parallèles au plan du géotextile (fig. 1).

Fig. 1 Lame mince réalisée dans le plan d'un géotextile non tissé aiguilleté.

Ces lames minces sont ensuite traitées et analysées avec un quantimètre. Celui-ci permet d'obtenir un certain nombre d'informations quantitatives sur les pores, notamment la porosité surfacique et la dimension des pores, en caractérisant chacun d'eux par son diamètre équivalent (diamètre du cercle de même aire que le pore) ou mieux par son diamètre "érodé", obtenu par érosions successives de chaque pore (ou dilatation des fibres). Ce diamètre érodé est comparable au diamètre du cercle inscrit dans le pore, mieux adapté au problème du passage des particules de sol.

On obtient ainsi une distribution porométrique de surface (Fig. 2) qui sera considérée comme caractéristique de la structure du géotextile, à condition que la lame mince puisse être tenue pour équivalente à une "nappe élémentaire", la nappe totale étant reproduite par empilement de "nappes élémentaires".

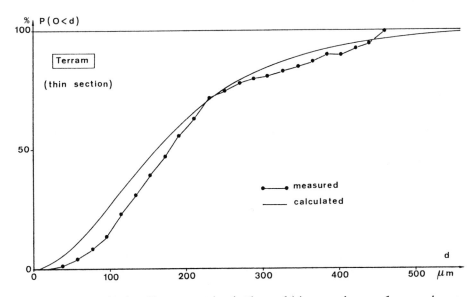

Fig. 2   Porométrie d'un non tissé thermolié mesurée sur lames minces. Comparaison avec la porométrie obtenue en utilisant la théorie des polyèdres poissoniens.

2.2. Approche théorique :

Les observations faites dans le plan du géotextile non tissés laissent supposer que la théorie mathématique des polyèdres poissoniens isotropes à deux dimensions (Matheron 1971) peut s'appliquer. Elle permet d'obtenir la granulométrie des cercles inscrits dans les pores entre les fibres d'une nappe élémentaire (assimilée à un plan) d'épaisseur égale au diamètre des fibres D .

Si λ est le nombre de fibres de direction donnée et si le géotextile est supposé orthotrope d'axe normal au plan de la nappe, λ est donné par (Gourc 1982) :

$$\lambda = 4 \ (1-n)/ \ (\pi^2 D)$$

où D : diamètre des fibres
    n : porosité du géotextile.

La granulomérie des pores est la fonction G(d), probabilité cumulée d'avoir un pore de diamètre inférieur à d :

$$G(d) = 1 - [\ 1 + \lambda \pi d/ \ (2 + \lambda \pi D)]^2 \ \exp \ (-\lambda \pi d)$$

La figure 2 montre une comparaison de la distribution porométrique obtenue par la mesure sur lame mince et celle calculée pour un géotextile non tissé. Le modèle théorique semble bien adapté pour décrire le milieu fibreux.

2.3. Application à la détermination théorique des propriétés hydrauliques :

a) Perméabilité normale k_n

La perméabilité normale de la nappe est déterminée, à partir de la porométrie calculée précédemment, en considérant le géotextile comme une succession de nappes élémentaires. Les pores sont alors assimilés à des cylindres dont la distribution théorique Q(d) est donnée par :

$$Q(d) = [G(d)]^{T_g/D}$$

où T_g est l'épaisseur du géotextile.

La perméabilité moyenne de la nappe est calculée en tenant compte de la perte de charge dans chaque cylindre, pondérée par la fonction répartition Q(d) (Millot 1986).
La figure 3 compare le modèle théorique aux résultats expérimentaux sur non tissés aïguilletés. Cette loi notée "C.G" convient assez bien aux fortes porosités, pour n >0,70.

b) Ouverture de filtration O_f

L'ouverture de filtration, dimension de la plus grosse particule susceptible de traverser le géotextile de part en part, est déduite de la courbe de répartition des pores selon des cylindres. On retient pour O_f le diamètre du cylindre tel que 95 % des cylindres soient de diamètre inférieur (le diamètre maximum théorique est infini).
La validité du modèle théorique a été vérifiée (Millot 1986) en réalisant une simulation de l'essai de tamisage hydrodynamique La probabilité de passage d'une particule au travers du géotextile est déduite de la courbe de répartition des pores selon des cylindres. Chaque cycle de tamisage est considéré comme un évènement (du point de vue probabilité). La figure 4 montre une comparaison du modèle

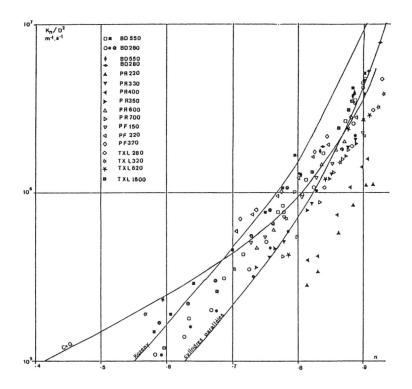

*Fig. 3   Lois théoriques de perméabilité normale et résultats expéri-
mentaux. Non tissés aiguilletés.*

théorique avec les résultats expérimentaux obtenus sur un non tissé
aiguilleté en fonction du nombre de cycles (Sunjoto 1986). La correspondance est satisfaisante, tant sur O_f (= D_{95}) que sur la masse de
passant μ_F à travers le géotextile. Le modèle ne prend pas en compte
l'interaction entre les particules, c'est pourquoi la simulation est
plus en accord avec l'essai où est utilisé un agitateur qui empêche
tout arrangement des grains au-dessus du textile.

Ceci est une première étape vers la simulation de la fonction
filtre. En effet, dans cette étude, les particules sont considérées
comme isolées et le colmatage éventuel n'est pas pris en compte. Des
modèles sont actuellement à l'étude pour prendre en compte l'interaction entre particules, notamment les particules piégées et les phénomènes de voûtes.

L'intérêt de cette étude théorique est important car elle permettra de prévoir le comportement hydraulique du système sol-géotextile
dans certaines conditions.

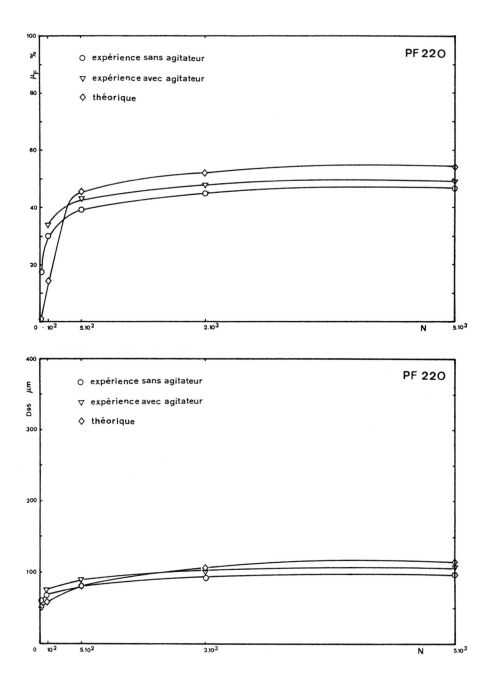

Fig. 4   *Simulation de l'essai de tamisage hydrodynamique. Variation de la masse de passant μ_F à travers le géotextile et de l'ouverture de filtration $O_f = D_{95}$ en fonction du nombre de cycles.*

120

3. Comportement du système sol-géotextile en filtration

Des essais systématiques ont été réalisés pour mettre en évidence les conditions critiques, conduisant à l'instabilité du système sol-géotextile mis en place dans de bonnes conditions :
- sol non en suspension dans l'eau,
- sol en contact avec le filtre, sous compression.

La figure 5 montre un schéma de principe de l'appareillage d'essai.

Différentes structures textiles et différentes granulométries de sols pulvérulents ont été testées sous différentes sollicitations hydrauliques et mécaniques (Sundias 1986).

Les paramètres mesurés, significatifs du fonctionnement du système, sont la masse de passant pendant la durée de l'essai et la variation de la permittivité de la zone filtrante (géotextile et sol adjacent).

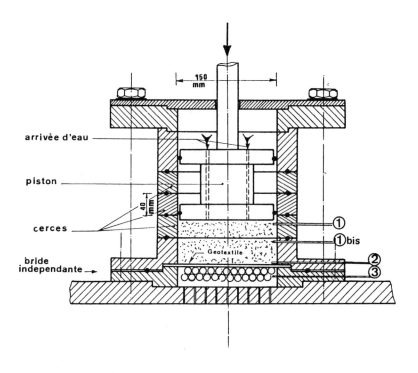

Fig. 5 Schéma de principe de l'appareillage de filtration. La pression interstitielle est mesurée aux points notés 1, 1 bis, 2 et 3.

3.1. Comportement du sol au contact d'une ouverture :

Le comportement du sol est mis en évidence par des essais réalisés avec des textiles tissés toile de monofilaments, dont la maille carrée est bien définie.

Le rôle des paramètres du sol (granulométrie, uniformité), de la contrainte de confinement, de la vitesse et de la durée de l'écoulement sur les conditions de stabilité du sol, est montré clairement:

Fig. 6 : La quantité de passant augmente avec la vitesse d'écoulement.

Fig. 7 : La contrainte de confinement favorise la stabilité du sol. La masse de passant diminue quand la contrainte de compression augmente.

Un sol pulvérulent à granulométrie étalée est plus sensible

Fig. 7 : au lessivage aux faibles compressions qu'un sol uniforme.

Fig. 8 : La rétention du sol est assurée par une ouverture inférieure à deux fois le d 85 du sol dans des conditions non critiques: contrainte de 100 kPa, gradient faible (de l'ordre de l'unité), sol uniforme.

Dans le cas des sols pulvérulents, la durée de l'écoulement (1 ou 7 jours) n'a pas d'influence sur la quantité de sol passant à travers le textile quand la condition Of/d 85 <2 est vérifiée.

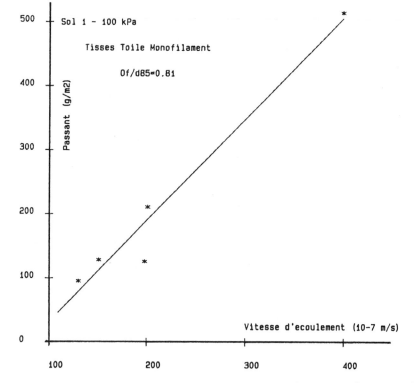

Fig. 6 Influence de la vitesse d'écoulement sur la masse de passant μ_F. Tissé toile de monofilament.

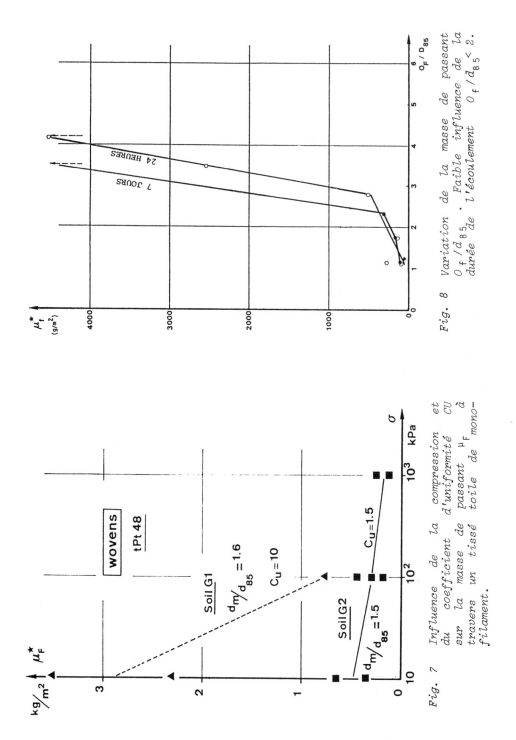

Fig. 8 Variation de la masse de passant O_f/d_{85}. Faible influence de la durée de l'écoulement $O_f/d_{85} < 2$.

Fig. 7 Influence de la compression et du coefficient d'uniformité CU sur la masse de passant μ_F à travers un tissé toile de mono-filament.

3.2. Influence de la structure du géotextile sur la rétention du sol

Le rôle du paramètre Of/d 85 a été mis en évidence précédemment. L'influence de la structure du géotextile a été montrée à la suite d'essais sur 24 h avec différents tissés de bandelettes et non tissés au contact de sols monoclasses (Fig. 9). L'utilisation de ces sols permet de faire varier le rapport Of/d 85 sans changement de la granulométrie pour un même géotextile.

La valeur de Of/d 85, limite de stabilité du sol pour les tissés toile de monofilament, semble réduite à 1 et non 2 comme sur la Figure 8, mais il faut remarquer que l'échelle utilisée pour la masse de passant μ_F n'est pas la même.

A même rapport Of/d 85, les tissés toile crin ont une moins bonne capacité de rétention que les tissés de bandelettes ou que les nontissés. Mais il faut noter plusieurs choses :
- les conditions de filtration sont peu critiques (i = 1, σ = 100 kPa),
- les tissés toile crin ont toutes leurs mailles de dimension égales ou supérieures à Of. Ces ouvertures sont en nombre sans doute plus grand que dans les nontissés et sûrement plus grand que dans les tissés de bandelettes (celles-ci sont plus larges que les filaments). Les essais de tamisage pour mesurer l'ouverture de filtration des géotextiles ne permettent pas d'obtenir d'information à ce sujet,
- pour certains géotextiles non tissés et tissés de bandelettes, la compression a pour effet de diminuer nettement l'ouverture de filtration (Dewitt 1985) de 30 à 40 % ce qui réduit le rapport Of/d 85 à prendre en compte.

3.3. Evolution du système sol-géotextile :

Des essais de plus longue durée (7 jours) ont été réalisés avec des géotextiles nontissés, aiguilletés ou thermoliés en se plaçant résolument dans le domaine "stable" observé avec les essais à 24 h, c'est à dire avec Of/d 85 < 1 (Machizaud 1982).

Les pertes de charge dans le sol et au voisinage du textile (textile compris) ont été mesurées au cours de l'essai. L'évolution de la permittivité de la zone filtrante Ψ_f et du sol en amont Ψ_s est corrélée aux quantités de passant obtenues à 24 h et 7 jours.

Voici deux exemples de comportement filtrant, obtenus avec un non tissé aiguilleté (O_f = 105 μm) en contact avec un sol pulvérulent :

a) Exemple 1 : Filtration d'un sol pulvérulent à granulométrie étroite (CU ≃ 1,5 ; d 85 = 100 μm). Sous compression très faible (σ_n = 10 kPa) et des gradients hydrauliques voisins de 0,5, un léger "colmatage", réduction de la permittivité de la zone filtrante, est observé (Fig. 10) et semble se stabiliser rapidement (moins de 48 h). La masse de passant n'a pratiquement pas augmenté :

73,5 g/m² à 24 h et 90 g/m² à 145 h

Le "colmatage" observé ne correspond donc qu'à la mise en place d'une structure stable de blocage des particules. Dans ces conditions, le géotextile remplit correc-

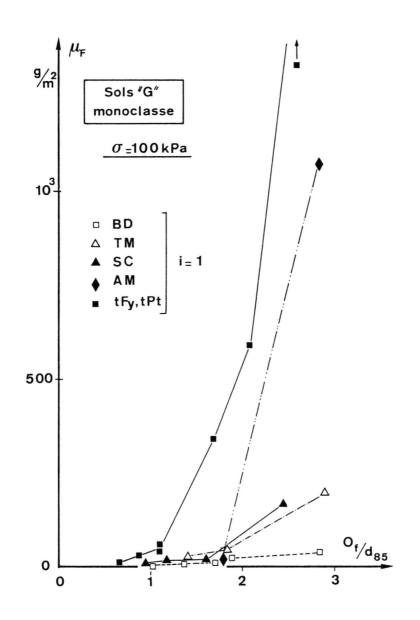

Fig. 9 *Influence de la structure du géotextile sur la masse de pas-sant* μ_f .

   BD : *Non tissé aiguilleté*
   TM : *Non tissé thermolié*
   SC : *Tissé de bandelettes*
   AM : *Tissé de bandelettes calendré*
   tFy, tPt : *Tissé toile de monofilaments*

tement son rôle, tant du point de vue de la rétention
que de la permittivité.

Bien que la compression soit faible, les conditions
de filtration sont peu critiques : Of/d 85 ≈ 1, gradient
moyen de 0,5.

b) Exemple 2 : Filtration d'un sol pulvérulent à granulométrie étroite
(CU = 10 ; d 85 = 100 µm). Avec les conditions de filtration σ_n = 10 kPa et i ≈ 20 un "lessivage" de la zone
filtrante est mis en évidence (Fig. 11) : La permittivité de cette zone est instable et a tendance à augmenter, tandis que la perméabilité du sol n'évolue pas.

Les mesures de passant effectuées dans des conditions
équivalentes montrent une augmentation très nette de
la masse de passant avec le temps de filtration :

74 g/m² à 24 h   et   693 g/m² à 165 h

Dans ce cas, les conditions de filtration peuvent être
considérées comme très critiques (faible compression,
gradient élevé) bien que Of/d 85 soit ≈ 1.

Une augmentation de la contrainte de confinement à
σ_n = 100 kPa et un gradient i = 9 montre un léger colmatage avec une diminution sensible de la masse de
passant : 306 g/m² à 175 h (Fig. 12).

La réduction de permittivité ne semble pas dangereuse
pour le système, ce qui a été confirmé par un essai
sur 1100 h (Fig. 13).

La mise en place d'une structure granulaire stable au voisinage
du filtre implique nécessairement une réduction de la permittivité
de la zone filtrante qui n'évoluera plus après stabilisation du sol.
Cette stabilisation sera donc fonction des conditions de filtration
(compression, gradient, Of/d 85).

Quand ces conditions sont favorables (peu critiques), la stabilisation a lieu rapidement car le sol est pulvérulent. Dans le cas
de sols à faible coefficient de consolidation, le temps de stabilisation est certainement plus grand, mais pas beaucoup plus dans la mesure où la zone concernée est de faible épaisseur.

4. Conclusion

Nous avons mis en évidence un certain nombre de conditions favorables ou défavorables à la stabilité du complexe sol-géotextile en
filtration.

Les résultats obtenus sont-ils significatifs du comportement
à long terme ? Ils n'apportent sûrement pas la solution à tous les
problèmes mais ils permettent de comprendre certains mécanismes.

Ces essais ont été réalisés avec un sol pulvérulent pour lequel
les caractéristiques mécaniques et hydrauliques mises en jeu au cours
des essais sont celles à long terme. Les indications obtenues sont
donc significatives. Cependant, si des mécanismes tels que le blocage
géométrique ou la formation de voûtes granulaires ont été pris en

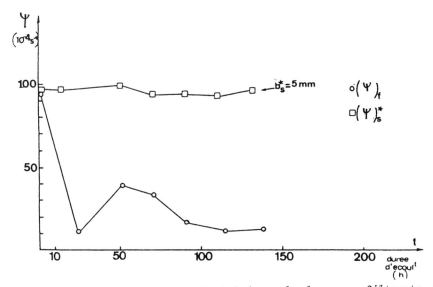

Fig. 10   *Evolution de la permittivité* Ψ_f *de la zone filtrante et*
Ψ_s *du sol en fonction du temps. Conditions de filtration*
peu critiques : i ≈ 0,3, σ_n = 10 kPa, sol à granulométrie
étroite, O_f/d_{85} ≈ 1.

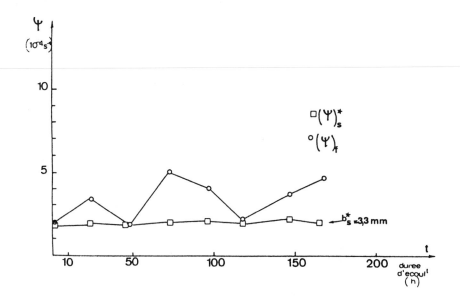

Fig. 11   *Evolution de la permittivité* Ψ_f *de la zone filtrante et*
Ψ_s *du sol en fonction du temps. Conditions de filtration*
critiques : i ≈ 20, σ_n = 10 kPa, sol à granulométrie étalée,
O_f/d_{85} ≈ 1.

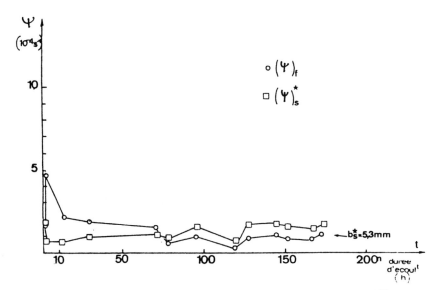

Fig. 12   *Evolution de la permittivité Ψ_f de la zone filtrante et Ψ_s du sol en fonction du temps. Conditions de filtration peu critiques : $i \simeq 9$, $\sigma_n \simeq 100$ kPa, sol à granulométrie étalée, $O_f/d_{85} \simeq 1$.*

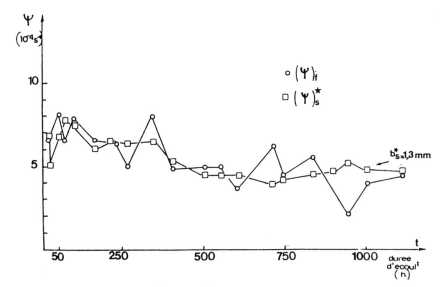

Fig. 13   *Evolution de la permittivité Ψ_f de la zone filtrante et Ψ_s du sol en fonction du temps. Conditions de filtration peu critiques : $i \simeq 6$, $\sigma_n \simeq 100$ kPa, sol à granulométrie étalée, $O_f/d_{85} \simeq 1$.*

128

compte dans ces simulations, les phénomènes d'adhérence de particules fines sur les fibres n'ont certainement pas eu lieu.

Quel type d'essai faut-il réaliser pour choisir un géotextile pour une application donnée ? Il est bien sûr conseillé d'utiliser le même sol qu'in situ et aussi de réaliser une simulation avec les mêmes conditions de compression et de vitesse d'écoulement que celles prévues sur le terrain. Il n'est pas souhaitable d'effectuer une simulation avec des conditions plus défavorables à priori, compression plus faible et vitesses plus élevées, surtout dans le cas de sols peu consolidés ou de géotextiles compressibles. Des essais réputés stables dans ces conditions ne sont pas une garantie à long terme dans la mesure où les mécanismes mis en jeu ne sont pas les mêmes: formation d'un "gâteau" si le sol est peu comprimé ou s'il n'est pas en contact avec le géotextile, absence de colmatage interne par adhérence si l'écoulement est trop rapide.

La durée de l'essai doit être suffisante pour permettre la consolidation du sol au voisinage du filtre. Si le système sol-géotextile ne présente pas d'évolution ni de la permittivité de la zone filtrante, ni de la masse de passant, on pourra considérer que le système est stable à long terme, sous réserve de la tenue du géotextile : compressibilité, fluage sous tension et vieillissement physico-chimique.

Références

Dewitt, P. (1985) Porométrie des géotextiles non-tissés aiguilletés. Mémoire de 3ème Année. ENITRTS. Strasbourg.

Gourc, J.P. (1982) Quelques aspects du comportement des géotextiles en Mécanique des Sols. Thèse de Doctorat d'Etat. Université de Grenoble.

Machizaud, Ch. (1982) Pouvoir filtrant des géotextiles. Thèse de Doctorat de Spécialité. Université de Grenoble.

Matheron, G. (1971) Les Polyèdres Poissoniens Isotropes. 3ème Symposium sur la fragmentation. Cannes.

Millot, F. (1986) Etude de la porométrie des géotextiles et applications. Thèse de Docteur Ingénieur. Université de Grenoble.

Sundias, E. (1986) Etude de la capacité de rétention des géotextiles. Thèse de Docteur Ingénieur. Université de Grenoble.

Sunjoto, S. (1986) La mesure de l'ouverture de filtration des géotextiles. Analyse des méthodes d'essais. Thèse de Docteur Ingénieur. Université de Grenoble.

MÉCANISMES DE COLMATAGE DES GÉOTEXTILES

A. L. ROLLIN
Ecole Polytechnique de Montréal

SOMMAIRE

Le phénomène de colmatage des géotextiles relève du comportement à long terme en filtration de ces matériaux. Il est essentiel que le géotextile puisse conserver ses propriétés initiales aussi longtemps que possible sinon une diminution de ses caractéristiques filtrantes entraînerait des travaux de réfection pouvant compromettre l'utilité technique et économique de l'ouvrage tout entier.

Le niveau de colmatage a une incidence directe sur la perméabilité du filtre. Les particules d'un sol entraînées par un courant d'eau peuvent être arrêtées en amont du filtre, entrer dans la structure du filtre et être emprisonnées ou bien passer au travers du filtre. Tout dépend de la granulométrie des particules, de la structure du filtre et des forces dynamiques de l'eau sur les particules. D'autres facteurs sont aussi très importants pour minimiser les risques de colmatage tels que les conditions de mise en oeuvre (le degré de saturation du sol et le niveau de contact entre le sol et le filtre), les conditions physico-chimiques dans les drains, les charges dans l'eau drainée (organismes, sédiments organiques, présence de fer et de sels dissous) et les cycles périodiques de drainage.

Il faut donc concevoir les ouvrages afin de favoriser l'arrêt des particules (formation d'un filtre naturel) et de s'assurer que les particules entraînées dans la structure des géotextiles durant la période initiale de filtration traversent entièrement le filtre.

De plus en plus de géotextiles sont utilisés dans des ouvrages d'assainissement ou dans des bassins de retenu de sédiments toxiques ou de déchets miniers. Ces particules de faibles dimensions sont souvent en suspension dans l'eau de telle sorte que le risque de colmatage est très élevé. Il faut donc sélectionner le géotextile capable d'opérer pendant la période de temps requise (période relativement courte). La limite entre la filtration et la microfiltration doit être établie de telle sorte que l'identification des éléments à retenir est nécessaire.

Le colmatage ferrique est une menace constante sur des sites à contextes géologiques contrastés. La précipitation du fer dans les drains peut s'expliquer par la simple modification des conditions d'oxydo-réduction dans les systèmes de drainage favorisant le passage du fer de l'état ferreux soluble à l'état ferrique insoluble. Cette modification s'accomplit à l'aide de l'intervention de microorganismes par oxydation directe ou par dégradation des complexes organo-minéraux libérant le fer sous forme d'hydroxydes ferriques. Durant les périodes sèches, l'air présent dans les systèmes de drainage favorise la précipitation ferrique à l'intérieur des géotextiles et des tuyaux drainants pouvant rapidement les colmater.

Cette contribution traitera des points suivants:
1) introduction: propriétés hydrauliques des géotextiles et importance du phénomène du colmatage.
2) les mécanismes de la filtration: la formation d'un filtre naturel et l'arrêt des particules en suspension dans l'eau.
3) les essais de simulation en laboratoire.
4) des exemples de colmatage in situ.
5) l'évaluation des risques de colmatage et les façons d'éviter ou de minimiser le colmatage:
    a) favoriser la formation d'un filtre naturel
    b) connaissance de la granulométrie des sédiments à retenir
    c) sélection judicieuse de la structure du géotextile
    d) utilisation d'une bonne technique de mise en place des systèmes de drainage

1) INTRODUCTION

1.1) PROPRIETES HYDRAULIQUES DES GEOTEXTILES

Les propriétés hydrauliques des géotextiles sont reliées a leurs fonctions de drainage et de filtration. Elles résultent généralement de leur structure poreuse constituée de fibres ou de filaments synthétiques sous forme de nappes tricotées, tissées ou non-tissées aiguilletées ou thermoliées. Ces propriétés sont présentées au tableau-1.

perméabilité normale ou permittivité
ouverture de filtration
perméabilité transversale ou transmissivité
mouillabilité

TABLEAU-1: PROPRIETES HYDRAULIQUES DES GEOTEXTILES

Ces propriétés sont déterminées par des essais effectués en laboratoire selon des tests normalisés. Cependant certaines de ces propriétés sont modifiées au cours de leur utilisation par le colmatage partiel ou total des géotextiles. Cette diminution des propriétés résulte de la présence de particules, de sédiments, de

matériaux organiques ou d'oxyde ferrique dans la structure des
géotextiles ou résulte de la formation d'une couche imperméable en
amont des filtres.

1.2) L'IMPORTANCE DU PHENOMENE DE COLMATAGE

Les géotextiles utilisés comme filtre et/ou couche drainante
dans les applications géotechniques, de drainage agricole, de retenue
de sédiments, d'écrans marins et autres doivent conserver leurs
propriétés initiales le plus longtemps possible car une diminution de
leurs caractéristiques peut compromettre l'ouvrage tout entier. Ainsi,
le drainage des sols, de remblais, de routes, de voies ferrées, de
barrages, et autres requiert des géotextiles retenant les particules
des sols tout en permettant à l'eau de s'écouler au travers de leur
structure. Le colmatage ayant une incidence directe sur la
perméabilité normale et transversale du filtre, il faut prévoir
l'inutilité des systèmes de drainage mis en place si le niveau de
colmatage des géotextiles et des tuyaux drainants devient trop élevé
(voir la figure-1).

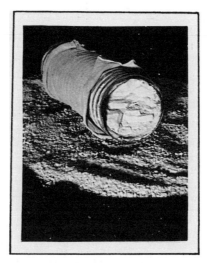

Figure-1: Exemple d'un drain colmaté.

Plusieurs travaux reliés à l'étude du colmatage des filtres
synthétiques installés dans des systèmes de drainage pour des ouvrages
en génie civil (Rollin (1983), Sotton (1981), Sotton (1982)) et pour
des drains agricoles (Broughton (1976), Rollin (1985), Stuyt (1986),
Cestre (1985), Dierickx (1982), Dierickx (1986), Williardson (1982))
ont été effectués pour identifier les facteurs prédominants. Ce
phénomène de colmatage est relié à une multitude de facteurs tels que
les conditions hydrauliques et géologiques existant aux sites

observés, la présence d'organismes et de minéraux dissous dans la phase aqueuse, les propriétés structurales des filtres et l'identification peu rigoureuse des éléments à retenir. Le colmatage est donc le résultat de plus d'un facteur de tel sorte qu'il est peu probable qu'une seule étude puisse identifier les mécanismes impliqués.

2) LES MECANISMES DE FILTRATION

Deux mécanismes de filtration sont connus, soient la formation d'un filtre naturel et l'arrêt de particules en suspension.

2.1) FORMATION D'UN FILTRE NATUREL

Dans les ouvrages géotechniques, le géotextile est installé dans un sol afin de le drainer et de le retenir en place pour favoriser sa stabilisation dans le temps.

2.1.1) ARRET PHYSIQUE

Dans les sols étalés, la structure des filtres doit être choisie pour retenir en amont de ceux-ci les plus grosses particules (95% passant). Cette couche de particules retenues à l'interface sol/géotextile retient alors à son tour des particules plus petites qui elles-mêmes retiennent des particules encore plus fines tel que schématisé à la figure-2. Suite à un certain temps d'utilisation, un filtre naturel est formé et l'entraînement des particules est stoppé. Une quantité de petites particules en conctact avec le filtre auront été entraînées dans la période initiale de filtration à l'intérieur du géotextile pour y demeurer piégées ou pour le traverser entièrement.

2.1.2) FORMATION DE VOUTES

Le mécanisme de formation de voûtes est reconnu pour les sols étalés ayant une proportion appréciable de particules argileuses. Cette formation est favorisée en plus par la présence d'une couche fibreuse en contact avec le sol (Rollin (1983)) . Les fibres de cette couche peuvent accomplir un travail similaire aux matériaux granulaires.

La conception de filtres possédant des caractéristiques de surface favorisant la formation des voûtes permet de retenir des particules plus petites que l'ouverture de filtration tel que defini par Fayoux (1977) et tel que démontré par Faure (1986). Pour fin d'exemple, un schéma d'une photographie d'une formation de voûtes est présenté à la figure-3.

133

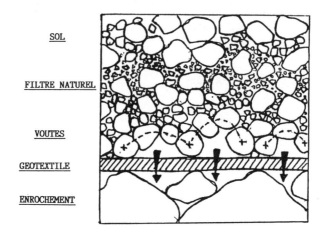

Figure-2: Mécanisme de filtration: arrêt physique.

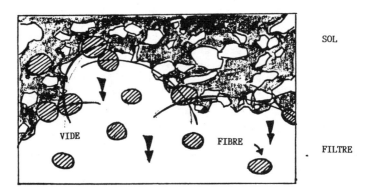

Figure-3: Mécanisme de filtration: formation de voûtes.

2.2) ARRET DE PARTICULES EN SUSPENSION

Dans certains ouvrages tels que les écrans marins ou les écrans pour l'arrêt du silt, les enceintes de retenue des déchets miniers et des sédiments toxiques et les ouvrages d'assainissement, les géotextiles doivent arrêter les particules en suspension dans une phase aqueuse. Une situation similaire peut être créée lors d'une mise en place non rigoureuse du géotextile (installation dans des conditions de saturation, protection non adéquate ou contact insuffisant entre le sol et le géotextile).

Pour ces ouvrages ou sous ces conditions, le risque de colmatage est très élevé puisque les particules sont entraînées indépendamment les unes des autres dans la structure des filtres (voir le schéma de la figure-4). Le mécanisme est alors similaire à celui rencontré en filtration industrielle. Le remplacement des filtres suite à une période d'utilisation doit être effectué ou la durée d'utilisation doit être prévue.

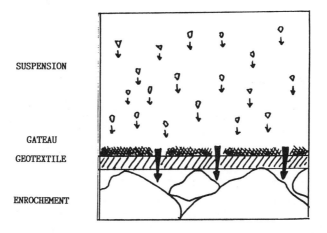

Figure-4: Mécanisme de filtration: suspension.

3) LES ESSAIS DE SIMULATION EN LABORATOIRE

Plusieurs essais en laboratoire ont été effectués pour simuler les conditions favorisant le colmatage des géotextiles utilisés dans les systèmes de drainage en utilisant deux types d'appareils (Barrington (1985), Bonnel (1985), Broughton (1976), Rollin (1980), Rollin (1985)): un perméamètre vertical ou horizontal à écoulement perpendiculaire au filtre et un système comprenent un tuyau drainant enveloppé d'une enveloppe synthétique pour simuler un écoulement radial (la description des appareils est présentée aux références). La variation de la perméabilité du système sol/filtre ou celle des débits d'eau drainée est observée dans le temps afin de prévoir le niveau de colmatage.

La difficulté d'interprétation des résultats de ces essais réside dans le choix des conditions d'opération soient a) le gradient hydraulique, b) la granulométrie et la nature du sol, c) le niveau de saturation du sol, d) le niveau de compaction du sol, e) la qualité de l'eau utilisée, et f) la direction de l'écoulement de l'eau. Les résultats publiés sont généralement fonction des appareils utilisés et des conditions sélectionnées. De plus, peu d'études ont permis de relier les caractéristiques des filtres utilisés aux niveaux de colmatage observés.

L'influence des conditions favorisant l'arrêt des particules, la formation des voûtes et la formation d'un filtre naturel tout en évitant la mise en suspension des particules d'un sol n'a pas été systématiquement étudiée. Les résultats obtenus lors des essais réalisés ne peuvent être généralisés.

Enfin l'étude en laboratoire du colmatage ferrique est très ardue à cause des conditions très particulières favorisant ce mécanisme: la culture des microorganismes, les cycles de drainage, la période d'observation très longue et les techniques d'analyse très complexes.

4) EXEMPLES DE COLMATAGE

Plusieurs exemples de colmatage ont été signalés (Dierickx (1986), Houot (1984), Rollin (1983), Sotton (1982)). Parmi ces cas, deux exemples sont discutés soient la retenue de sédiments toxiques dans des enceintes et le colmatage ferrique des systèmes de drainage.

4.1) RETENUE DE SEDIMENTS TOXIQUES

La déposition de sédiments toxiques au fond des lacs, bassins, lagunes et canaux est chose courante de nos jours. Les sédiments déposés sont généralement constitués de particules de sols, de matières organiques, de macromolécules synthétiques et de métaux toxiques tels que le zinc, le chrome, le plomb, le mercure, le chrome, le nickel et le cuivre. Des courbes caractéristiques de tels sédiments recueillis au fond d'un bassin fluvier sont présentées à la figure-5.

L'isolement des sédiments s'effectue selon des méthodes disponibles tels le dragage ou le recouvrement (voir les figures 6 à 8). Dans les deux cas, un géotextile peut être utilisé pour retenir en place les sédiments ou pour les contenir dans une enceinte. Il doit retenir les éléments tout en laissant passer l'eau durant une période de temps suffisamment longue pour compléter l'ouvrage.

Les molécules organiques et les métaux toxiques étant associés aux particules les plus petites, le géotextile devra retenir les particules les plus fines ayant une densité voisine de celle de l'eau. Le mécanisme de rétention des matériaux est donc relié à la filtration de particules en suspension dans une phase aqueuse.

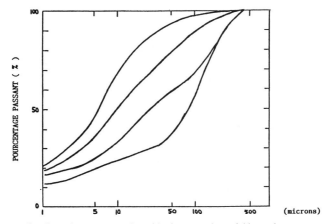

Figure-5: Courbes granulométriques de sédiments.

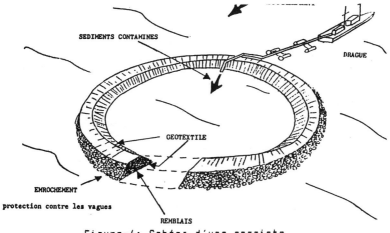

Figure-6: Schéma d'une enceinte.

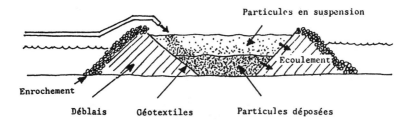

Figure-7: Schéma des mécanismes de retenue dans une enceinte.

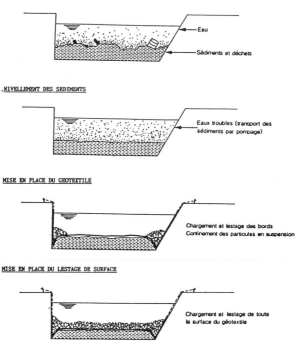

ETAT INITIAL DU CANAL

— Eau

— Sédiments et déchets

.NIVELLEMENT DES SEDIMENTS

Eaux troubles (transport des
sédiments par pompage)

MISE EN PLACE DU GEOTEXTILE

Chargement et lestage des bords
Confinement des particules en suspension

MISE EN PLACE DU LESTAGE DE SURFACE

Chargement et lestage de toute
la surface du géotextile

Figure-8: Recouvrement de sédiments déposés dans un canal.

Pour documenter cette application, les résultats d'un programme d'essais en laboratoire effectués à l'EPM à l'aide d'un perméamètre horizontal sont présentés (voir figures 9A et 9B). Une série de géotextiles ayant des ouvertures de filtration variant de 40 à 140 microns ont été utilisés et les pourcentages de sédiments retenus ont été enregistrés en fonction de leur ouverture de filtration (voir tableau- 2). Les résultats ont démontré que le niveau de colmatage augmente en fonction du degré de retenue obtenu. Par exemple, le géotextile pouvant arrêter au delà de 99.5% des sédiments s'est colmaté rapidement avec comme résultat une diminution de sa perméabilité de 0.04 à 0.00006 cm/s.

Il faut donc prévoir le colmatage des géotextiles devant arrêter les sédiments toxiques, les déchets miniers et les particules de silt. Le succès de leur utilisation réside dans la prévision de la période de service requise pour compléter l'ouvrage.

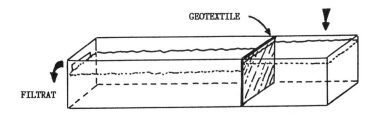

Figure-9A: Schéma du perméamètre horizontal.

Figure-9B: Le perméamètre horizontal.

SEDIMENT	LE POURCENTAGE PASSANT					
	G-1	G-2	G-3	G-4	G-5	G-6
S-1	1.0	–	–	–	–	1.0
S-2	2.0	1.0	–	2.5	0.1	1.0
S-3	–	–	–	–	–	0.6
S-4	0.5	–	0.2	–	–	0.3
S-5	2.0	–	–	–	–	0.5

Tableau-2: Capacité de rétention de géotextiles.

4.2) LE COLMATAGE FERRIQUE

Le colmatage ferrique des systèmes de drainage se produit dans plusieurs régions du monde (Alcock (1976), Cestre (1985), Ford (1979), Houot (1984), Ivarson (1978), Rollin (1984), Stuyt (1986), Thornburn (1976)). Ce problème est très sérieux et devient une menace pour les sites où du fer à l'état ferreux (soluble dans l'eau) est transformé à l'état ferrique (insoluble) par: oxydation directe, dégradation de complexes organo-minéraux résultant de l'activité de microorganismes ou de conditions géologiques favorables à une réaction d'oxydo-réduction. La précipitation de ces oxydes entraîne à long terme le colmatage des filtres et des tuyaux de drainage.

L'analyse du niveau de colmatage de géotextiles recueillis in situ peut être effectuée à l'aide d'une technique optique. Tel que présenté aux figures 10 à 12, des sections de filtres receuillis sont observées sous des agrandissements différents. On observe des régions noires constituées de d'oxyde ferrique et des régions blanches représentant des particules du sol qui occupent entièrement les vides de la structure du géotextile.

DIRECTION DE L'ECOULEMENT

PARTICULES DU SOL

OXYDES FERRIQUES

GEOTEXTILE COLMATE

AGRANDISSEMENT 100X

Figure-10: Sol et géotextile prélevés: colmatage ferrique.

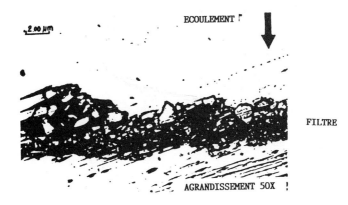

Figure-11: Colmatage ferrique d'un géotextile.

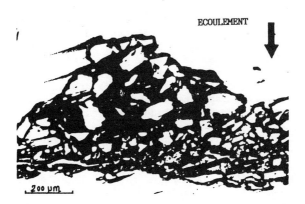

Figure-12: Colmatage ferrique d'un géotextile: agrandissement 100X.

L'examen plus détaillé des sections de géotextile situées au dessus des fentes des tuyaux annelés démontre la présence de chemins préférentiels tel que schématisé à la figure-13. Lors de la progression de la précipitation de l'oxyde dans la structure du géotextile, l'eau doit, sous le gradient hydraulique établi, se forcer un chemin à travers une couche de plus en plus imperméable. Les canaux ou chemins préférentiels apparaissent alors et peuvent subsister tant qu'un drainage est effectué sous une charge hydraulique importante. D'autre part, la précipitation est accélérée par la présence d'oxygène dans les systèmes. La période d'utilisation d'un système de drainage est alors plus courte sous des conditions de cycle de drainage irrégulier.

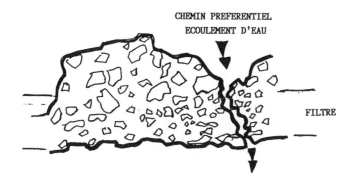

CHEMIN PREFERENTIEL
ECOULEMENT D'EAU

FILTRE

Figure-13: Schéma d'un géotextile colmaté: agrandissement 100X.

5) L'EVALUATION DES RISQUES DE COLMATAGE ET LES FACONS DE MINIMISER LE COLMATAGE

L'évaluation des risques de colmatage est un point qu'il ne faut pas ignorer lors de la sélection d'un géotextile devant être utilisé en filtration. Elle s'accompagne d'une description précise et détaillée du travail que le filtre devra accomplir et du milieu dans lequel il doit travailler. La dimension des éléments à retenir, le niveau de retenue requis, le taux de drainage espéré et la durée d'utilisation prévue doivent être déterminés en premier lieu. Par la suite les conditions hydrauliques et géologiques existantes, la qualité de l'eau à drainer, la fréquence des cycles de drainage, le niveau de compaction du sol prévu dans l'ouvrage et la procédure de mise en place devront être établis. Ces facteurs influencent grandement le risque de colmatage d'un géotextile de telle sorte qu'il est possible à partir des données recueillies d'évaluer ces risques, de sélectionner le géotextile le plus performant et ultimement d'éviter le colmatage.

On devra favoriser la formation d'un filtre naturel en diminuant la perméabilité des filtres, en s'assurant de la présence de fibres libres en surface et en utilisant un critère de filtration adéquat. On devra également protéger le filtre durant sa mise en place en le recouvrant le plus rapidement possible, en compactant le sol sur le filtre, en s'assurant de ne pas laisser d'espace entre le sol et le filtre et en utilisant une couche granulaire au besoin. On devra aussi s'assurer que l'installation n'est pas effectuée dans des conditions de saturation. Le géotextile devra être choisi pour une durée d'utilisation réaliste surtout lorsque les particules à retenir sont en suspension et des systèmes de lavage à rebours (pour le décolmatage) devront être prévus au besoin. Une surface de drainage plus grande pourra être prévue pour diminuer les forces dynamiques sur

142

les éléments à retenir. Enfin, le colmatage ferrique pourra être
diminué en conservant les systèmes de drainage constamment remplis
d'eau à l'aide de trop pleins. Le géotextile choisi devra permettre le
passage d'une quantité de fines particules entraînées à la période
initiale de filtration.

BIBLIOGRAPHIE

- ALCOCK M., (1976), "A Survey of Ochrous Land Drainage Sites in
    England and Wales", FDEU Techn. Bull., vol 76, (1).
- BARRINGTON S., (1985), "The Sealing of Soils by Manure", Ph.D.
    thesis, Macdonald College, McGill University.
- BONNEL R., Broughton R.S. and Bolduc G., (1985), "Les essais de
    matériaux filtrants pour les tuyaux de drainage en terrain
    sablonneux", comptes rendus du 12 e colloque de génie rural,
    Université Laval, Québec.
- BROUGHTON R.S., Damant C., Ami S. and English B., (1976), "The Soil
    Retention and Water Flow Performance of Some Drain Tube Filter
    Materials", CPTA annual meeting, Point Clear, Alabama.
- CESTRE T., (1985), " Revue des critères d'appréciation des risques
    de colmatage minéral des drains agricoles", CEMAGREF, B.I. no.
    325.
- DIERICKX W. and Yuncuogly H., (1982), "Factors Affecting the
    Performance of Drainage Envelope Materials in Structural
    Unstable Soils", Agric. Water Management, vol 5, 215.
- DIERICKX W., (1986), "Field Experience and Laboratory Research on
    Drainage Envelopes", Proc. Int. Sem. on Land Drainage,
    Helsinki, 51, Finland .
- DIERICKX W., (1986), "Model Research on Geotextiles Blocking and
    Clogging in Hydraulic Engineering", Proc. III rd Int. Conf.
    on Geotextiles, 775.
- FAURE Y., Gourc J.P., Brochier P. et Rollin A.L., (1986),
    "Interaction sol-géotextile en filtration", Proc. III rd Int.
    Conf. on Geotextiles, 1207, Vienna.
- FAYOUX D., (1977), "Filtration hydrodynamique des sols par les
    géotextiles", comptes rendus du colloque international sur
    l'emploi des textiles en géotechnique, vol 2, 329, Paris.
- FORD H.W., (1979), "Characteristic of Slime and Ochre in Drainage
    and Irrigation Systems", ASAE, vol 22, (5), 1093.
- HOUOT S., Cestre T. et Berthelin J., (1984), "Origine du fer et
    conditions de formation du colmatage ferrique", XII congrès
    int. des irrigations et du drainage, Fort Collins.
- IVARSON K.C. and Sojak M., (1978), "Microorganisms and Ochre
    Deposits in Field Drain of Ontario", Can. J. Soil Sc., vol 58,
    1.
- ROLLIN A.L., Estaque L. et Lafortune G., (1980), "Programme
    d'analyse de géotextiles utilisés comme écran marin ", rapport
    technique Ecole Polytechnique, CDT-P-901.
- ROLLIN A.L., (1983), "Les mécanismes de colmatage des géotextiles
    non-tissés: analyse de structures colmatées", revue
    association suisse des professionnels de geotextiles, mars .

- ROLLIN A. et Brochier P., (1984), "Analyse de filtres prélevés sur des tuyaux de drainage agricole", rapport techn. Ecole Polytechnique, mai.
- ROLLIN A.L., Broughton R.S. and Bolduc G., (1985), "Synthetic Envelope Materials for Subsurface Drainage Tubes", CPTA annual meeting, Fort Lauderdale.
- SOTTON M., (1981), "Le vieillissement et la durabilité des géotextiles", congrès Index, session 7.
- SOTTON M., Leclercq B., Fedoroff N., Fayoux D. et Paute J.L., (1982), "Contribution à l'étude du colmatage des géotextiles: approche morphologique", 2 e congrès int. sur les géotextiles, Las Vegas.
- STUYT L.C.P.M., (1986), "A Non-Destructive Morphological Study of Mineral Clogging of Drains", Proc. Int. Sem. on Land Drainage, Helsinki, 90, Finland.
- THORBURN A.A. and Trafford B.D., (1976), "Iron Ochre in Drains: a Summary of Present Knowledge", FDEU Techn. Bull., vol 76, (1).
- WILLARDSON L.S., (1982), "Exit Gradients at Drain Openings", Proc. 2 nd Int. Drain Workshop, 198, Washington D.C..

ETUDE DE L'INTERFACE SOL-GÉOTEXTILE EN RELATION AVEC LA RÉTENTION DES PARTICULES

J. M. RIGO
Institut de Génie Civil, Université de Liège

1. Introduction

Dans les applications des géotextiles où les fonctions hydrauliques ont
un certain rôle à jouer, il a été mis précédemment en évidence le rôle
néfaste que peut jouer sur ces fonctions le colmatage des géotextiles
par des particules en provenance du sol. Ce colmatage peut se réaliser
soit à l'amont du géotextile, soit dans le géotextile mais également à
l'aval de celui-ci par blocage de l'ensemble du système drainant.
Si des particules du sol se sont logées dans le géotextile ou à
l'aval de celui-ci, elles ont dû forcément passer par la zone d'interface entre le sol et le géotextile.

Des recherches menées dernièrement au Laboratoire des Matériaux de
Construction de l'Université de Liège ont porté sur l'étude de la zone
d'interface entre le sol et le géotextile.
Nous considérons, en effet, que cette zone d'interface est le point de
passage obligé pour les particules de sol si celles-ci ne sont pas suffisamment stabilisées.
La méthode développée à Liège comporte deux étapes :
- dans la première, on étudie spécifiquement le maillage de contact
  entre le sol et le géotextile;
- dans une seconde étape, des essais de filtration sont réalisés, qui
  mettent en relation les résultats obtenus dans le cadre de la première étape, avec le comportement réel des géotextiles.

2. Méthode du maillage de contact

Cette méthode consiste tout d'abord en un examen par microscope de
l'interface entre un géotextile et une plaque de verre; le géotextile
étant sollicité transversalement par des charges variables.

La figure 1 montre un schéma du dispositif d'essai utilisé.
Comme indiqué à cette figure, le géotextile est pris en sandwich entre
deux plaques de verre; ces plaques de verre étant appliquées l'une
contre l'autre à l'aide d'un système de bras de levier. Un dispositif
microscopique est focalisé sur la zone d'interface verre-géotextile.
Des clichés peuvent être réalisés à l'aide d'un appareil photographique
pour diverses pressions transversales exercées sur le géotextile. Les
clichés sont ensuite analysés manuellement.
Les fibres apparaissant manifestement à l'interface entre le verre et
le géotextile sont reportées manuellement sur un papier calque. Ceci
définit le maillage de contact entre le géotextile et les plaques de
verre.

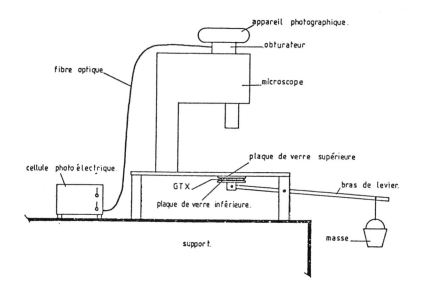

Figure 1 : schéma de l'appareillage

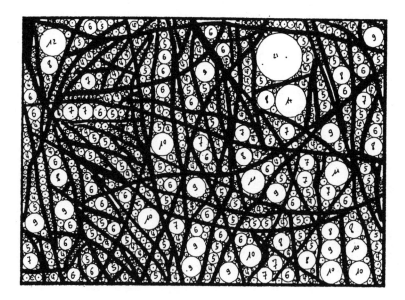

Figure 2 : approche manuelle du maillage
de contact

La figure 2 donne un exemple de résultat obtenu. Les éléments de surface définis à cette figure et limités entre eux par les fibres de contact sont ensuite remplis progressivement de cercles. Ce remplissage
se réalise par ordre décroissant de diamètre de cercle, jusqu'à remplissage quasi complet de ces surfaces complexes. La population des cercles
inscrits est alors analysée et classifiée par tranches de diamètre.
Cette réduction des données permet donc de définir un certain nombre de
classes de cercles et, pour chaque classe, l'établissement d'une fréquence d'observation. Ce diagramme des fréquences est alors assimilable
à la courbe granulométrique d'un sol hypothétique, en contact avec le
géotextile.

La figure 3 montre le résultat de ce genre de travail. Elle donne les
courbes granulométriques de maillage de contact pour un géotextile
donné et pour diverses pressions transversales. Il est à remarquer sur
cette figure que la courbe caractéristique d'un produit est fonction
de la pression transversale appliquée à celui-ci. Le diamètre moyen de
maillage de contact est donc dépendant de la pression transversale ap-
pliquant le géotextile sur une surface.
Ces courbes permettent de définir, pour chacune des pressions, des ouvertures de filtration caractéristiques des géotextiles.

Nous avons décidé de retenir, pour la suite des travaux, la valeur correspondant au diamètre pour lequel le pourcentage de grains de dimensions inférieures serait de 95 % (O_{c95}).

Le tableau 1 donne quelques valeurs obtenues sur des géotextiles pour
cette valeur, pour diverses pressions. Ces résultats ont été mis en
parallèle avec les résultats obtenus dans le cadre du tamissage hydrodynamique (méthode C.E.M.A.G.R.E.F.) ainsi qu'avec les résultats obtenus par la méthode théorique développée par le Professeur A. ROLLIN
à l'Ecole Polytechnique de Montréal.
Il est à remarquer au tableau 1 la très bonne correspondance entre les
résultats obtenus à haute pression transversale par la méthode du maillage de contact et les résultats obtenus dans le cadre de la méthode
hydrodynamique.
Nous n'avons pas, à ce jour, obtenu d'explication quant à cette similitude; nous nous contentons actuellement de la constater.
Des études et des discussions de ces résultats devront avoir lieu pro-
chainement entre les Universités de Liège, Grenoble et Montréal.

La méthode de maillage de contact permet donc de définir pour chaque
géotextile envisagé une ouverture caractéristique de ses pores en contact avec le sol pour diverses pressions transversales.
La première étape vient de nous montrer que cette valeur d'ouverture
caractéristique est fortement dépendante de la pression d'application
du géotextile contre le sol.
Il est donc très important pour la suite de prendre en considération la
pression latérale d'application du géotextile sur le sol pour l'étude
du comportement en filtration des géotextiles.

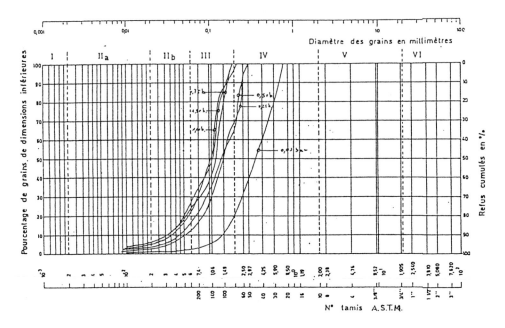

Figure 3 : courbes granulométriques de maillage de
contact pour diverses pressions transversales

Tableau 1 : détermination de la porométrie par les différentes méthodes

Géotextile	Maillage de contact			Tamisage hydrodyn.	Méthode théoriq.	Autres laboratoires	
	Oc95 à 0,03 bar	Oc95 à 0,25 bar	Oc95 à 1,5 bar	Ov95	ā	fitrat. d95	Fayoux D95
MANTA lainé PP recyl.	650	270	...170	165	501,2		
MANTA lainé	300	230	140	150	197,3		
MANTA non lainé PP r.	425	270	180	175	543,8		
MANTA non lainé	350	210	140	150	208,0		
BIDIM U 64	310	160	95	80	290,6	60	59

3. Relation entre le maillage de contact et la rétention des particules en filtration par les géotextiles

3.1. Principe

La méthode de maillage de contact développée plus haut a mis en évidence la sensibilité des caractéristiques de rétention aux fines particules des géotextiles par rapport à la pression d'application de ceux-ci sur un support.

La seconde partie de ce travail a essayé de chiffrer les effets de ce phénomène. Le principe en est le suivant : un géotextile est sollicité transversalement par une pression mécanique; il est également surmonté d'une couche d'un sol à définir. Ce sol, et donc le complexe sol-géotextile, est soumis à une pression hydrostatique. Les quantités d'eau et quantités de particules traversant le géotextile sous cette sollicitation combinée sont récupérées et analysées.

3.2. Appareillage

La figure 4 montre une coupe dans une cellule qui a été utilisée dans le cadre de cette expérimentation. Comme indiqué sur cette figure, le géotextile est posé sur une grille métallique renforcée. Le géotextile est surmonté de billes de verre de 4 mm de diamètre qui remplissent tout le corps de la cellule. A la partie supérieure de la cellule, un dispositif comprenant une membrane d'étanchéité en caoutchouc permet la mise en pression des billes de verre et donc l'application d'une pression transversale mécanique sur le géotextile.
Par ailleurs, les vides laissés entre les billes sur une hauteur de 1 cm, compté à partir du géotextile, sont remplis à l'aide d'un sol à déterminer. Des ouïes latérales permettent une arrivée d'eau dans le corps de la cellule et donc l'application d'une charge hydrostatique sur le complexe sol-géotextile. La cellule a un diamètre intérieur de 25 cm. Le gradient hydraulique utilisé est fixé à 30.
Le sol étant mis en place à sec, l'ensemble de la cellule une fois monté est tout d'abord plongé dans un récipient contenant de l'eau pendant une heure. Les cellules sont ensuite retirées de l'eau et le gradient hydraulique est alors appliqué, ce qui définit le temps de début d'essai. L'eau s'écoulant au travers du complexe sol-géotextile est filtrée et récoltée. Il est donc possible de suivre en permanence la quantité de fines particules passées au travers du géotextile ainsi que la perméabilité du complexe sol-géotextile.

La figure 5 donne un schéma plus général du dispositif d'essai.

Le choix des sols mis en présence de géotextiles est réalisé de la manière suivante : la méthode du maillage de contact a permis de définir la courbe granulométrique d'un sol hypothétique en contact avec le géotextile. Cette courbe sert de référence au choix des sols retenus.

La figure 6 montre le principe du choix des sols.
Sur cette figure, on a reporté en pointillé la courbe représentative du maillage de contact du géotextile, pour une pression transversale définie. Pour cette même pression transversale, on choisit ensuite un

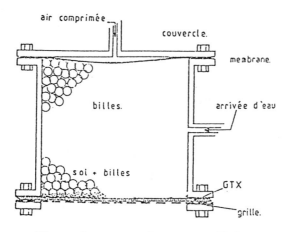

Figure 4 : coupe dans une cellule

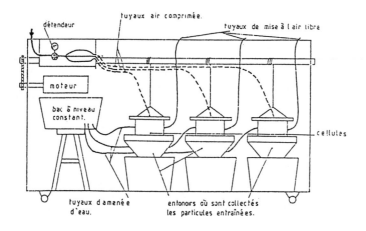

Figure 5 : schéma de l'appareillage

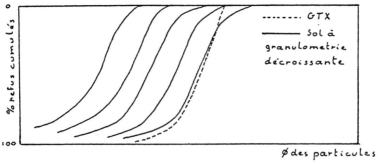

Figure 6 : sol à granulométrie
de plus en plus fine

150

ensemble de sols dont les courbes granulométriques s'écartent de plus
en plus de celles caractéristiques du géotextile jusqu'à obtenir le
phénomène de lessivage au travers du géotextile; phénomène de lessivage défini ci-après.
La durée des essais est fixée à 48 heures.

3.3. Résultats obtenus
Les figure 7, 8 et 9 donnent diverses allures de résultats que l'on
peut obtenir au cours de ces manipulations. Sur chacune d'elles, on a
reporté la courbe de perméabilité du complexe sol-géotextile en fonction du temps ainsi que des diagrammes rectangulaires représentant la
quantité de particules passées pendant un laps de temps donné.

Trois types de comportement distincts peuvent être obtenus.
Tout d'abord (figure 7), après un certain temps de stabilisation, la
quantité d'eau passant au travers du complexe sol-géotextile augmente
brutalement; on a, à ce moment, affaire au phénomène de lessivage.
On obtient ce genre de comportement pour des sols à granulométrie extrêmement petite.

La figure 8 donne l'allure des résultats lorsque l'on rencontre un phénomène de colmatage. La quantité d'eau passant au travers du complexe
eau-géotextile diminue jusqu'à s'annuler; la quantité de particules
passant au travers du géotextile suit la même allure.

Enfin, la figure 9 montre les résultats obtenus lorsqu'il y a stabilisation des phénomènes. Après une période de mise en place et une
légère augmentation, la perméabilité du complexe sol-géotextile diminue pour se stabiliser à une valeur non nulle. Parallèlement, la quantité de particules passant au travers du géotextile diminue jusqu'à
s'annuler; c'est le cas de figure que tout système drainant doit
pouvoir atteindre.

Les figures 10, 11 et 12 donnent les quantités de sol passées au travers du complexe sol-géotextile entre la 24ème et la 48ème heure en
fonction du rapport des dimensions caractéristiques du géotextile et
du sol. Pour le géotextile, c'est la valeur caractéristique Ω_{c95} pour
une pression déterminée qui est retenue. Pour le sol, nous
avons fait le choix du d_{85}.

Les diagrammes donnent les résultats pour l'ensemble des géotextiles
investigués pour les pressions de 0,03 bar, 0,25 bar et 1,5 bar.
Sur ces divers diagrammes, à côté de chaque point représentant un résultat, il a été ajouté une flèche. Lorsque cette flèche est dirigée
vers le haut, cela signifie qu'au moment de la prise de mesure à la
48ème heure, le débit continuait à augmenter; lorsque la flèche est
dirigée vers le bas, à ce même moment, le débit était en diminution.
Lorsqu'il n'y a aucune information, cela signifie que le débit était
stabilisé.

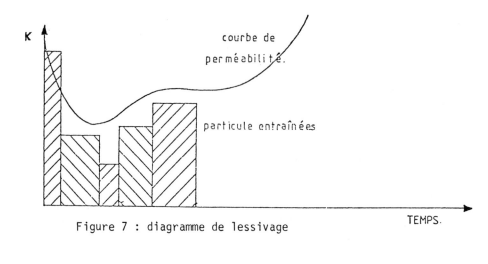

Figure 7 : diagramme de lessivage

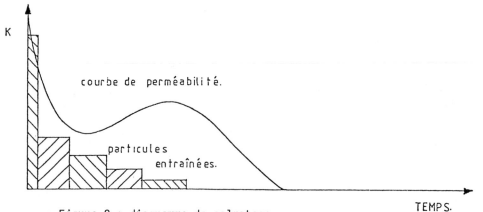

Figure 8 : diagramme de colmatage

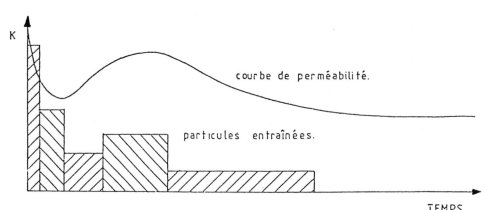

Figure 9 : diagramme exprimant le cas idéal en filtration

3.4. Analyse des résultats

Les figures 13, 14 et 15 sont à mettre en rapport respectivement avec les figures 10, 11 et 12.

Les figures 13 à 15 présentent des ajustements de type exponentiel qui ont été réalisés pour chaque famille de géotextiles investigués.

En comparant ces trois dernières figures, il est possible de mettre à nouveau en évidence l'influence de la pression transversale appliquée sur le géotextile (exprimée ici par le terme O_{c95}) sur la capacité de rétention en fines particules de sol des géotextiles.

Par ailleurs, les figures 10 à 12 ont montré qu'il existait pour l'ensemble des géotextiles investigués une quantité de sols critiques au-delà de laquelle les débits étaient constatés en augmentation systématique, donc cas où nous nous trouvions en face de phénomènes de lessivage. Cette valeur critique a été fixée et constatée à 200 milligrammes par mètre carré pour 24 heures. Les courbes obtenues aux diagrammes 13 à 15 peuvent être mises en équation par traitement statistique et on a obtenu les allures de courbes suivantes :

$$M = a \; e^{O_{c95}/d_{85}} \cdot b \qquad\qquad a = f_1 \, (P) \quad \text{et} \quad b = f_2 \, (P)$$

ou encore :

$$a \cdot b = e \, P + d$$

$$b^2 = e \, P^2 + f \, P$$

D'une manière plus générale, il est donc possible d'écrire cette loi de la manière suivante :

$$M = f_1 \, (P) \cdot e^{O_{c95}/d_{85}} \cdot f_2 \, (P)$$

3.5. Utilisation

Les résultats de l'analyse menée ci-avant nous permettent d'établir les recommandations suivantes : en partant du principe qu'un géotextile jouant office d'élément filtrant pour un système drainant peut laisser passer une quantité de matière déterminée, le dimensionnement du géotextile pourra être mené de manière à limiter la quantité de particules traversant le géotextile en fonction des données obtenues sur site, à savoir : la pente du terrain à drainer, le diamètre des particules en contact, les débits que l'on constate, les longueurs de système drainant, etc...

Grâce à l'équation établie ci-dessus, grâce à la connaissance de la nature du sol, et donc de son d_{85}, grâce à la connaissance de la pression d'application du géotextile sur le terrain, il sera possible de déterminer O_{c95} en connaissant la valeur de m, quantité de particules pouvant traverser le géotextile sans provoquer le colmatage ou le bouchage de l'ensemble du système drainant.

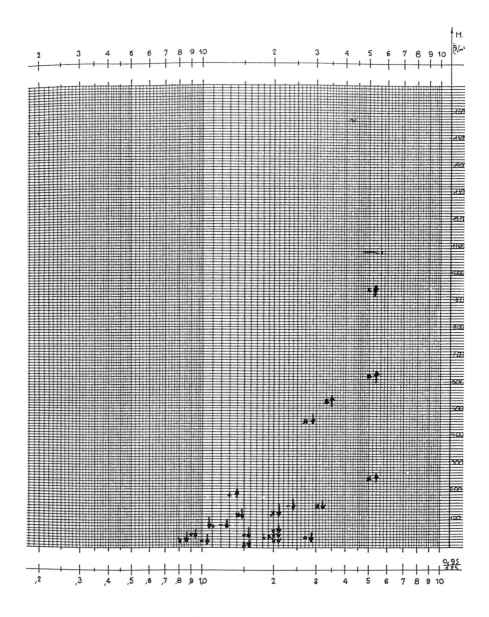

Figure 10 : quantité de sol passée au travers du géotextile
entre la 24e et la 48e heure, en fonction du rapport
O_{c95}/d_{85} pour la pression de 0,03 bars

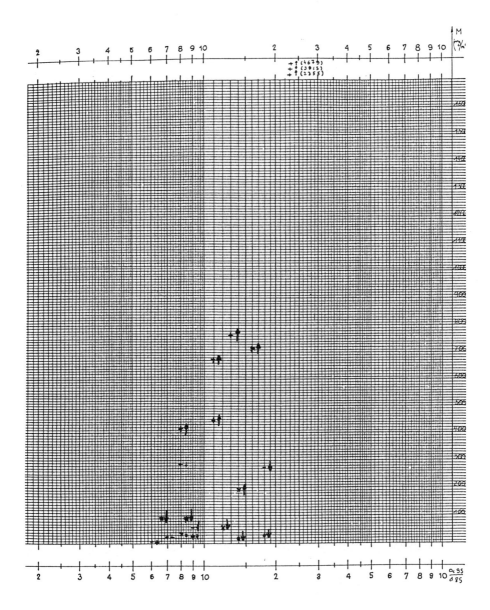

Figure 11 : quantité de sol passée au travers du géotextile
entre la 24e heure et la 48e heure, en fonction du
rapport O_{c95}/d_{85} pour la pression de 0,25 bars

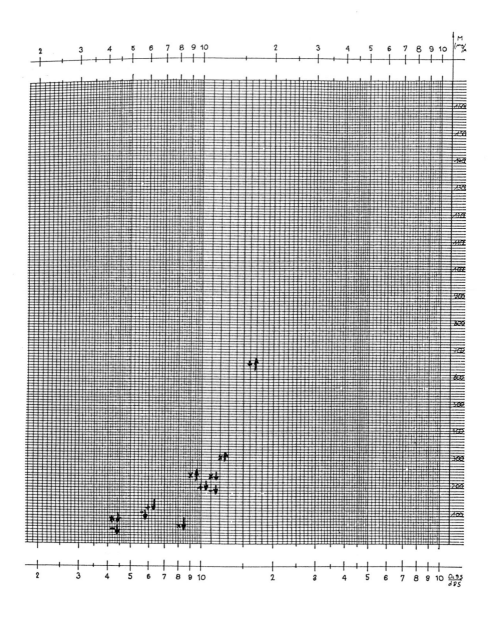

Figure 12 : quantité de sol passée au travers du géotextile entre la 24e heure et la 48e heure, en fonction du rapport O_{c95}/d_{85} pour la pression de 1,5 bars

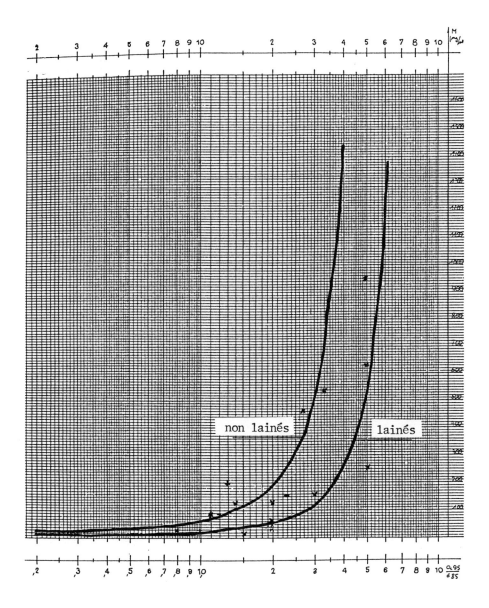

Figure 13 : courbes ajustées sur les essais à 0,03 bars

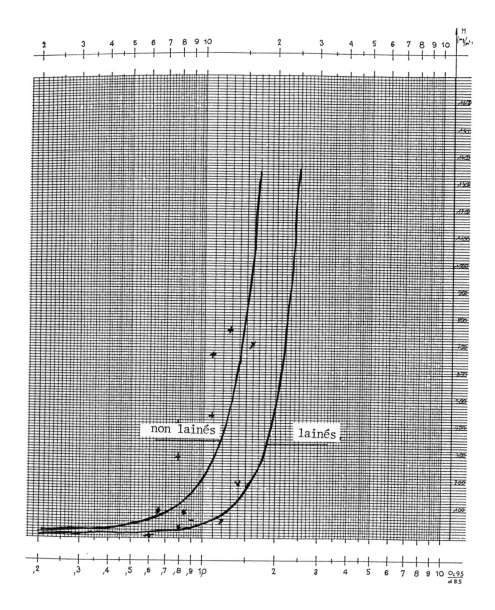

Figure 14 : courbes ajustées sur les essais à 0,25 bars

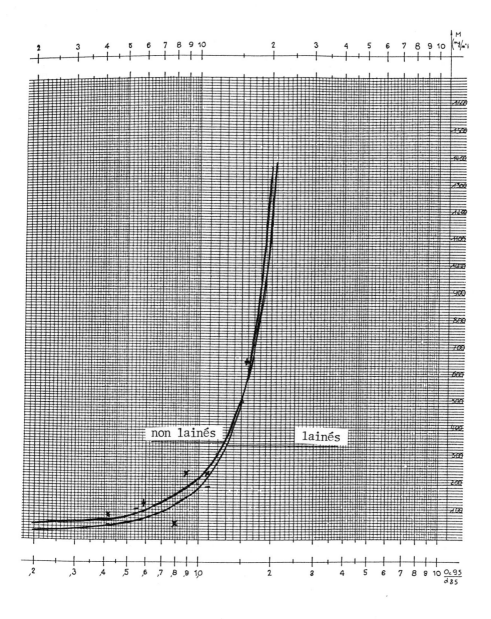

Figure 15 : courbes ajustées sur les essais à 1,5 bars

4. Conclusions

En conclusion de cette étude, il peut être affirmé qu'il sera nécessaire à l'avenir de prendre en considération la pression d'application du géotextile sur le sol pour l'établissement des critères de filtration.
Par ailleurs, il a été démontré clairement que ces critères de filtration doivent également prendre en considération la nature de la structure qui est constituée.
Nous avons mis en évidence le danger que représente une quantité trop importante de particules pouvant passer au travers d'un géotextile car l'afflux de ces particules en un certain nombre de points de concentration de débit peut provoquer un colmatage et un bouchage complet du système drainant.
Il apparaît également de toute première importance que le géotextile ait les capacités de déformation suffisantes pour pouvoir s'adapter au profil non régulier des tranchées drainantes.
Ces géotextiles auront donc de préférence une grande déformabilité pour des sollicitations de faible valeur.

PROBLÈMES LIÉS À LA PRÉDICTION DU COMPORTEMENT À LONG TERME DES MATÉRIAUX POLYMÈRES

J. VERDU

Département Matériaux, Ecole National Supérieure d'Arts et Métiers, Paris

INTRODUCTION

Grâce à un effort de recherche très soutenu depuis un quart de siècle, nous disposons de deux stocks importants de données sur le vieillissement des matériaux organiques.

Le premier concerne les données fondamentales sur les mécanismes de vieillissement. Les principaux obstacles d'ordre analytique ou conceptuel ont été pour la plupart franchis grâce au développement et à la relative banalisation de techniques comme la spectrophotométrie par transformée de Fourier, l'analyse microcalorimétrique, les techniques chromatographiques, etc ..., et aux progrès dans le domaine de la physico-chimie macromoléculaire, en particulier la chimie à l'état solide.

Le deuxième stock de données est l'ensemble énorme, mais très disparate, de résultats expérimentaux sur le comportement à long terme des matériaux industriels et en particulier sur l'évolution de leurs propriétés d'utilisation : résistance mécanique, aspect, etc.

Bien sûr, compte tenu de la vaste combinatoire offerte par la diversité des environnements, des mécanismes d'altération, des matériaux et surtout le caractère très évolutif de ces derniers, nous nous devons d'accroître encore ces stocks de connaissances. Il nous semble cependant que dans les années qui viennent, un effort de synthèse particulièrement important devra être fourni, autrement dit, de plus en plus de chercheurs devront consacrer une partie non négligeable de leur activité à établir des liens aussi nombreux et étroits que possible entre ces deux ensembles de données. Ceci exigera un large décloisonnement des activités (Industriels/universitaires, chimistes/physiciens/mécaniciens, etc ....).

Plutôt qu'une revue des connaissances, nous proposerons une revue des "méconnaissances" dans les domaines du vieillissement thermique et hydrolytique, en focalisant notre attention sur les aspects mécaniques qui intéressent tout particulièrement les utilisateurs de géotextiles.

Avant d'aborder ces points particuliers, nous définirons ce qui devrait, selon nous, être la démarche de tout spécialiste du vieillissement.

POLYMERE(S)	. IRREGULARITES STRUCTURALES
IMPURETES (restes de catalyseur)	. CONTAMINATION EVENTUELLE
ADJUVANTS	. EVAPORATION . EXSUDATION . CONSOMMATION . PRODUITS DE REACTION
MORPHOLOGIE	. ORIENTATION . CRISTALLINITE . STRUCTURE PEAU-COEUR . DISTRIBUTION SPATIALE DES ADDITIFS
GEOMETRIE	. EPAISSEUR . SURFACE SPECIFIQUE
Paramètres "Matière"	Paramètres "Mise en Oeuvre"

Fig. 1 Paramètres "Matériau".

ATMOSPHERE	. OXYGENE (confinement ?) . HUMIDITE HR HR = f(t)
OU MILIEU	. NATURE P_H, ions ...
TEMPERATURE	. T = f(t)
CONTRAINTES	. σ = f(t)
RAYONNEMENTS	. SPECTRE I = f(t)

Fig. 2 Principaux Paramètres "Milieu".

LA DEMARCHE GENERALE

L'utilisateur est avant tout demandeur d'un modèle cinétique décrivant l'évolution dans le temps d'une ou de plusieurs propriétés du matériau qui est défini par sa structure, sa composition et sa morphologie (Fig. 1). Dans le cas du vieillissement thermohydrolytique, les principaux paramètres du modèle seront la température, l'hygrométrie et, dans certains cas, les contraintes mécaniques. Ces paramètres sont susceptibles de varier dans le temps. Cette variation peut constituer en elle-même une cause de vieillissement (chocs thermiques ou hygro-thermiques ...) (Fig. 2).

Pour parvenir à ses fins, l'utilisateur pourra éventuellement utiliser des données acquises sur le terrain mais le plus souvent il devra réaliser des essais de vieillissement accéléré pendant lesquels il déterminera périodiquement les caractéristiques mécaniques. Pour donner une base scientifique au modèle cinétique d'évolution de ces propriétés, il sera conduit, le plus souvent, à suivre simultanément l'évolution de la structure et de la composition du matériau (Fig. 3).

CARACTERISTIQUES
d'UTILISATION

. ESSAI de TRACTION

. ESSAI de FLUAGE, FATIGUE

. DUREE de VIE sous CHARGE

CARACTERISTIQUES
PHYSICO-CHIMIQUES

. VISCOSIMETRIE à l'ETAT FONDU

. VISCOSIMETRIE EN SOLUTION

. GPC

. SPECTROPHOTOMETRIE INFRA-ROUGE

. ANALYSE THERMIQUE

. MICROSCOPIE

. ANALYSE SOL-GEL

. ANALYSE EXTRACTIBLE (adjuvants)

Fig. 3 Principaux Types d'Essais
Réalisés en Vieillissement.

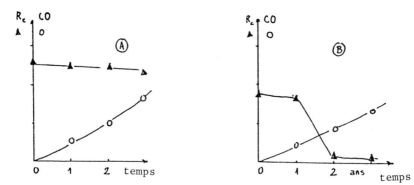

Fig. 4a   Photo-Oxydation et Résistance au Choc de Profilés PVC rigide
A. Température d'extrusion : 205 °C   B. Température d'extrusion : 180 °C

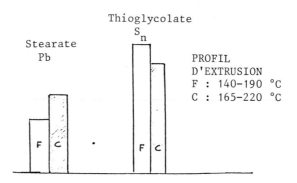

Fig. 4b   Vitesse de Photo-Oxydation de Compounds PVC
extrudés en fonction de la Température d'Extrusion.

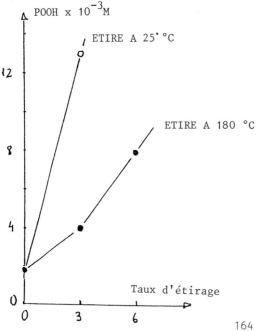

Fig. 5a   Concentration en Hydropé-roxydes à la demie-vie (50 % de l'allongement à la rupture initial). Photo-Oxydation de Fibres PP d'après D.J. CARLSSON, A. GARTON et D.M. WILES ACS Chem. Ser. 169, 56, (19)

Les conditions d'expérimentation en laboratoire imposeront éventuellement l'utilisation d'échantillons différant sensiblement, au moins par la forme, du matériau utilisé en pratique.

Enfin viendra l'exploitation des résultats de vieillissement accéléré et la mise en forme du modèle de comportement à long terme.

Ici, le praticien devra prendre conscience du fait qu'il établit dans le cas le plus général, un modèle et non une loi physique, l'extrême complexité des phénomènes et notre relative méconnaissance des relations entre la structure et le comportement mécanique rendant très délicat le passage entre le microscopique (l'acte chimique élémentaire, par exemple la coupure de chaîne) et le macroscopique (par exemple la résistance à la rupture). Le modèle devra donc contenir le minimum d'empirisme (utilisation maximale des concepts de cinétique chimique et physique), et le problème de ses limites de validité devra faire l'objet de la plus grande prudence.

Des questions se posent à tous les niveaux de cette démarche, nous allons en poser quelques unes qui nous paraissent cruciales.

QU'EST-CE QU'UN MATERIAU ?

Pour un non initié, c'est un nom commercial : Kevlar, Nylon, Dacron, etc ...

Pour un spécialiste de la chimie macromoléculaire, c'est un mélange de macromolécules, d'adjuvants et de charges. Il sait éventuellement que ce mélange a été partiellement transformé par l'opération de mise en oeuvre : les macromolécules ont été légèrement oxydées ou dégradées par le passage à température élevée, les stabilisants ont été consommés en partie, certains additifs ont pu s'évaporer, d'autres exsuder, etc ...

Pour un spécialiste du vieillissement, c'est un objet pratiquement unique car il sait :

- que ces modifications de structure et de composition, même apparemment légères, peuvent avoir des répercussions importantes sur le comportement à long terme. Exemple : le PVC rigide (Fig. 4),

- que les conditions de mise en oeuvre déterminent la morphologie au sens large (cristallinité, orientation, excès de volume libre, etc ...) et que cette morphologie détermine étroitement les conséquences des processus chimiques au plan des propriétés mécaniques. Exemple : les fibres de polypropylène (Fig. 5), (1).

On voit ici que l'utilisation de systèmes modèles ou simplifiés (par exemple films minces pour une étude spectrophotométrique), si elle est très utile dans la recherche fondamentale pour l'identification des mécanismes, est sujette à caution lorsqu'il s'agit de prédiction du comportement mécanique à long terme.

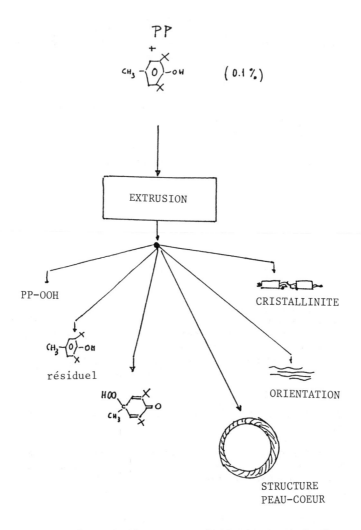

Fig. 5b Paramètres Contrôlant la Durabilité
Exemple du PP.

QUEL TEST DE CARACTERISATION CHOISIR ?

Posons-nous d'abord la question : Quelles sont les modifications structurales susceptibles d'induire une modification du comportement mécanique ? Nous en voyons deux types essentiels dans le cas des matériaux fibreux :

1) Les coupures statistiques de chaînes :

Elles peuvent résulter de l'oxydation (Fig. 6)

* Amorçage :

Décomposition thermique d'une
structure thermolabile   ———> R$^\bullet$ (radicaux)

* Propagation :

R$^\bullet$ + O$_2$ ———> RO$_2^\bullet$ (très rapide)
RO$_2^\bullet$ + PH (polymère) ———> RO$_2$H + P$^\bullet$
P$^\bullet$ + O$_2$ ———> PO$_2^\bullet$
PO$_2^\bullet$ + PH ———> PO$_2$H + P$^\bullet$ (Etc...)
                (dépend surtout de l'énergie de
                liaison P-H)

* Ramification

POOH ———> PO$^\bullet$ + OH$^\bullet$
                              ↘coupure de chaîne éventuelle

POOH + POOH ———> POO$^\bullet$ + PO$^\bullet$ + H$_2$O

* Terminaison

P$^\bullet$ + P$^\bullet$
POO$^\bullet$ + P$^\bullet$ }———> Produits inactifs
POO$^\bullet$ + POO$^\bullet$
                      ——➤ En particulier P=O + PHO

Fig. 6 Schéma "Standard" des Mécanismes
d'Oxydation Radicalaire en Chaîne

ou de l'hydrolyse   (Fig. 7).

Polyamides :

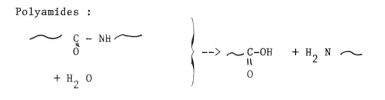

Polyesters

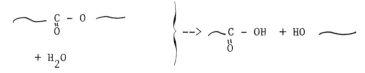

NB :   Groupe ester dans la chaîne :
        Polyesters linéaires : PET, PBT, Polycarbonate
        Polyesters tridimensionnels : Polyestères insaturés
        Polyuréthannes Polyesters
        Epoxy réticulés par anhydrides

Fig. 7   Coupure Statistique de Chaine
              par Hydrolyse.

2)   La plastification par l'eau absorbée :

Rappelons que l'eau ne pénètre que la phase amorphe, d'où
influence du taux de cristallinité. Les effets de l'absorption
d'eau sont les suivants :

a – Gonflement de polymère d'où génération de contraintes internes
    résultant de gonflements différentiels macroscopiques (en régime
    transitoire de sorption et désorption) et microscopiques (à
    l'interface amorphe-cristallin). Au cours du vieillissement
    naturel, la variation cyclique de l'hygrométrie peut se traduire
    par une fatigue à long terme (2). Ces problèmes sont parfois
    critiques dans le cas des composites ils devraient l'être beaucoup
    moins dans le cas des polymères non chargés.

b – Diminution de la température de transition vitreuse. Les polycon-
    densats les plus courants : polyamides, polyesters, ont des
    températures de transition vitreuse relativement basses :
    50-80 °C. L'effet de la plastification par l'eau peut les amener
    au voisinage de la température d'utilisation et se traduire donc
    par une modification notable du comportement mécanique, en
    particulier de la résistance à la fissuration (Fig. 8).

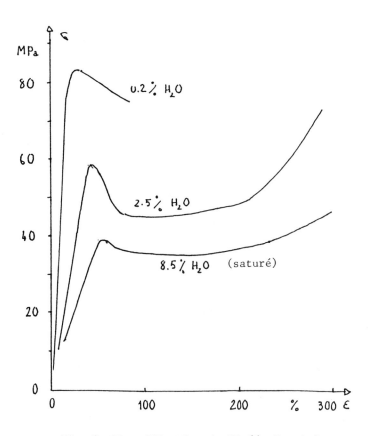

Fig. 8 Plastification de PA 66. Essai de
Traction à 23 °C. Pièce Injectée.

En l'absence de réaction chimique (hydrolyse), les effets de la
plastification sont réversibles, autrement dit les propriétés initiales sont restaurées après dessiccation. D'autre part, les effets
n'évoluent plus dès lors que le matériau est saturé (Fig. 9). Ces deux
caractéristiques permettent de dissocier expérimentalement les effets
physiques et chimiques de l'eau.

On peut donc proposer la démarche suivante :

1) Détermination de la masse moléculaire après vieillissement

par viscosimétrie en solution, chromatographie sur gel
(généralement difficile sur les matériaux utilisés pour la
réalisation de fibres), ou plus simplement mesure de l'indice de
fluidité (rappelons que la viscosité à l'état fondu dépend de la
masse molaire selon une loi du type :

$\eta = KM^{\alpha}$ où $\alpha = 3,4$ pour de nombreux polymères).

Deux possibilités se présentent :

---- La masse moléculaire diminue au cours du temps

---- La masse moléculaire est stable. Dans ce cas, l'endommagement résulte nécessairement d'un processus physique.

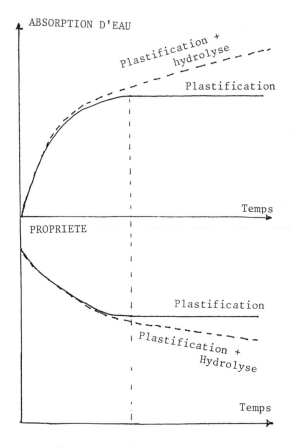

Fig. 9   Effets Physiques et Chimiques
de l'Absorption d'Eau.

2)   Etude gravimétrique

Elle conduit aux observations représentées sur la Fig. 9.

3) <u>Analyses Physico-Chimiques Diverses</u>

Elles sont surtout intéressantes dans le cas des polyoléfines :
dosage des groupes C=O résultant de l'oxydation par spectrophotométrie IR, dosage chimique des hydroperoxydes, dosage des
antioxygènes résiduels, etc ...

4) <u>Etude Mécanique</u>

En l'absence de plastification, seules les propriétés à la
rupture sont affectées (Fig. 10), il est donc inutile de déterminer le module d'élasticité ou les propriétés au seuil d'écoulement. Si ces derniers évoluent, on peut envisager soit une
plastification (Fig. 8), soit une restructuration morphologique
profonde assez peu probable dans le cas des fibres et qui
pourrait le cas échéant être mise en évidence par microscopie,
microcalorimétrie différentielle ou diffraction X. De façon
générale, la réaction de coupure de chaînes et/ou la plastification, qui augmentent la mobilité macromoléculaire, favorisent
une post-cristallisation (Fig. 11).

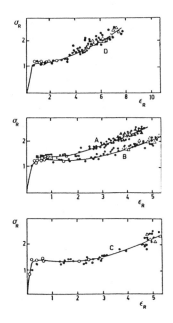

Fig. 10 Photo-Oxydation de films PEbd
Points : Enveloppe de Rupture
Courbe : Courbe de Traction Initiale

171

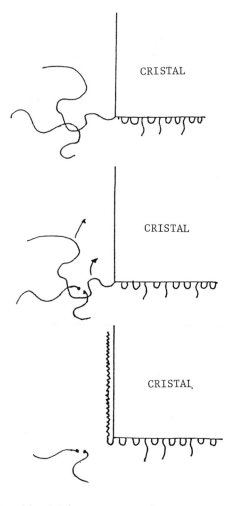

Fig. 11   Schématisation d'un Processus
de Chimicristallisation

NB. : Du fait de la superposition des effets des processus physiques
et chimiques, un essai de caractérisation mécanique après
exposition à long terme ne peut être valablement exploité que si
les échantillons sont conditionnés dans l'état de référence
prévu pour la caractérisation initiale.

COMMENT EXPRIMER LA CINETIQUE ?

Dans le cas de la réaction de coupure de chaîne, puisque chaque coupure crée une nouvelle chaîne, on peut écrire :

$$N_t = \frac{1}{\overline{M}_{nt}} - \frac{1}{\overline{M}_{no}}$$

où N_t est le nombre de coupures au temps t, $\overline{M}_{nt}$ et $\overline{M}_{no}$ les masses moléculaires moyennes en nombre au temps t et au départ de l'exposition.

Les variations de Nt en fonction du temps peuvent être traitées par les équations de la cinétique chimique. Un exemple est donné en Fig. 12 pour les polyesters.

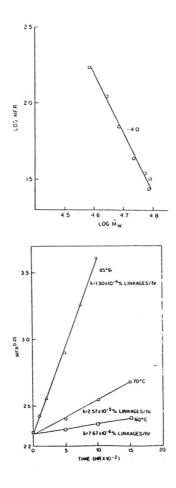

Fig. 12 Hydrolyse du PBT à 95 % HR d'après la Réf. (4). En haut : Etalonnage de la mesure d'indice de fluidité : MFR = $f(\overline{M}_w)$
En bas : Cinétique d'hydrolyse à 60, 70 à 95 °C

L'équation d'Arrhenius est généralement applicable avec des réserves qui seront faites au chapitre suivant. Dans le cas où la température varie (vieillissement naturel), on pourra faire une prédiction à partir de la température de l'essai isotherme équivalent (Tu) en écrivant :

$$\tau \exp. \left(\frac{-B}{T_u}\right) = \int_o^\tau \exp. \left(\frac{-B}{T(t)}\right) dt$$

soit :

$$T_u = \frac{-B}{Ln\left[\frac{1}{\tau} \int_o^\tau \exp.\left(-\frac{B}{T(t)}\right)dt\right]}$$

où B est la pente du diagramme d'Arrhenius déterminée par des essais de vieillissement artificiel isothermes, τ est la période du cycle de variation de température (généralement τ = 1 an) et $T(t)$ est la variation de température (données climatiques sur le site d'exposition).

On observera que cette température dépend de l'énergie d'activation (B) du processus, autrement dit qu'elle est caractéristique du matériau.

KAWKINS et coll. (5) ont donné un exemple d'application de cette démarche au cas du polyétylène.

En ce qui concerne les essais de vieillissement sous contrainte, il n'existe malheureusement pas de loi physique faisant l'objet d'un consensus général. L'école soviétique (6) adopte la relation proposée par ZHURKOV :

$$\Delta t = A \exp. \left(\frac{(E - B\sigma)}{RT}\right)$$

où σ est la contrainte et B un coefficient ayant la dimension d'un volume molaire (volume d'activation), mais nous n'avons pratiquement aucune indication sur la façon dont pourraient varier les paramètres de cette équation lorsque le polymère se dégrade.

On notera la similitude entre l'équation de ZHURKOV et celle d'EYRING qui décrit les relations entre contrainte, vitesse de déformation et température, et qui devrait en principe bien s'appliquer aux matériaux fibreux dans leur domaine d'utilisation.

En portant la contrainte réduite σ/T en fonction du logarithme de la vitesse de déformation, on obtient des graphes semblables à celui de la Fig. 13, dans lesquels on met en évidence l'existence d'une transition entre deux modes différents de déformation, correspondant par exemple à une transition ductile-fragile. Cette transition se déplace lorsque le matériau se dégrade et la température correspondante semble varier de façon monotone avec le temps (7), ce qui est particulièrement intéressant pour une éventuelle extrapolation.

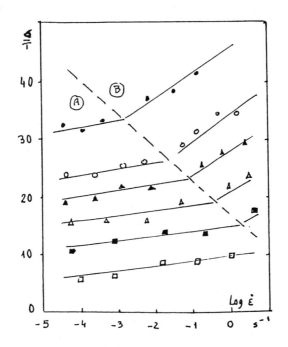

Fig. 13 Diagramme d'Eyring pour le PP.
Régions (A) et (B) —> Mécanismes
d'endommagement différents.

Au plan fondamental, une interprétation structurale de la variation du volume d'activation avec le vieillissement serait probablement fort intéressante. Malheureusement, la lourdeur de l'expérimentation a jusqu'à présent rebuté les chercheurs.

Dans le cas où le vieillissement est dominé par l'absorption d'eau, il existe, au moins pour les verres organiques, des méthodes d'approche intéressantes (8), mais elles ne semblent pas transposables au cas des fibres pour lesquelles nous sommes encore à court de solutions générales.

Le problème de la variabilité des résultats des tests de caractérisation est crucial, Philips (9) en a donné un exemple frappant dans le cas du vieillissement sous charge des matériaux composites.

Soit $\overline{\sigma_R}$ la contrainte à la rupture moyenne d'un lot d'éprouvettes et σ la contrainte appliquée : $\sigma = 0,5 \; \overline{\sigma_R}$ dans le cas étudié. L'écart type sur la détermination de σ_R est de 13 %, ce qui signifie que le lot comporte des éprouvettes telles que $\sigma / \sigma_R = 0,40$ ou $\sigma / \sigma_R = 0,66$.

Par régression linéaire, l'auteur détermine une loi empirique de durée de vie (t), du type :

$$\sigma / \overline{\sigma_R} = A - B \; Logt$$

où A et B sont des constantes.

Avec la dispersion initiale observée, l'auteur trouve par extrapolation de cette loi, des durées de vie pouvant varier entre 10^6 et 10^{11} secondes. Peu d'utilisateurs pourraient se satisfaire d'une incertitude aussi grande, il est donc particulièrement important de rechercher un test de caractérisation aussi peu dispersé que possible. Ces problèmes sont particulièrement critiques dans le cas des essais mécaniques.

QUELLES SONT LES LIMITES DE VALIDITE DE LA CINETIQUE ?

C'est l'une des questions fondamentales qui se posent au praticien, on peut la poser sous une autre forme : Sur quelle base justifier la validité d'une extrapolation de résultats de vieillissement accéléré ?

Dans le cas d'un phénomène aussi complexe que le vieillissement, il n'est en général pas possible d'apporter une réponse physique rigoureuse à cette question. Seul le verdict de l'utilisation serait indiscutable mais il est bien sûr hors de question de l'attendre, surtout dans le cas de matériaux de construction où des durées de vie supérieures ou égales à dix ans sont monnaie courante.

Nous ne savons donc pas exactement ce qu'il faut faire, par contre nous savons, dans certains cas, ce qu'il ne faut pas faire.

1) Le facteur température

L'un des points importants à cet égard concerne les transitions physiques et mécaniques du matériau, on peut l'énoncer sous forme d'une recommandation :

Les températures de transition, en particulier température de transition vitreuse, température de fusion (dans le cas des polymères semi-cristallins), températures de transition mécaniques dans le cas d'essais mécaniques, constituent autant de frontières qu'une extrapolation ne devrait franchir qu'avec la plus extrême prudence.

Cette recommandation est d'autant plus importante que l'élévation de température est généralement le moyen le plus commode d'accélérer le vieillissement.

Considérons successivement les différents domaines physiques délimités par les principales températures de transition :

a) Le domaine vitreux (T < Tg)

Dans la phase amorphe, les mouvements moléculaires de grande amplitude sont "gelés", la fraction de volume libre est faible, la diffusion des réactifs (oxygène, eau ...), qui dépend de ces deux facteurs, est relativement lente, les processus de vieillissement contrôlés par la diffusion ou faisant intervenir des réactions intermoléculaires sont donc fortement ralentis.

Ces caractéristiques tendent à disparaître au-delà de la transition vitreuse, ce qui est relativement bien mis en évidence par des études d'oxydation de polymères complètement amorphes comme les résines epoxy (Fig. 14) ou même par l'hydrolyse de polymères semi-cristallins comme les polyesters (4).

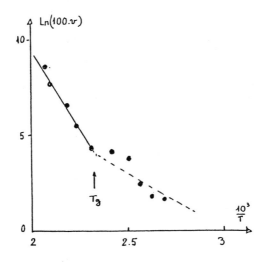

Fig. 14 Diagrammes d'Arrhénius pour la Formation de Groupes Oxygénés dans des Réticulats Epoxyde-Amine.Noter la Rupture de Pente à Tg.

L'état vitreux est par ailleurs caractérisé par son instabilité thermodynamique, et donc par son potentiel d'évolution spontanée, en l'absence de tout agent extérieur, qui dépend étroitement des conditions de mise en oeuvre, et en particulier de la vitesse de refroidissement au terme de l'opération de mise en forme. Ce phénomène, appelé vieillissement physique, a fait l'objet d'un remarquable ouvrage de STRUIK (10). Nous n'y reviendrons donc pas sauf pour noter que réaliser un vieillissement accéléré à T>Tg revient à négliger les effets du vieillissement physique, lequel peut pourtant se traduire par une augmentation notable de la contrainte au seuil d'écoulement (par ex. 10 - 20 % pour le polycarbonate), une diminution non moins notable de la résilience et une diminution considérable de la complaisance en fluage.

Le comportement mécanique ne varie pas nécessairement de façon monotone dans tout le domaine vitreux, un mode d'endommagement donné pouvant prédominer ou non en fonction essentiellement de la température et de la vitesse de sollicitation (Fig. 13). A chaque type d'endommagement va bien sûr correspondre un modèle cinétique propre.

b) **Le domaine compris entre la température de transition vitreuse et la température de fusion (polymères semi-cristallins)**

Nous sommes ici en présence d'une dispersion de cristallites dans une matrice caoutchoutique donc mobile. Au plan du vieillissement, les difficultés proviennent essentiellement de ce que nous sommes en présence d'un matériau "morphologiquement vivant" : Les contraintes internes, les orientations dans la phase amorphe, ont tendance à se relaxer rapidement. Les segments de chaîne stéréoréguliers qui étaient piégés dans la phase amorphe par un effet de trempe lors de la mise en oeuvre vont être libérés et vont pouvoir s'incorporer à la phase cristalline.

Les coupures de chaînes, comme on l'a déjà vu, peuvent jouer le même rôle (chimi-cristallisation).

Ces restructurations morphologiques, qui vont toutes dans le sens d'une augmentation de la cristallinité, s'ajoutent bien sûr aux effets directs du vieillissement, en particulier aux coupures de chaînes, ce que nous pouvons écrire sous la forme de l'équation :

Vieillissement Accéléré à T>Tg = Vieillissement + Recuit

Ces phénomènes devraient bien sûr être d'autant plus importants que la fraction initiale de phase amorphe est elle-même importante.

Notons que pour certains polymères couramment utilisés sous forme de fibres (polyamides, polyester), Tg est, comme on l'a vu, relativement proche de la température ambiante. L'effet plastifiant de l'eau absorbée entraîne une diminution de Tg et peut de ce fait faire "basculer" le comportement du polymère d'un domaine dans l'autre à une température voisine de l'ambiante.

c) **Le domaine liquide** $(T > T_F)$

Prenons l'exemple du test bien connu de stabilité thermique des polyoléfines par calorimétrie différentielle (DSC).

Le principe est simple : il est basé sur la mesure de la période d'induction en exposition isotherme dans l'air ou dans l'oxygène. A la fin de cette période, la brusque accélération des processus d'oxydation se traduit par l'apparition d'un exotherme sur le thermogramme (Fig. 15).

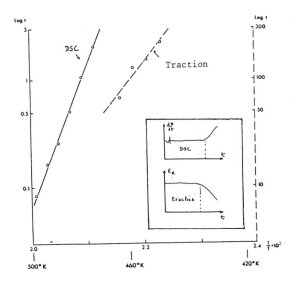

Fig. 15 Diagrammes d'Arrhénius pour la Thermo-Oxydation du PE d'après M. JORQUERA ENCINA (Thèse D3C PARIS VI 1984)

Malgré la sensibilité des appareils actuels, ceux-ci ne peuvent guère délivrer un signal observable à des températures inférieures à 200 °C, les vitesses d'oxydation, autrement dit de dégagement de chaleur, étant trop faibles au-dessous de

179

cette température. Les périodes d'induction obtenues de cette
manière sont essentiellement liées aux performances chimiques
des anti-oxygènes présents et obéissent en général assez bien à
la loi d'Arrhénius, ce qui permet en principe de réaliser des
extrapolations à plus basse température.

Les essais de vieillissement à long terme réalisés à l'état
solide (< 110 °C pour le PE, < 160 °C pour le PP) conduisent
cependant à des durées de vie notablement différentes (généralement inférieures), de celles prédites à partir des résultats
de DSC (11).

L'une des raisons analysée par BAIR (12) est liée à la solubi-
lité du stabilisant dans la matrice polymère, plus élevée à
l'état liquide qu'à l'état solide, ne serait-ce que parce que
la fraction de phase amorphe qui contient pratiquement la
totalité des adjuvants est supérieure.

L'autre raison apparaît lorsque l'on réalise des études de la
cinétique d'oxydation du polymère pur de part et d'autre de la
température de fusion, par exemple dans le cas du PP par
chimiluminescence (Fig. 16).

Bien que la cinétique globale d'absorption d'oxygène soit
apparemment peu modifiée par la fusion, la part relative des
différents mécanismes peut varier de façon importante. S'il
s'agit par exemple des coupures de chaînes, on peut s'attendre
à une modification radicale du comportement mécanique à long
terme. Nous reviendrons sur ce problème dans le prochain
chapitre.

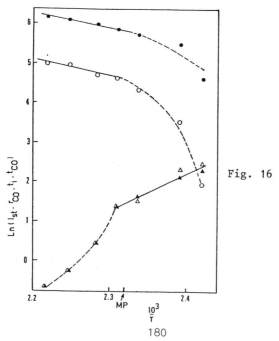

Fig. 16

2) Les autres facteurs

Prenons le cas des sollicitations en fatigue cyclique de polymères semi-cristallins. Les essais statiques avaient révélé l'existence de mécanismes de rupture, par exemple intra ou intersphérolitiques, chacun d'eux prédominant dans un domaine de vitesses de sollicitation bien déterminé (13).

SCHULTZ a proposé le traitement des cinétiques sur la base de la loi d'EYRING en partant de l'hypothèse que deux types de sites d'amorçage de l'endommagement ayant des caractéristiques différentes : énergie et volume d'activation, peuvent être impliqués (14). Nous avons récemment montré que ces concepts pouvaient s'appliquer à la fatigue du polypropylène (15).

Le mode d'accélération le plus courant des essais de fatigue consiste en une augmentation de la fréquence de sollicitation et de l'amplitude de contrainte ou de déformation. D'après ce qui précède, on voit que, là aussi, une limite existe, c'est celle au-delà de laquelle le mode d'endommagement prédominant devient différent de ce qu'il est en vieillissement naturel.

Examinons maintenant le cas de la fatigue à amplitude de déformation constante en présence d'humidité. L'eau plastifie la phase amorphe, (qui gouverne pour une grande part la déformabilité du matériau) et tend donc à diminuer l'amplitude de la contrainte induite, ce qui aura dans certains cas un effet favorable sur la durée de vie. On voit qu'en l'occurrence un facteur réputé "dégradant" sur la base d'essais statiques peut jouer un tout autre rôle dans certaines conditions de fatigue. La plastification par l'eau peut par ailleurs faire basculer la rupture d'un régime cinétique à l'autre.

Y A-T-IL UNE CORRESPONDANCE ETROITE ENTRE CINETIQUE DE DEGRADATION CHIMIQUE ET CINETIQUE D'EVOLUTION DES PROPRIETES MECANIQUES ?

Ayant vérifié qu'au plan des mécanismes de dégradation chimique et d'endommagement mécanique, les conditions d'essai de vieillissement accéléré étaient valables, et ayant acquis les résultats d'essai, nous devons maintenant modéliser la cinétique d'évolution (ou la durée de vie) des propriétés mécaniques.

La démarche qui s'impose consiste à faire l'hypothèse qu'à un état structural donné (déterminé par analyse physico-chimique) correspond un état mécanique donné (éventuellement prévisible par les relations structure-propriétés -par exemple propriétés mécaniques-masse moléculaire -bien établies pour la plupart des polymères industriels).

Nous verrons que l'essentiel des problèmes réside dans la façon dont on appréhende cet état structural.

Considérons d'abord le problème sous l'angle des relations structure-propriétés mécaniques en partant de l'hypothèse la plus simple d'une dégradation homogène d'ordre zéro :

$$N_t = \frac{1}{\overline{M}_{nt}} - \frac{1}{\overline{M}_{no}} = Kt \tag{I}$$

Des considérations de volume libre, ou simplement l'hypothèse qu'une extrémité de chaîne est une "microamorce de rupture", conduisent de nombreux auteurs, après FLORY, à proposer pour la dépendance de la contrainte à la rupture avec la masse moléculaire, la relation suivante :

$$\sigma_R = \sigma_{R\infty} - \frac{A}{\overline{M}_n} \tag{II}$$

où $\sigma_{R\infty}$ et A sont des constantes.

En combinant les équations (I) et (II), on arrive à :

$$\sigma_{Ro} - \sigma_{Rt} = K.A.t \tag{III}$$

soit

$$\sigma_{Rt} = \sigma_{Ro} - K.A.t$$

On voit que dans ce cas (idéal) il est facile d'exprimer la variation de contrainte à la rupture en fonction du temps et de la constante de vitesse de la dégradation chimique à condition de connaître la pente A de la droite $\sigma_R = f(1/\overline{M}_n)$.

Il est cependant assez rare que l'on observe une variation monotone de la contrainte à la rupture avec le temps d'exposition. Dans de nombreux cas, on observe dans un premier temps une relative conservation des propriétés, suivie par une chute rapide et catastrophique indiquant que l'on vient de franchir une transition (dont on rappellera qu'elle dépend de la vitesse de sollicitation).

Les relations structure-propriétés nous apprennent que cette transition s'opère lorsque la masse moléculaire devient inférieure à M_c (masse moléculaire moyenne critique), au-delà de laquelle il n'y a plus de possibilité d'enchevêtrement des macromolécules (16). Dans les cas favorables, par exemple celui de l'hydrolyse du polycarbonate (17), on observe expérimentalement que la transition ductile-fragile intervient bien à une masse moléculaire moyenne indépendante des conditions d'exposition ($M \simeq 3.10^4$ dans le cas du polycarbonate).

L'équation (I) devient alors :

$$\frac{1}{M_c} - \frac{1}{M_o} = K.\Delta t \qquad\qquad (IV)$$

où Δt est la durée de vie, le passage de l'état ductile à l'état fragile constituant le critère de fin de vie.

La durée de vie est donc : $\Delta t = \dfrac{1}{K} \left(\dfrac{1}{M_o} - \dfrac{1}{M_o} \right)$

Dans les relations (III) et (IV), on peut exprimer K en fonction des conditions d'exposition, généralement sous la forme :

$$K = K_o \ (HR)^\alpha \ . \ \exp.(- \frac{E}{RT})$$

où HR est l'hygrométrie relative, α un exposant proche de l'unité, déterminé expérimentalement et E l'énergie d'activation de la réaction d'hydrolyse.

On voit qu'a priori il est possible de prédire, sans empirisme, l'évolution de propriétés physiques -en particulier mécaniques- sur la base de données physico-chimiques : les mesures de masse moléculaire et les relations masse moléculaire-propriétés, en utilisant le formalisme de la cinétique chimique.

Cette approche a cependant ses limites, essentiellement liées au caractère hétérogène de la dégradation.

Pour des raisons de contrôle de la cinétique par la diffusion des réactifs ou d'hétérogénéité du milieu (phase amorphe/phase cristalline), la dégradation est souvent confinée dans une zone superficielle de l'échantillon et toujours dans la phase amorphe (Fig. 17).

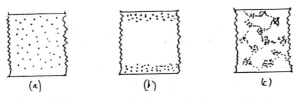

Fig. 17.1 Distribution des Actes Chimiques de
Dégradation dans un Matériau
(a) Distribution homogène
(b) Attaque superficielle
(c) Attaque préférentielle des microdomaines.

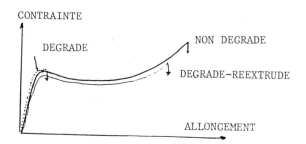

Fig. 17.2   Courbes de Traction d'un PE Oxydé,
Influence du Recyclage.

Or, pour des raisons évidentes, les méthodes conventionnelles d'analyse physico-chimiques ne donnent accès qu'à des valeurs moyennes
intégrées dans l'ensemble du volume de l'échantillon ou, tout au
moins, dans une fraction importante de celui-ci.

Il est clair que, du point de vue mécanique, un échantillon comportant
simultanément des domaines fortement dégradés et des domaines peu ou
non dégradés n'est pas équivalent à un échantillon dans lequel la
dégradation est homogène. La preuve en a été fournie depuis longtemps
par l'expérience suivante :

Un échantillon extrudé de polyoléfine dont l'allongement à la rupture
initial est 800 %, est oxydé à l'état solide jusqu'à ce que son
allongement à la rupture atteigne une valeur inférieure à 100 %. Il
est ensuite fondu et réextrudé sous la forme initiale. Ses propriétés
mécaniques retrouvent alors presque leur niveau initial (Fig. 17).

Explication : La présence de domaines très dégradés dans l'échantillon
vieilli facilite fortement l'amorçage de la rupture. La mise en oeuvre
à l'état fondu redistribue de façon homogène les extrémités de chaînes
dans la masse, d'où la restauration quasi totale des propriétés
mécaniques.

Ici, on conçoit que l'approche précédente, fondée sur les relations
structure-propriétés, s'applique seulement à l'échantillon réextrudé,
ce qui est purement académique.

Les preuves de l'influence de la morphologie sur la localisation des
actes chimiques sont établies depuis longtemps, en particulier dans le
cas de l'oxydation (18).

L'hétérogénéité de la dégradation dans l'épaisseur a également été
montrée dans certains cas, par exemple par analyse de coupes microto-
miques ou par l'étude de matériaux multicouches (19).

L'analyse de l'évolution des propriétés mécaniques, lorsqu'elle est suffisamment détaillée, montre bien qu'il s'agit d'un phénomène d'accumulation d'amorces de rupture (3).

Cependant le nombre total d'observations de ce type est encore extrêmement limité et en tous cas très loin d'être suffisant pour que des lois fiables de comportement en soient tirées. Nous nous trouvons donc devant deux verrous à faire sauter :

- Les difficultés et la lourdeur d'une analyse "cartographique" de la dégradation,

- La prédiction des propriétés mécanique d'un matériau ayant subi une dégradation hétérogène.

Il s'agit de véritables défis, tant au plan de l'analyse physicochimique qu'au plan de la mécanique de la rupture.

CONCLUSION

Nous avons tenté d'évoquer brièvement quelques problèmes importants se posant, à l'heure actuelle, aux praticiens du vieillissement des matériaux polymères.

Certains de ces problèmes : l'analyse des mécanismes élémentaires, la simulation du vieillissement naturel et son expertise, ont déjà été largement abordés dans une grande variété de cas de figure et nous disposons pour les résoudre d'outils relativement performants.

D'autres, par contre, en particulier le passage du microscopique au macroscopique (de la chimie aux propriétés physiques), sont encore loin d'être résolus et devront polariser, dans les années qui viennent, l'attention d'un nombre croissant de chercheurs. La lourdeur des moyens à mettre en oeuvre, et le caractère fondamentalement multidisciplinaire de ces problèmes sont tels qu'ils ne pourront être résolus que par des groupes importants associant probablement plusieurs laboratoires industriels et universitaires.

REFERENCES

(1) D.J. CARLSSON, A. GARTON et D.M. WILES ACS Chem. Ser. 169, 56 (178)

(2) M. VARNA Die Makromol. Chem. 130, 261 (1969)

(3) J. PABIOT et J. VERDU, Polym. Eng. Sci. 21, 32 (1981)

(4) P.G. KELLEHER, R.P. WENTZ, M.Y. HELLMAN et E.H. GILBERT, Polym. Eng. Sci. 23, 537 (1983)

(5) W.L. HAWKINGS, M.G. CHAN et G.L.LINK, Polym. Eng. Sci. 11, 377, (1971)

(6) V.S. KUKSENKO et V.P. TAMUZS, Fracture Micromechanics of Polymer Materials", MARTINUS NIJHOFF PUB. Londres, 1981

(7) ROUX, Physique des Matériaux, CSTB, n° 188, p. 292

(8) D.C. WRIGHT et K.V. GOTHAM, Polym. Eng. Sci. 23, 135, (1983)

(9) M.G. PHILIPS, Composites 14, 270, (1983)

(10) L.C.E. STRUIK, "Physical Aging in Amorphous Polymers and Other Materials", Elsevier-Amsterdam, 1973

(11) M. JORQUERA ENCINA, Thèse de 3ème cycle, Paris 6, Février 1984

(12) H.E. BAIR, Polym. Eng. Sci. 13, 435, (1973)

(13) A. SANDT, Kunststoffe, 72, 791, (1982)

(14) J.M. SCHULTZ, Polym. Eng. Sci. 24, 770, (1984)

(15) J.P. TROTIGNON et J. VERDU, J. Appl. Polym. Sci. - A paraître

(16) H.H. KAUSCH in "Interrelations between Processing, Structure and Properties of Polymeric Materials", J.C. SEFERIS and P.S. THEOCARIS Eds p. 363, Elsevier-Amsterdam, 1984

(17) R.J. GARDNER et J.K. MARTIN, J. Appl. Polym. Sci, 24, 1269, (1979)

(18) L. REICH et S. STIVALA in "Autoxidation of Hydrocarbons and Polyolefins", p. 385, Marcel DEKKER NY, (1969)

(19) K. PERENYI et J. VERDU, Matériaux et Techniques 3, 69, (1981)

EVOLUTION DES CARACTÉRISTIQUES MÉCANIQUES ET PHYSICOCHIMIQUES DES GÉOTEXTILES PRÉLEVÉS DANS QUELQUES OUVRAGES

B. LECLERCQ
Institut Textile de France, Paris

1 - Introduction

Les géotextiles peuvent-ils avoir une durée de vie au moins égale à celle des ouvrages dans lesquels ils sont placés ? Telle est la question que peut se poser le concepteur ou l'ingénieur. Pour tenter d'apporter quelques éléments de réponse à cette interrogation, on peut considérer d'une part les polymères entrant dans la fabrication des géotextiles ainsi que les agressions auxquelles ils peuvent être soumis.

Actuellement, les polymères rencontrés dans les géotextiles sont essentiellement les polyoléfines (polyéthylène et polypropylène), le polyester et, à un degré moindre, les polyamides. Par leur structure chimique, ces polymères, et plus particulièrement les polyoléfines à cause de leur caractère paraffinique, présentent une bonne résistance aux agents chimiques. Néanmoins, il est bien connu des chimistes que les polyesters et les polyamides obtenus par réaction de polycondensation mettant en jeu l'élimination de molécules d'eau sont susceptibles de s'hydrolyser lorsque les conditions de pH sont fortement acides ou basiques. Tous ces polymères sont sensibles à l'oxydation. Celle-ci, mise à part l'action d'agents chimiques, peut être initiée soit thermiquement (thermooxydation), soit par des rayonnements (photooxydation). Sur le plan fondamental, les mécanismes de ces réactions ont déjà fortement été étudiés. On admet également que ces polymères ne sont pas biodégradables.

Les géotextiles sont, pour la plupart, formés de polymères fibreux qui ont subi un certain étirage au cours de leur fabrication. Ces étirages ont induit une certaine orientation des chaînes macromoléculaires et une certaine cristallinité. Il en résulte que ces polymères ne sont pas dans un état thermodynamiquement stable et qui, au cours de leur durée de vie, auront tendance à évoluer vers un état thermodynamique plus stable. Il faut toutefois observer que cette évolution ne pourra se faire qu'à des vitesses très lentes compte tenu du fait que les macromolécules sont plus ou moins figées à l'état solide.

Les géotextiles étant utilisés dans le sol et à des températures modérées, on peut admettre que la thermooxydation restera faible, voire négligeable. Il en est de même pour la photooxydation, sauf pendant la période de mise en oeuvre ou lorsque le géotextile est placé en surface du sol. Mise à part l'action des microorganismes, les agressions auxquelles pourront être soumis les géotextiles dans le sol peuvent être de deux ordres :

- chimique : oxydation pouvant être éventuellement catalysée par des sels métalliques et hydrolyse pour les matériaux à fonctionnalité ester ou amide

- physique : fluage ou fatigue sous l'action des contraintes. Il y a lieu de vérifier comment les variations de structure interne des polymères peuvent influer sur ces mécanismes de fluage et/ou de fatigue. Il y a lieu de ne pas oublier les agressions localisées pouvant conduire à des amorces de déchirures pouvant modifier les performances des géotextiles.

Comme il n'existe pas de relation directement identifiable entre les caractéristiques mécaniques d'un polymère et les paramètres de structure qui peuvent influer sur elles (masse moléculaire, polydispersité, cristallinité, orientation), pour suivre la durabilité des géotextiles il est important de suivre en fonction du temps :

- les caractéristiques mécaniques tant sur le plan du matériau que sur les fibres ou fils le composant afin de faire la part des sollicitations localisées (perforation, frottement...)

- les paramètres structuraux
  . masse moléculaire et polydispersité par mesure des masses moléculaires en nombre M_n et en poids M_w
  . orientation et cristallinité par analyse infrarouge, et si nécessaire, par rayons X.

L'analyse infrarouge peut, dans certains cas, permettre de mettre en évidence la formation de groupements fonctionnels pouvant résulter d'une oxydation. En outre, par analyse chromatographique, il est possible de suivre l'évolution de la concentration de certains adjuvants (antioxydants ou stabilisants UV dans les polyoléfines).

Les enseignements que peuvent fournir ces diverses techniques seront illustrés par l'examen de géotextiles prélevés dans divers ouvrages.

2 - Prélèvements des géotextiles

Lors d'une enquête menée par les laboratoires des Ponts et Chaussées en 1978, environ 200 utilisations de géotextiles ont été recensées dans divers ouvrages. Après une sélection prenant en compte la représentativité des conditions d'emploi, la nature du polymère constituant le géotextile, l'ancienneté de l'ouvrage, et les possibilités de prélèvements, une trentaine de géotextiles ont été extraits suivant un protocole bien déterminé (1, 2, 3).

La répartition de l'utilisation dans les divers ouvrages retenus est indiquée dans le tableau 1 . Ces géotextiles sont des nontissés polyester ou polypropylène.

Tableau 1. Géotextiles par types d'ouvrages

Types de Géotextiles	Remblais	Pistes et couches de forme	Filtres - Drains	Autres
Polypropylène	1	1	3	-
Polyester	4	6	7	3

Le temps depuis lequel ces géotextiles étaient dans les ouvrages s'étale de 5 à 10 ans.

Pour être en mesure d'apprécier l'évolution des géotextiles, un point essentiel à considérer est celui des échantillons témoins de référence pour obtenir des valeurs de références. Ces dernières ont été obtenues soit par les données des producteurs sur les matériaux de l'époque, soit à partir d'échantillons contemporains des géotextiles mis en oeuvre et conservés dans des conditions suffisamment précises.

3 - Evolution des caractéristiques des Géotextiles

La première constatation, avant toutes mesures de caractéristiques des échantillons prélevés, est empirique, mais est cependant importante. Tous les Géotextiles ont été retrouvés en place dans les ouvrages dans lesquels ils avaient été mis quelque 5 à 10 ans plus tôt. Même si certains présentent des perforations provoquées par des matériaux à angles vifs, ou si d'autres sont traversés par des racines, les constatations faites sur les lieux indiquent qu'ils ont rempli les rôles qu'on attendait d'eux, et qu'ils pourraient les remplir encore longtemps. Les géotextiles ont donc bien résisté aux sollicitations de mise en oeuvre et de fonctionnement des ouvrages, ainsi qu'aux contraintes dues aux milieux environnants. L'examen visuel des échantillons prélevés n'a pas révélé d'attaque par des microorganismes.

3.1 - Evolution des caractéristiques mécaniques

L'évolution des caractéristiques mécaniques des échantillons prélevés par rapport à celle des témoins est représentée par les figures 1 et 2. Sur la figure 1, sont corrélées les pertes de résistance de la nappe ΔRG à celles des fibres qui composent les géotextiles ΔRF, tandis que sur la figure 2, sont reliées les pertes d'allongements des nappes correspondant à leurs pertes de résistances ΔALG aux pertes d'allongements des fibres ΔALF. Les pertes de résistances et d'allongements tant sur fibres que sur nappes ont été obtenues par des essais de traction.

Sur le diagramme représentatif de l'évolution des résistances (Fig 1) les sites de prélèvement peuvent être répartis en quatre zones. La zone 1 comprend des sites dont les géotextiles présentent des pertes de résistances inférieures à 30 %. Ils correspondent à l'emploi de géotextiles dans des pistes, des drains ou des barrages de faible hauteur (inférieure à 3 mètres) tels que Saint Angel Combresol et Cheverny et référencés respectivement par les points AC et CH. La zone 2 correspond à des sites où les pertes de résistance des géotextiles sont comprises entre 30 et 50 %, alors que les pertes de résistance des fibres restent limitées, inférieures à 20 %. Ces sites sont des remblais dans lesquels les géotextiles ont du être soumis à des sollicitations localisées importantes lors du compactage. Au moment du prélèvement , il a été noté sur ces échantillons des perforations provoquées par les éléments de recouvrement conduisant à une perte de caractéristique mécanique de la nappe. C'est le cas des remblais de Caen (C 16), Gandelain (G) et Saint Clair de la Tour (CT).

Dans la zone 3, les pertes de résistance des nappes et des fibres sont du même ordre et sont comprises entre 30 et 50 %. Les observations et les photographies faites au cours du prélèvement de Noyalo référencé No montrent que le géotextile, qui était en contact avec un sol mou,s'est déformé sous le poids du remblai et est marqué de très nombreuses empreintes dues à la couche d'apport 20-40 sans qu'il y ait eu de perforations. Le fait que le géotextile ait travaillé sur le plan mécanique, ce qui est d'ailleurs confirmé par les études de structure qui seront examinées au point suivant, peut expliquer cette diminution de caractéristiques mécaniques. Le géotextile prélevé au Montet référencé L.M est apparu fortement décohésionné. Cela n'est certainement pas dû à un défaut d'aiguilletage du géotextile lors de sa fabrication, mais est attribuable à une exposition trop prolongée à la lumière avant le recouvrement par le matériau d'apport sur l'accotement de la route où il a été prélevé. Il en est de même pour le géotextile prélevé au barrage de Maurepas (M4) et situé sur le parement amont d'un remblai en terre où la protection avait été endommagée.

Dans la zone 4, on retrouve des géotextiles dont les pertes de résistance sont supérieures à 50 %, alors que celles des fibres restent inférieures à 30 %. Cette zone correspond à des géotextiles qui ont subi d'importantes agressions dues aux intempéries. C'est notamment le cas des sites Algérie (A1 et TA8) et Valcros (V11 et V12). L'examen microscopique des échantillons a mis en évidence des ruptures de filaments au niveau des points d'aiguilletage. Ces ruptures ont pour résultat de diminuer la cohésion du matériau et expliquent les pertes de résistance. On notera de plus que les points A (1) et TA (8) situés en dehors et à droite de la zone 4 correspondent aux caractéristiques des fibres qui ont été prélevées en surface des échantillons A1 et TA8 et dont les pertes de résistances sont supérieures à 50 %. Ils font ressortir l'action néfaste des intempéries

et plus particulièrement l'action néfaste des radiations ultraviolet-
tes.

L'échantillon C correspond à un géotextile qui avait été utilisé
pour la construction d'un chemin dans la région de Carentan où il a
été recouvert d'une couche de 25 cm de grès quartzites concassés
0/30 mm. La stabilité de surface du chemin est assurée par un clou-
tage 40/70 en matériau de même nature de 5 cm d'épaisseur, recouvert
d'une émulsion et d'un gravillonnage. Le géotextile prélevé compor-
tait de nombreuses perforations responsables de la perte importante
de résistance. Cet emploi de géotextile est l'exemple d'un sous-
dimensionnement de la structure du chemin ,compte tenu de la qualité
des matériaux d'apport et de la nature du trafic. Une épaisseur plus
importante aurait sans doute diminué cet effet de perforation.

Le diagramme reflétant l'évolution des caractéristiques d'allongement
des géotextiles par rapport à celui des fibres (fig. 2) présente une
allure identique à celle des résistances (fig. 1).

Fig. 1 - Pertes de résistances géotextiles/fibres

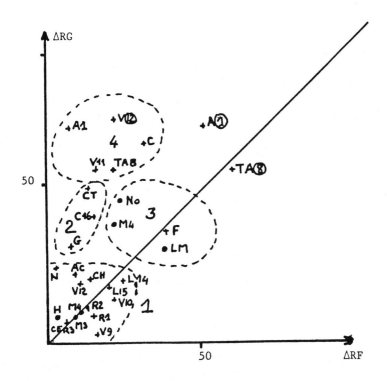

191

Fig. 2 - Pertes d'allongement géotextiles/fibres

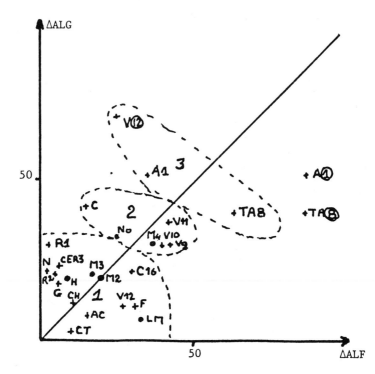

Il ne présente que 3 groupes car les éléments du groupe 2 du diagramme des résistances sont venus s'intégrer à ceux du groupe 1.

Le groupe 3 du diagramme des allongements ne contient que les éléments
du groupe 4 du diagramme précédent correspondant à des géotextiles
qui ont été soumis à une action intense de la lumière et par suite des
ultraviolets. Les pertes d'allongements dans ce cas sont supérieures
à 50 %.

Dans le groupe 2 du diagramme des allongements, on retrouve les éléments du groupe 3 de la figure 1 auxquels se sont ajoutés les échantillons prélevés à Valcros (Vll, Vl0, V2) ainsi que Carentan (C).

Dans les éléments du groupe 1, certains éléments tels que Caen,
Le Montet, Saint-Clair de la Tour, Saint Angel Combresol respectivement référencés C16, LM, CT, AC, sont caractérisés par des pertes

d'allongements plus faibles que les pertes de résistances (groupes 1 et 2 de la figure 1). Dans ce dernier groupe, les cas de Redon 1 et Redon 2 sont particulièrement intéressants puisque les variations d'allongements à la rupture correspondent essentiellement à l'allongement qu'ont subi les géotextiles, du fait de l'orniérage qui a été constaté lors du prélèvement (Fig. 3).

Fig. 3 - Orniérages de Redon 1 (R1) et Redon 2 (R2)

Redon 1   Redon 2

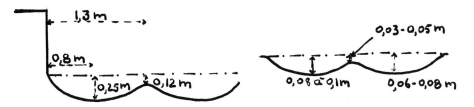

Le géotextile R2 qui était placé sous le même matériau que Redon 1, mais sous une couche plus épaisse a subi la déformation la plus faible.

3.2 - Evolution des caractéristiques chimiques

Considérant qu'une oxydation du polyester se traduirait par une coupure de la chaîne macromoléculaire, l'évolution chimique des échantillons de polyester a été suivie par le dosage des groupes terminaux acides en prélevant les éléments fibreux tant dans toute l'épaisseur de la nappe qu'à sa surface supérieure ou inférieure (Tableau 2).

Si l'on excepte Neufchatel, Cheverny et Saint Clair de la Tour, où les augmentations de groupes terminaux COOH sont supérieures à 50 %, les autres semblent n'avoir subi que des modifications chimiques très faibles sous l'influence de leur environnement. Dans le cas de Cheverny, on peut expliquer cette augmentation des groupes COOH par un colmatage ferrique important mis en évidence lors de l'observation microscopique de lames minces obtenues à partir de coupes sur des carrotages sol-géotextiles. Les éléments ferriques incrustés sur les fibres, et qui ne se détachent pas par simple rinçage à l'eau, ont vraisemblablement perturbé le dosage en conduisant à une valeur par excès du nombre de COOH. A Neufchatel, le géotextile est placé entre le fond de forme et le matériau de remblai qui est un phosphogypse. On peut admettre que ce géotextile s'est donc trouvé dans un milieu à pH fortement acide qui a pu provoquer une légère hydrolyse du polyester, qui se traduit par une augmentation des groupes terminaux. Lors du prélèvement sous le remblai de Saint Clair de la Tour qui avait été construit sur un marécage, l'eau se trouvait au niveau du géotextile. Ce seul renseignement n'est pas suffisant pour expliciter

les causes d'une telle présence de groupes terminaux. Dans le cadre
de ces résultats, il est à noter qu'il n'y a pas de corrélations
apparentes entre l'augmentation des groupes terminaux et la variation
des caractéristiques mécaniques.

Tableau 2 - Groupes COOH Terminaux

	Nombre COOH x 10^{-6} Epaisseur totale	Nombre COOH x 10^{-6} Face supérieure	Nombre COOH x 10^{-6} Face interne
Témoin actuel	43,5		
Redon Témoin	51		
Redon 1	48	52,6	52,6
Redon 2	53,3	60	53,4
Beauvallon	56,9		
Carentan	53,7	53,7	56,2
Grandelain	47	47,7	49,9
* Neufchatel	64,9	51,9	74,1
Saint-Flour	45		
Saint Angel	51,9	61,8	56,3
* Cheverny	68	62,7	60,6
* Saint Clair de la Tour	63,4	62	59,4

3.3. - Evolution des caractéristiques structurales
Les caractéristiques structurales ont été appréhendées soit par ana-
lyses infrarouges, soit par rayons X.

Les résultats correspondant à deux échantillons de polyester sont
donnés dans le tableau 3 dans lequel l'indice cristallin infrarouge,
l'orientation générale et l'orientation cristalline sont définis
par :

$$\text{Indice cristallin} = \frac{\text{Intensité de la bande à 975 cm}^{-1}}{\text{Intensité de la bande référence à 795 cm}^{-1}}$$

Orientation générale = Rapport dichroïque de la bande à 875 cm^{-1}

Orientation cristalline = Rapport dichroïque de la bande à 975 cm^{-1}

Tableau 3 - Caractéristiques structurales de géotextiles Polyester

	Cristallinité RX	Indice cristallin IR	Orientation générale	Orientation cristalline
Témoin	55,3	52,7	31,8	36
Saint-Flour	53,1	49,1	29,2	36
Redon 1		50,4	29,9	37
Redon 2		50,9	28,8	35,5

Ces deux échantillons sont situés dans la zone 1 de la figure 1 et présentent des pertes de caractéristiques mécaniques inférieures à 30 %. Ces échantillons avaient cependant subi un certain niveau de contraintes comme en témoignent les orniérages des pistes Redon 1 et Redon 2 (figure 3). Les éléments du tableau 3 indiquent que les variations de structures sont négligeables. On peut tout au plus noter une légère tendance à la diminution de l'orientation générale. On peut donc admettre que ces géotextiles ont bien supporté les contraintes auxquelles ils avaient été soumis, et on peut suggérer qu'après consolidation du sous-sol le géotextile n'a pratiquement plus travaillé.

Le comportement de deux géotextiles polypropylène est rapporté dans le tableau 4 où les paramètres mesurés sont :

$$\text{Indice cristallin} = \frac{\text{Intensité de la bande à 846 cm}^{-1}}{\text{Bande de référence à 975 cm}^{-1}}$$

Orientation générale = Rapport dichroïque de la bande à 975 cm^{-1}

Orientation cristalline = Rapport dichroïque de la bande à 846 cm^{-1}

Ces deux géotextiles se trouvent dans la zone 3 de la représentation de la figure 1 .

Tableau 4 - Caractéristiques structurales de géotextiles Polypropylène

	Cristallinité X	Indice cristallin	Orientation générale	Orientation cristalline
Témoin	53,5	0,92 ± 0,02	35,5 ± 1,1	70,4 ± 1,2
Noyalo	44,1	0,74 ± 0,02	40,6 ± 1,4	64,3 ± 2,3
Maurepas 2	50	0,97 ± 0,07	34,4 ± 1,1	68 ± 3,2
Maurepas 3	42,7	0,91 ± 0,06	39,4 ± 3,1	77,9 ± 3,1
Maurepas 4	43,1	1,05 ± 0,07	37,1 ± 3,1	77,5 ± 3,2

Le géotextile NOYALO montre une diminution de la cristallinité, qu'elle soit mesurée par Infrarouge ou Rayons X, une augmentation de l'orientation générale et une diminution de l'orientation cristalline qui sont attribuables à un fluage. Ceci est corroboré par les observations faites lors du prélèvement. Le sol mou sur lequel le géotextile avait été étendu. s'était déformé sous le poids du remblai.

Sur le site de Maurepas, l'échantillon M_2 est placé en parement amont d'un barrage en terre et a subi peu de pertes mécaniques. Il présente seulement une très légère diminution de l'orientation cristalline. Les échantillons M_3 et M_4 ont été soumis à des contraintes mécaniques plus sévères et à l'action de la lumière. Les importantes pertes de caractéristiques mécaniques sont accompagnées d'une décristallisation du polymère observé par rayons X, mais qui n'est pas corrélée par l'observation infrarouge. Ceci est dû au fait que rayons X et infrarouges ne mesurent pas exactement les mêmes domaines. L'infrarouge prend en effet en compte les zones smectiques que ne prennent pas les rayons X. On enregistre une augmentation de l'orientation cristalline.

4 - Conclusions

La faible érosion chimique observée sur les échantillons prélevés met en évidence la bonne résistance des géotextiles à l'enfouissement. Les pertes de résistances mécaniques sont modérées (en général inférieures à 30 %). L'action de la lumière ou de contraintes localisées importantes conduisant à des perforations provoque au contraire des chutes de caractéristiques qui pourraient conduire à la destruction du géotextile. L'analyse des variations structurales, qui paraissent limitées, en fonction des contraintes (fluage notamment) est encore trop partielle pour permettre des prévisions du comportement des polymères. Il n'en reste pas moins que l'expérience pratique fait apparaître un bon comportement d'ensemble des géotextiles.

Références

Sotton, M., (1981) Ageing and Durability of Geotextile - Index 81 Amsterdam p. 1-15

Sotton, M., Leclercq, B., Paute, J.L., Fayoux, D., (1982) - Quelques éléments de réponses au problème de la durabilité des Géotextiles - 2ème Congrès International des Géotextiles - Las Vegas - p. 553-558

Leclercq, B., Sotton, M., (1984) - La durabilité des Géotextiles - Index 84 - p. 1-10.

PROBLEMS RELATING TO LIGHT DEGRADATION AND SITE TESTING OF GEOTEXTILES – INTERIM RESULTS OF AN INTERNATIONAL WEATHERING PROGRAMME

P. R. RANKILOR *Manstock Geotechnical Consultancy Services Ltd., Manchester*

SUMMARY

This paper describes the setting up of an international weathering programme to empirically assess the relative degradation of a wide range of commercially available geotextiles in substantially different environments. The problems of establishing weathering stations in the U.K., north of the Arctic Circle, in the South China Sea, and in the New Mexico desert, are described. Some initial results from the first two and a half years of weathering are described, revealing some remarkably rapid strength losses in certain geotextiles over a short time scale.

1. INTRODUCTION

The weathering programme described in this paper is a privately funded project, intended to examine, in a practical way, the multiple variations in weathering and degradation which can occur when a wide variety of commercially available geotextiles are subject to substantially varying environmental conditions. The variables being examined included the following:-

1. Differences in environment.
    a) temperature ranges from -40C to +40C
    b) insulation ranging from none to desert conditions
    c) exposure above ground as against burying beneath ground as against immersion in the sea.
2. Time - degradation periods varying from 1 to 10 years.
3. Orientation of samples exposed to sunlight, varying through 360 degrees.
4. Variations in size and shape of textile fibre
    (specific surface area, diameter, tape cross section, strips up to 25mm wide).
5. Variations in type of textile polymer
    (polypropylene, polyethylene, polyester, polyamide, polyvinylidene).

In considering this work, recognition must be given to the fact that all samples tested internationally, were taken from the same batches and were therefore directly comparable in behaviour with one another and with control samples tested in the laboratory without being exposed to weathering.

Although research work has been undertaken over many years on plastics in general, it has generally involved the exposure of large blocks of material where the specific surface area is extremely small and where the relative volume of the sample is very large. Examples include the testing of plastic pipe for use as submarine cable; for architectural purposes; for anchor chains and boat construction; for paints; etcetera. In the case of geotextiles, not only is the specific surface area of the material extremely large, but the true dimension of fibre cross sections, in relation to ultra violet light penetration, is small. Therefore, it is likely that, given any two geotextiles made from an identical polymer, the relative dimensions of the individual component fibres will be important in governing the way in which the overall fabric weathers and decomposes. It has been interesting to observe from the experimental work, that the actual methods of construction of the individual fibres and fabrics also appear to govern the way in which they respond to stress and thus open themselves up to additional degradation.

Furthermore, it is interesting to report that scanning electron microscope work has revealed that some of the control polymers had deteriorated physically, over a period of three years, even though not exposed to U.V. light or weathering of any kind. There are so many variables within the possible scope of a weathering programme, that usually such programmes are restricted to one particular location, with one orientation (usually south) for the materials, and either a restricted range of products or else a restricted range of polymer types. However, in this case, because many variables have been taken into account, it must be recognised that there is a consequential difficulty in obtaining values of high statistical or interpretative reliability, from such a limited number of tests. An intrinsic part of this assessment programme was, therefore, the development of a set of simple tests, designed to support the pragmatic observations and to provide numerical indications of the likely order of variation of degradation in different materials in different environments.

It is intended that this information can be used subsequently, as guide line parameters within which to establish more rigorously definable weathering conditions and against which to compare results using standard test procedures when these have been produced by appropriate International Standards committees. Also, the development and proving of the simple non-standard tests may provide an economic way of monitoring geotextile deterioration in small scale as well as large scale, high responsibilty structures. Ultimately, it is hoped that these results may be used to calibrate artificial accelerated weathering tests for the forecasting of deterioration of new polymers in different real environmental situations.

2. DEVELOPMENT OF A SUITABLE TEST STATION LAYOUT AND FABRIC EXPOSURE METHOD.

It was decided to establish a limited number of stations in widely differing climatic and environmental conditions. In the general sense, it was intended to have one station in the temperate climate of Europe; one in desert conditions resembling the civil engineering environment of Middle East; one in the tropical environment of Java, to represent work in tropical conditions, and one in the Arctic, to represent environments such as the northern oil fields.

It took approximately two years to obtain suitable sites in each of these areas, before the full testing programme could be established. The greatest difficulty was not actually in locating suitable areas, or appropriate contacts in these areas, but in finding sites which were both exposed and at the same time would be undisturbed and vandal-proof for a period of up to 10 years. It was pointless starting out with the establishment of a site if at least there was not a current indication that a ten year research period could be achieved.

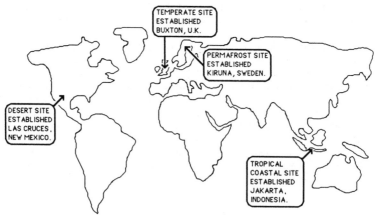

Fig. 1 - **GEOGRAPHICAL DISTRIBUTION OF ESTABLISHED ENVIRONMENTAL WEATHERING SITES FOR GEOTEXTILES**

Fig.1 shows the location of the four sites finally chosen. The first to be established was situated in peat lands on the exposed Pennine Hills near Buxton in the U.K. The second was set up in Indonesia, in the sea in a private harbour just north east of Jakarta city. The third was established north of the Arctic Circle at a small village called Kiruna, where the specimens were established in a permafrost peatland environment. Finally, the last installation obtained was in the sand desert of New Mexico set at an altitude of some 2500 m., where ultra violet radiation would be extremely strong and where the diurnal temperature range is high. After much consideration of how to establish a simple station that would be both inexpensive and yet would take into account a large number of different site variables, it was decided to adopt the simple expedient of wrapping the geotextiles around square posts and placing them half-buried in the ground. Figs.2 & 3 illustrate the mounting techniques and the proposed burial/exposure arrangement. Fig.4 shows the proposed land array and Fig.5 the marine intertidal exposure arrangement.

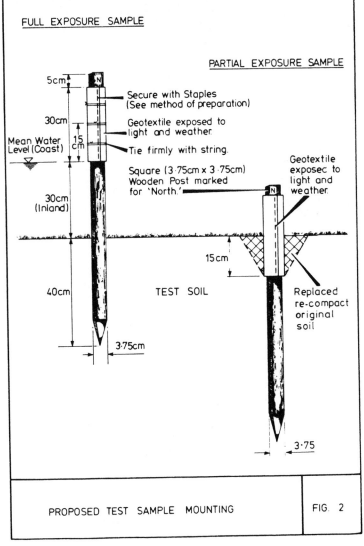

FULL EXPOSURE SAMPLE

PARTIAL EXPOSURE SAMPLE

5cm

Secure with Staples
(See method of preparation)

30cm

Geotextile exposed to
light and weather.

Mean Water
Level (Coast)

15
cm

Tie firmly with string.

Square (3·75cm x 3·75cm)
Wooden Post marked
for 'North.'

Geotextile
exposec to
light and
weather.

30cm
(Inland)

TEST SOIL

15cm

40cm

Replaced
re-compact
original
soil

3·75cm

3·75

PROPOSED TEST SAMPLE MOUNTING

FIG. 2

199

Geogrids are to be left flat and not wrapped around the stake. They should be fastened by a procedure similar to A.1 - 5 above. Staple centre of geogrid firmly and check for a secure fix, using double rows of staples. In addition, secure geogrid firmly to stake with at least 3 double strands of the polypropylene string. Geogrid to be flat and stand out from the stake with long axis east-west.

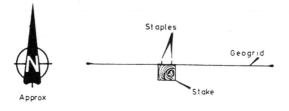

Fig. 3 -   PLAN VIEW GEOGRID

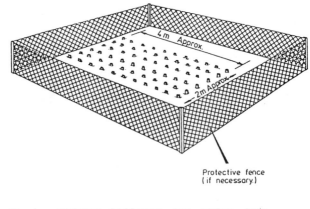

Fig. 4 -   TYPICAL PROPOSED SOIL BURIAL SITE

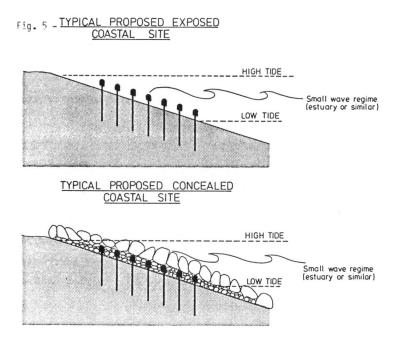

Fig. 5 _ TYPICAL PROPOSED EXPOSED
COASTAL SITE

HIGH TIDE

Small wave regime
(estuary or similar)

LOW TIDE

TYPICAL PROPOSED CONCEALED
COASTAL SITE

HIGH TIDE

Small wave regime
(estuary or similar)

LOW TIDE

The objectives of wrapping each textile around a square post of approximately 35mm side dimension, were as follows:-

1. So that 50% of the sample could be buried in the local soil and be subjected to biodegradation.
2. 50% of the sample could be exposed to ultra violet radiation and sub-aerial degradation.
3. So that each face of the sample could be directed toward north, south, east and west respectively to make an overall assessment of the effect of insolation direction.
4. So that one section of the geotextile would overlap another section and give an indication of the extent of ultra violet protection afforded by the geotextile when wrapped around itself.
5. So that samples could be placed in marine situations easily and be covered by stones or not as necessary.
6. So that samples could be moved easily.
7. So that the entire array of samples would occupy very little space even though each sample should be separated from its neighbour sufficiently so as not to interfere with one another's exposure to light.

Fig. 6 shows a typical array at Kiruna Sweden. The Indonesian installation was beneath the sea, below the low tide range. In Indonesia, the author was advised that wooden stakes would be impractical, because they would be destroyed by boring animals. The samples were therefore wrapped on plastic tubes and placed in a large diameter concrete pipe. However, although they were placed in a private harbour, they were broken into and the majority were stolen for no apparent reason. Only half a dozen out of 90 samples were left to recover and the entire installation had to be re-established. Therefore, the testing programme has available only a limited number of samples for testing at this stage. However, a one and a half year delay in a ten year programme is considered acceptable.

Fig. 6

A further set of samples were lost when arrangements were made to set a weathering station in Saudi Arabia, and the personnel concerned were repatriated as a result of the reduction in oil production in the Middle East. During the change of staff, the samples were lost and the project abandoned in that area. A full set of 90 samples had been kept in reserve for such occurrences, and it is a serious lesson learned from this particular research project, that considerably more sets of samples are needed both for control purposes and to recover from loss situations, than might be considered at first sight.

3. GEOTEXTILES AND GEOGRIDS SELECTED FOR TESTING.

Sixteen different products were selected for testing on the basis of representing a full cross-section of different polymer materials and fabric construction types.

The following is a list of the particular items chosen:-
Typar - Du Pont Polypropylene - non-woven, heat bonded.
Terrafix - Kenross Naue Polyamide - needle-punched felt on scrim.
Polyfelt - Chemie Linz Polypropylene - needle-punched felt.
Terram - ICI Polyethylene/polypropylene - non-woven, heat melded.
Bidim - Rhone-Poulenc Polyester - needle-punched.
Lotrak - Don & Low plc Polypropylene - woven.
Propex - Amoco Polypropylene - woven tape.
Hate - Heusker Synthetic Polyester - needle-punched felt on scrim.
Filter X - Carthage Mills Polyvinylidene - woven.
Polyfilter X - Carthage Mills Polypropylene - woven. Hi Strength - UCO Polyester - woven.
Tensar GM1 - Netlon Ltd Polypropylene - mono-directionally orientated geogrid.
Netlon CE131 - Netlon Ltd Polyethylene - extruded mesh.
Tensar SR2 - Netlon Ltd. Polyethylene - mono-directionally oriented geogrid.
Paraweb - ICI Polyester fibres in polyethylene sheath - strip webbing.
Fibretain - Pilkington Araldite & Glass fibre - composite strip.

As can be seen, this list represents all the generally-available geotextile and geogrid constructions and a wide range of polymers. The particular points of interest are as follows:-

1. Geogrids. These were chosen because they are widely used in the world markets throughout every type of climatic zone. The Netlon mesh is used, amongst other things, for rock slope protection, which is a fully uv exposed end use. Similarly, although the Tensar SR2 is primarily a ground reinforcing grid, it has been used in the past for the manufacture of gabions and other polyethylene products are now similarly used for this purpose. The Netlon product is made from polypropylene which has been extruded and joined whilst still in a highly plastic state. The Tensar product is made from a plain sheet of polyethylene with holes punched in and subsequently extended to align the molecules. The effects of weathering and exposure on these two products are therefore of interest, both in terms of their end uses and because they represent the more-classical type of plastic exposure trial in which the specific surface area is low.

2. Non-wovens. A number of non-woven fabrics have been chosen for this weathering programme, varying from very thick needlepunch to thin heat welded products. Terram 1000 was chosen because its method of manufacture relies on an external fibre sheath of polyethylene melting and forming the fibre-to-fibre bond whilst an internal polypropylene core remains intact. The affect of weathering and stress on the sheath is of particular interest. For a comparison, Typar was chosen as a similar heat-welded product, to examine the affect of weathering on the welded junctions, being the intersection points of simple mono component filaments.

3. Woven Fabrics. Within the range of woven fabrics the test samples include tapes of different profiles and materials.

4. Webs and Strips. The largest components within the test were included in this section. In particular, a single strip of Paraweb webbing was included for testing and a strip of Pilkington's Fibretame which is used in the ground as a synthetic soil reinforcing strip.

4. SCOPE OF OBSERVATIONS AND OBJECTIVES.

The programme intends to assess the deterioration of the various materials in a simplistic and empirical form by means of a series of very simple tests and observations. The objective is to develop a simple and inexpensive test approach to assessing the field deterioration of standard fabrics in different environments. It is hoped that the test results will provide a base figure against which other international results can be compared and which will provide the basis of a growing test result library. Scanning electron micrographs were made which demonstrate clearly some of the early significant observations. The micrographs shown in this paper were taken during October 1986, at which time the control samples were already 3.5 years old. Therefore 'ageing' had already started! This adds an interesting dimension to the project, the results demonstrating that simple storage in good conditions does not prevent some degradation of geotextiles prior to their utilisation in the field. Therefore, the age of the fabric before weathering tests commence, is of significance both to test programmes and to civil engineering design specifications.

Fig.7 shows the splits in the control samples result in the fibrillation of the tapes after tensile testing. This splitting is an interesting feature since it dominates the failure mechanism. The tapes stretch by stress redistribution into unfibrillated strands. Only one broken fibril could be found, for example, in this test specimen after testing to failure. Fig.8 was taken after 2 years ageing + 1.5 years exposure in Sweden and after tensile testing. These photos show that there is a subtle but significant difference in the failure mode between the controls and the weathered samples. The fibrillation in the weathered samples goes one step further and the fibrils themselves break into minor sub-fibrils which split off and curl in stress relief.

Fig.8 shows a non-woven 'bi-component filament' control specimen after testing. It is interesting to note that this photograph is three times the scale of Fig 7. Note the great difference in dimensions and Specific Surface Area. Their appearances are markedly different. The polyethylene sheaths have been peeled off the polypropylene cores and have curled up under stress relaxation. The fragmentation of the sheaths in the bond areas is quite severe. Failure of the test samples has occurred without the breaking

Fig. 7

Fig. 8

Fig. 9

of the individual fibres. No broken fibres could be found for examination! This casts some interesting light on the state of this textile during its degradation process and in particular, on the pre-conceptions of the manufacturers as to the roles of the polyethylene sheath in the function of the product. It is apparent that the sheaths join the fibres well in terms of the manufacturing process, but since they fail under stress rather than the core filaments themselves, do they provide as much tensile strength as the fabric might possess if the main filaments had been bonded? On the other hand, the ability to strain considerably without rupturing the individual filaments could impart a resilience which might otherwise not be there.

Fig.9 shows a different type of heat welded non-woven geotextile, being a single-component type composed of polypropylene. The effect of tensile testing on this single-component filament sample has been to delaminate the body of the sample, pulling the component fibres apart and revealing the casts of the heat-formed junction points. This suggests that the weld junctions are sometimes not real welds, but semi-adhesive contact points generated during softening. This highlights the manufacturing problem of trying to balance the effectiveness of the weld, with too much softening which would result in the de-alignment of the polymer molecules, with consequent weakening.

5. PRELIMINARY TEST RESULTS

In order to obtain as many test samples as possible, and in order that each test should be representative of a different environment, each geotextile sample was divided up as shown in Fig.10.

Fig. 10 – Method of sub-dividing and labelling geotextile samples for tensile testing.

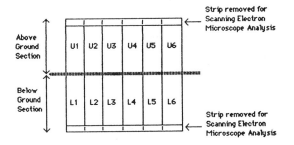

Samples strips 1 - 5 to be tested, with strips U6 and L6 to be retained as a single strip for other testing purposes.

In the case of the Tensar samples, they were separated into individual tensile strips and tested accordingly and the Netlon samples were cut into unit strips and tested similarly. Of course, in principle, this procedure of reducing the size of test sample, goes against the current trend. However, since, in this testing programme, we do not require to determine the actual ultimate breaking strength of the products, the smaller, more numerous strip samples give a better assurance that the relative changes observed are real. The consistent test result scatter confirms that this approach is correct.

In accordance with Fig.10, small scale samples were tested. Geotextile sample widths were approximately 30 mm. and length 100 mm. maximum. Subsequent to the tensile testing, a scanning electron microscope study was undertaken with photographic record, to assess details of failure mode on the microscopic scale. This was particularly interesting, since it demonstrated that in certain fabrics no threads broke at all during failure - only bonding failure was observed.

Fig.11 shows some of the initial tensile test results on two fabrics. The upper graph represents a woven polypropylene product, whilst the lower represents a non-woven product made of the same material. The 1.5 year figures are from Sweden, whilst the 1 and 2 year figures are from Buxton, UK. A relatively rapid fall in strength can be seen in the woven sample exposed to light, but very little fall off in strength is observed for the part of the samples buried in the ground. The non-woven geotextile exhibited a lesser fall off in strength in comparison with the woven .

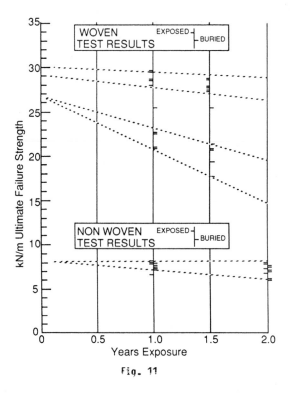

Fig. 11

6. CONCLUSIONS.

This work is in the early stages, but already, the simple approach to the study has proved to be suitable, producing a method of test which provides closely spaced results, attributing reliability to assessments in strength reduction. The use of the scanning electron microscope to study samples both before and after testing has proved useful in suggesting failure mechanisms and in describing the condition of the samples prior to testing.

The author is grateful to the manufacturers, for their donations of materials and permission to use them in this programme.

THE ROLE OF THERMO-OXIDATIVE AGEING IN THE LONG-TERM BEHAVIOUR OF GEOTEXTILES

J. D. M. WISSE

Plastics and Rubber Research Institute TNO, Delft

Introduction

In the past five years an increasing interest has been observed into the technical lifetime of geotextiles in hydraulic structures. Among these geotextiles, polypropylene fabrics and non-wovens are taking an important part in bank and bed protection structures. This interest is enhanced to a major extent by large scale applications of geotextiles, such as has been done in the Netherlands Delta Works, especially in the Eastern Scheldt Storm Surge Barrier Project, which was recently put into use officially.

The circumstance that an OPEN instead of a closed barrier should be build, did arise high durability demands for the bottom protection mattresses and the geotextiles in it. In the original plan the mattresses should keep their functional values during a period required for the completion of a closed dam, i.e. 5 years. In the final plan the mattresses should keep their functional values permanently, i.e. during the minimum expected life-time of the storm surge barrier, which was set extremely high (at 200 years).

At that time, in 1976, it became clear that 'conventional' geotextiles would almost certainly not meet this requirement. The development of special, so-called 'low-leach' stabilised polypropylene fabrics was started, and in the period 1978-1979 the first 'heavy duty' mattresses were laid on the sea bottom.

This development is, of course, equally important for all those cases, where a long technical life-time of the geotextile is required.

In the following a concise overview is given of several aspects which we consider to play a role in the durability of polypropylene geotextiles, and which therefore must be taken into account in assessing an expectation value for their technical lifetime.

Long term mechanical strength

In practice, the geotextile must keep its mechanical strength durir ;
a foreseeable, sufficiently long period. If a polypropylene yarn is
kept on a constant tension level, the yarn will soon or later fail.
At what time this will happen is dependent on the kind of polypropylene itself and the tension level.

This aspect has been investigated on PP-yarns which were used for the
fabrics applied in the block-mattresses in the Eastern Scheldt. Long
term tensile strength tests were done at 90°C and 110°C, from which
the results at 110°C are shown in Fig. 1. In this graph the points
represent the time to mechanical failure of the PP yarn, obtained at
different constant loads F, ranging from about 15 up to 80% of the
short term tensile breaking load F_T at the same temperature.

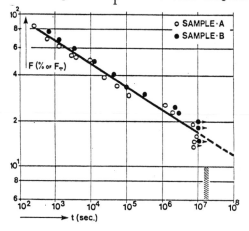

Fig. 1.   Time to mechanical failure of two samples polypropylene
           splitfilm yarns (1900 tex) under constant load at 110°C.
           The shaded area represents the time interval where the
           ovenlife of the yarns may be expected.

From the graph it appears that the time needed for the occurrence
of mechanical failure under a constant load F is given by a straight
line relationship, when F is plotted against log time: the lower the
load F, the longer the time to failure will be.

At lower loads, however, a second cause of failure becomes important, namely failure through thermo-oxidative degradation. In this
particular case, at 110°C, this type of degradation can be esti-
mated to happen at about 2.10^7 sec. (about 230 days).
This time interval where the thermo-oxidative degradation of the
yarns leads to embrittlement and loss of mechanical strength is
represented in Fig. 1 by the shaded area.

In fact this means that, at that time, embrittlement of the polypropylene may be expected to occur anyway, IRRESPECTIVE of the height
of the load. In other words, at relatively low tension levels a pure

mechanical break-down at very long times will not occur anymore, because failure of the material through thermo-oxidation of the PP will take place in an EARLIER Stage.

Quite similar results have been obtained at 90°C as well.

If one would try to make an estimate of how similar long term mechanical failure lines would probably look like at lower temperatures, this would yield something like the scheme given in Fig. 2.

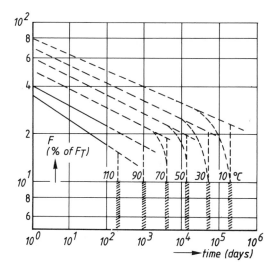

Fig. 2.   Time to mechanical failure of PP yarns (schematically).

In this schematic diagram only the full drawn lines at 110 and 90°C are experimentally established, the other dotted lines are estimates, starting from a known short time breaking force at that temperature.

Although this is only a scheme, it gives a fair idea of how the mechanical failure lines are thought to be 'terminated' by the time intervals where embrittlement due to thermo-oxidation has to be expected. It demonstrates clearly that at LOW load levels the thermo-oxidative stability of the polypropylene will be the overruling, determining factor for the durability of the PP-fabric.

In many applications permanent load levels are indeed restricted to a relatively low percentage value (e.g. F smaller than 10% of F_T), as it was also the case with respect to the blockmattresses in the Eastern Scheldt. For this reason the thermo-oxidative stability of the polypropylene used in the blockmattresses has become a major topic in the durability-study of this bottom protection structure.

Thermo-oxidative degradation

The basis phenomenon in the oxidative ageing process is constituted by a sequence of characteristic radical chain reactions. The end result of oxidation is that the mechanical properties deteriorate rapidly and the geotextile becomes brittle and cracks.

In order to reduce the oxidative break-down of the polymer so-called anti-oxidants are added. These anti-oxidants act as interruptors of the radical chain reactions or eliminate reaction products which could otherwise produce new reactive radical structures.

The anti-oxidants must meet three explicit requirements: they should provide a high stability with respect to thermo-oxidative degradation, they should not cause difficulties in the extrusion process and the subsequent stretching process in manufacturing the PP-split-film yarns, and the stabilisers should have a high resistance against leaching by water.

From these aspects we will discuss the assessment of the thermo-oxidative stability and the resistance against leaching in some more detail.

Tests for the evaluation of thermo-oxidative ageing

At ambient temperatures thermo-oxidation proceeds extremely slowly; it therefore becomes experimentally apparent only at higher temperatures. For this reason the determination of the resistance of polymers against thermo-oxidative ageing is commonly done by means of accelerated heat ageing tests at 100-150°C, the so-called 'oven tests'.

We have done these tests in 200 l Heraeus ovens Type T 5060 EK, which have a cubic space, without forced circulation of the air. Tests have been executed at a large range of different elevated temperatures, using lengths of PP-yarn or suitable test specimens of the PP-fabric. The time needed to cause embrittlement and mechanical failure of the PP-specimen (called 'ovenlife') was established by controlling the specimens at regular time intervals for embrittlement.

On the basis of these ovenlife values obtained, an extrapolation has to be made to lower temperatures, in order to obtain an estimate of the embrittlement time at the temperature of the surroundings in real practice, which represents in effect the durability of the PP geotextile.

In general it is found that the natural logarithm of the embrittlement time is, in the first approximation, inversely proportional to the absolute temperature T, represented by the so-called Arrhenius formula:

ln (ovenlife) = a constant + (ΔH/R).(1/T)

In this relationship ΔH represents the apparent activation energy of the thermo-oxidation reaction, R equals the gas constant and T is the absolute temperature.

Experience shows that this relationship is only valid within a relatively limited temperature range, namely that within which it can be shown or can be assumed that the reaction mechanism remains unchanged. It turns out that this is only reasonably valid for a limited number of systems.

An example of how this relationship looks like is given in Fig. 3.

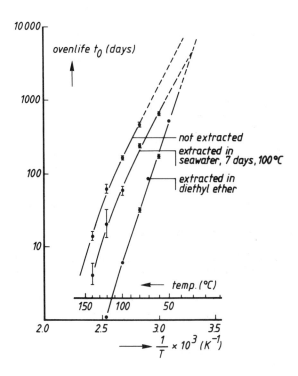

Fig. 3.   Time to mechanical failure of non-woven spunbonded polypropylene sheet, by heat-aging in an oven, as a function of temperature.

In this graph the ovenlife of a PP non woven is given as a function of the reciprocal absolute temperature 1/T. Three lines are given: the non-woven as such, the non-woven extracted in seawater during 7 days at 100°C, and the non-woven extracted in diethyl ether.

The diethyl ether extracted material (which is hence unstabilised) shows indeed a linear relationship up to very low temperatures, so that from these data a rather reliable estimate of the embrittlement time at ambient temperature can be made. The not extracted material as well as the seawater extracted material show a slightly curved line, turning off towards relatively shorter ovenlife times at lower temperatures.

In general it must be taken into account that the activating energy, ΔH, is not strictly temperature independent. Oven tests should, therefore, be carried out at as many different temperatures as possible and also at temperatures as low as possible in order to reduce the great uncertainties attached to extrapolation over tenths of degrees.

Both extractions, done prior to the oventest, reduce the thermo-oxidative resistance of the material to a considerable extent. In fact these three lines demonstrate in an accelerated way the effect of a partial leaching of the anti-oxidant by the seawater, and the possibly complete leaching of the anti-oxidant on the long term, respectively.

Leaching of stabiliser package

Apparently, the actual thermo-oxidative stability and hence the technical service life of geotextiles in hydraulic engineering also depends to an important extent on the extractability of the anti-oxidants.

This is also demonstrated in Fig. 4, where the ovenlife of the earlier mentioned PP non-woven at 120°C is given as a function of the time of preceding extraction in sea water at 50°C.

Since the stabiliser package used is not leach resistant against water the thermo-oxidative stability is reduced in a rather short time.

Anti-oxidant systems used in hydraulic structures should, therefore, preferably be 'low-leach', i.e. leach-resistant.

Recently we have started an investigation into the condition of the PP fabrics and PP non-wovens in the earliest block mattresses used in the Eastern Scheldt, where 'conventional' general-purpose anti-oxidants were applied. An example of analytical results concerning the concentration of applied anti-oxidants in the PP-yarns from the original fabric and from samples collected after 9 years from the sea bottom is given in Table 1.

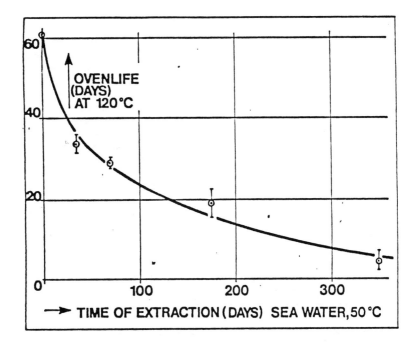

Fig. 4.   Time to mechanical failure of non-woven spunbonded polypropylene sheet by heat-ageing in an oven at 120°C, plotted against the time of preceding extraction in sea water
at 50°C.

Table 1.   Decrease of anti-oxidants (% w/w) in PP yarns of block
mattress fabrics (first generation, not low-leach stabilised).

		Original	After 9 years

WARP			
	Ionol	0.043	0.017
	Irganox 1010	0.0102	<0.0005
WEFT			
	Ionol	0.072	0.013
	Irganox 1010	0.0134	<0.0005

The obtained results show that certain frequently applied 'end use' anti-oxidants which are supposed to provide a long term protection against oxidation, such as Irganox 1010, may be completely washed out after a period of only 9 years on the sea bottom. The additive Ionol is mainly a 'processing stabiliser', meant to prevent polymer oxidation during the processing phase, and has only a minor significance in providing a long term protection against oxidation.

Similar results have been obtained for the PP non-woven, as is shown in Table 2. Here the main anti-oxidant is constituted by Topanol CA, which shows a major decrease in 9 years. The third component, Cyasorb UV 531, is known in the first place as a UV-absorber, although from other research it appears that it also possesses some anti-oxidant potential.

Table 2. Decrease of anti-oxidants (% w/w) in PP non-woven.

	Original	After 9 years
Ionol	0.004	0.004
Topanol CA	0.062	0.007
Cyasorb UV 531	0.370	0.274

The above mentioned results could mean that the expected life-time of these fabrics and non-wovens will on the long term be essentially equal to fabrics and non-wovens which have not been stabilized with anti-oxidants at all. In practical site conditions in bank and bed protections, for instance at locations on the separation of water and air, this may lead to problems within 20 years.

Retarding effect of water environment

Fortunately, the permanently under-water-applications such as the block mattresses have the advantage that thermo-oxidative ageing takes place more slowly under water than in the atmosphere. This is due to the lower oxygen content in water compared with air, which is about 1/7 of the oxygen content in air. The time to embrittlement in water will be accordingly longer. The relationship between oxidation velocity and the oxygen content in water is not known exactly. As a rule the delay factor is assumed to be at least 4, based on measurements of the (photo-)oxidation velocity of PP at different oxygen concentrations. Further research in establishing this factor is in progress.

Influence of ferric clogging

Iron clogging of geotextiles, for instance in drains, is a phenomenon which is already known for a long time. Besides the fact that this may impair the hydraulic functions by reducing the water permeability of e.g. filter fabrics, iron sediments have also a pronounced negative effect on the thermo-oxidative resistance of the polypropylene.

In behalf of the already mentioned investigation into the earliest block mattresses used in the Eastern Scheldt, many samples of fabric and upper lying non-woven were collected by divers from the sea bottom. Visual inspection of the samples yields a typical image of ferric oxide deposition on the fabric and non-woven, which can be met throughout all samples. It appears that ferric oxide deposition occurs on the UNDER side of fabric and non-woven.

Close-ups of the iron sedimentation patterns show stripes in the warp direction, which is probably connected to waving by cross-contraction of the fabric, as a result of exerted loads in the warp direction during the sinking operation of the block mattresses on location.

It is generally known that compounds of certain transfer metals like iron, manganese and copper have a catalysing effect on the thermo-oxidative degradation of polypropylene. One of the characteristics of the oxidation mechanism is that hydrogen peroxides are formed during oxidation, which itself split again into free radicals which in turn produce further radical reactions. While such splitting reactions normally require fairly high temperatures, they can take place also at lower ambient temperatures when transfer metal compounds are present.

We have been able to demonstrate this negative influence by means of an oventest on a sample PP geotextile from a 10 years old bank protection construction, where the polypropylene was contaminated with iron oxide stripes, caused by rusting steel wire around wooden fascines lying upon the PP fabric.
It appears that in the oven test the sample geotextile degrades in the first place on the spot where the iron oxide was present.

Recent investigations have shown that the reduction in thermo-oxidative resistance is dependent also on the AMOUNT of iron compound present on the geotextile. To that purpose we have made oxygen absorption measurements on unstabilised PP yarns at 150°C. During this test the amount of oxygen absorbed is recorded continuously. The obtained induction time is a measure for the oxidative stability of the PP-yarn.

An example of the results is given in Fig. 5.

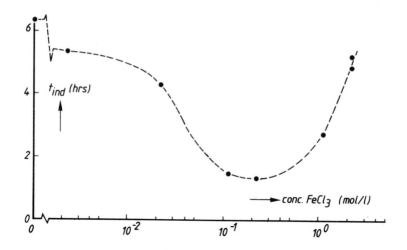

Fig. 5.

Several test specimens were prepared by soaking yarns for 2 hours in aqueous ferric chloride solutions of different strength (up to 2.2 mol/l), and subsequently drying the yarns freely suspended in the air. In this way a series of iron concentrations could be brought up onto the yarns which afterwards could be checked on the exact iron content.

In this figure the measured induction time is given as a function of the concentration of the ferric chloride solutions.

From the graph it can be seen that a maximum reduction factor in the oxidative stability of about 5 was found. At higher iron concentrations the reduction in thermo-oxidative resistance becomes smaller again. Apparently, two competitive mechanisms are involved.

These results show that iron contamination may become important in making estimates for the technical life-time of geotextiles. Our investigation into the condition of first generation block mattresses in the Eastern Scheldt has shown that iron oxide contamination on fabrics and non-wovens of the block mattresses is a generally occurring phenomenon. Iron contents up to 6% w/w were observed. It may therefore be expected that iron contaminations related to the MAXIMUM reduction factor must be taken into account.

CONCLUSIONS

E. LEFLAIVE
Laboratoire Central des Ponts et Chaussés, Orly

Conclusions

The conclusions to be drawn from the seminar are presented with respect to workshops held during the first day and to the different aspects of long term behaviour of geotextiles.

1 - Workshops conclusions

The three groups of producers, users and researchers met separately and an interesting result has been the converging conclusions expressed by the groups at the end of the sessions.

These common conclusions can be summarized as follows :

- The need for a complete and precise identification of products by manufacturers, to avoid any misinterpretation of observations made on material behaviour and to enable users to make good use of experience gained in the past.

- The need to clarify the respective levels of responsability of producers and users. Producers must be responsible for the technical characteristics of their products measured according to standard testing methods ; users must require these data on materials. Users are responsible for the working conditions in which materials are used.

- The need for more case history data and field observations.

217

- The need for a better information on research.

More specifically some groups stressed additionnal points :

- The wide range of durability requirements involved in the various applications of geotextiles.
- The need to clarify concepts and terms such as life duration, service duration, etc. with respect to the producer and the user points of views.
- The need for the monitoring of works with an appropriate instrumentation.
- The need to develop research efforts on the soil-geotextile interface phenomena.

2 - Mechanical function

From the discussions on the mechanical function of geotextiles the following conclusions were drawn :

- The need for a better knowledge of the mechanical properties of geotextiles in relation with their manufacturing conditions and with their internal structure (micromorphology), in order to understand their possible long term evolution and to identify the parameters that are significant for their long term behaviour.

  In this respect, users are not really apprehensive but are essentially ignorant about the production and the physics of the materials and have a reaction of prudence due to this ignorance.

- Principles of calculation methods must be examined and discussed.

  Two basic approaches are used :

  . calculation of stresses and strains in service ;
  . evaluation of failure conditions with the application of factors of safety.

The discussion dealt with the problem of knowing which one is more realistic according to the present knowledge available on soil mechanics and on the behaviour of reinforced systems and which one would be the best to answer the user's needs. The significance of mixed approaches must also be clear.

As a matter of fact, both basic approaches are necessary to the engineer, because he needs to predict the most probable behaviour of the structure and he also needs to evaluate what may happen if one or another assumption made in the design is not fulfilled. In other words, he needs to predict the most probable situation and, at the same time, to envisage potential critical or even catastrophic situations.

Calculation methods presented during the seminar and devised to take into account geotextile strain, including time-dependent strain, are necessary for a better understanding of the behaviour of geotextile reinforced structures. However uncertainties of such methods should not be underestimated because soil deformation calculations are not very reliable and because soil-geotextile interface mechanics are not well known. It should also be remembered that design methods to be used in practice will have to be simple enough for a wide application.

3 - Hydraulic function

Research on clogging phenomena has been developing during recent years and hydraulic behaviour of soil-geotextile systems begins to be understood, although a number of questions still need further study such as :

- effect of installation conditions on the behaviour of filters and, more generally, influence of contact conditions between soil and geotextile (geometry, stresses...) ;

- three-dimensional approach of filtration ;

- influence of soil dispersivity.

If a filter has been operating satisfactorily for a certain time such as a year or so, it does not seem that there is a risk to encounter long terms problems in the physical behaviour of the soil geotextile system, as long as microorganisms are not involved and/or geotextile ageing does not occur.

4 - Ageing

Ageing is a change of properties in time. It must be distinguished from time-dependent properties of a material. If the properties of a material, including the time-dependent properties, do not change, there is no ageing.

Ageing is related to morphological changes in the material or to structural changes in the macromolecules or to composition modifications. These changes are due both to past history of the material, including in the first place production history, and to present conditions : stresses, environment...

The study of ageing of oriented polymer fibres is less complex than for non oriented polymers.

If a material has a tendency for ageing, a number of its properties will be modified with time. Therefore, the measurement of these properties must take into account the age of the product at the time the tests are made. This is to be considered specially for creep, because ageing tends to modify creep rate. Creep characteristics measured on a brand new product and on an aged sample will be different.

Two approaches are possible for the study of ageing of geotextiles :

- a global, or systemic, approach,
- an analytical approach.

The global method starts with statistics on geotextile ageing from field observations. The objective of such an approach is to obtain a synthetic view of the present situation with respect to geotextile ageing.

An important conclusion of the seminar is that statistical data and case histories are presently insufficient to have a reliable overview of the situation. The collection of such data should be organized and developed.

The analytical approach deals with the study of specific ageing processes that may either be assumed from present scientific knwowledge or observed on field samples. The results of the global approach must be used to adjust the analytical approach.

5 - Final comments

The conclusions of the seminar can be summarized as follows :

- field observations and sampling must be developed ;

- we must know precisely the materials we are working with ;

- cooperation of producers, users and researchers is necessary.

Both RILEM and IGS are in a position to stimulate action to implement these conclusions.

However, it must be remembered that any result on geotextiles will be efficient as long as specific geotechnical problems raised by the use of geotextiles, such as soil-geotextile interface phenomena, soil dispersivity, etc. are studied concurrently.

o°o

Index

The page numbers refer to the opening page of the paper in which the reference is to be found.

222